THE REAL
CHEESE
COOKBOOK

THE REAL
CHEESE
COOKBOOK

Edited by
Catherine Cravell

WINDWARD

Executive Managers	Kelly Flynn
	Susan Egerton-Jones
Art Editor	Ruth Levy
Editor	Elizabeth Pichon
Editorial Assistant	Fiona Thomas
Production	Peter Phillips

Edited and designed by the Artists House
Division of Mitchell Beazley International Ltd
Artists House
14–15 Manette Street
London W1V 5LB

This edition published 1987 by
WINDWARD
an imprint owned by W.H.Smith & Son Limited
Registered No 237811 England Trading as WHS Distibutors
St John's House, East Street, Leicester LE1 6NE

"An Artists House Book"
© Mitchell Beazley Publishers 1981 and 1987

A–Z Cheeses have been selected from
The Mitchell Beazley Pocket Guide to Cheese
by Sandy Carr

ISBN 0 7112 0475 6

Typeset by Hourds Typographica, Stafford.
Reproduction by La Cromolito s.n.c., Milan.
Printed in Spain by Printer Industria Grafica SA, Barcelona.
D.L.B. 812-1987

We are especially grateful to
Editions Atlas for allowing us to
use the illustrations on pages
30, 32, 38, 39, 41 & 42.

CONTENTS

INTRODUCTION

There are many hundreds of cheeses made throughout the world. Some are available locally, others are widely exported. Today we have the opportunity to enjoy many of them. A big range is now available and the greater the demand for different varieties, the more likely we are to see the range increased.

This book explores the best and most interesting cheeses of the world. Most you will be very familiar with, and many more will be less well known. If this book introduces you to just one new cheese that becomes a favourite, then it will have accomplished its mission. The first part of the book is a fully descriptive list of cheeses from around the world organized alphabetically within its recognizable type – Fresh, Hard, Soft, Blue, etc. In the second part of the book over 200 recipes explore ways of using cheese in cooking for all occasions: whether as part of a dish, a snack, or the main ingredient of a meal. Naturally, cheese is often of special interest to vegetarians but the vegetarian section here will also be useful for anyone interested in cooking meatless meals, if only infrequently. Even in desserts cheese comes into its own: the textures and flavours of the Fresh cheeses provide an endless variety of choice. Many of the recipes which use a specific cheese can also be taken as a guide for experiment with other cheeses. This book is intended both to encourage experiment and increase understanding of the varied world of cheeses, and to, in turn, enjoy them all to the full.

The weights and measures used in this book are American and metric. All cups and spoons are American (not British). The metric equivalents have been rounded up for convenience. Stick to one set of measurements when following a recipe, don't use a combination of the two. The American standard cup holds 8 fluid ounces, and is obtainable in Britain from large stores. A satisfactory alternative, however, is to find any large cup, bowl or jug which will hold exactly 8 fluid ounces, and keep it for use with American recipes. The following table for liquid measures is a useful guide for those in Britain who have not yet turned metric!

American	British
1 Teaspoon	1 Teaspoon
1 Tablespoon	1 Dessert Spoon
$\frac{1}{2}$ cup	6 Dessert Spoons or 4 Fluid Ounces
$\frac{2}{3}$ cup	$\frac{1}{4}$ pint
1 cup	8 Fluid ounces
$2\frac{1}{2}$ cups	1 pint or 20 Fluid Ounces

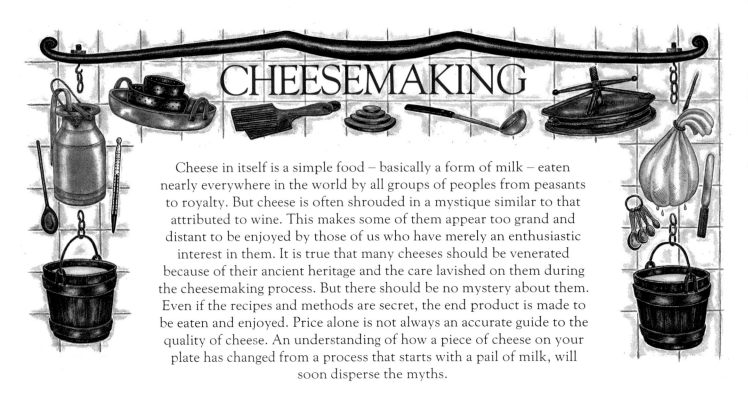

CHEESEMAKING

Cheese in itself is a simple food – basically a form of milk – eaten nearly everywhere in the world by all groups of peoples from peasants to royalty. But cheese is often shrouded in a mystique similar to that attributed to wine. This makes some of them appear too grand and distant to be enjoyed by those of us who have merely an enthusiastic interest in them. It is true that many cheeses should be venerated because of their ancient heritage and the care lavished on them during the cheesemaking process. But there should be no mystery about them. Even if the recipes and methods are secret, the end product is made to be eaten and enjoyed. Price alone is not always an accurate guide to the quality of cheese. An understanding of how a piece of cheese on your plate has changed from a process that starts with a pail of milk, will soon disperse the myths.

Cheese is not a new food. It's history goes back into the distant mists of time. So far back, in fact, the true origins are not clear. The Greeks believed it was a gift of the Olympian gods, the miracle of milk being transformed into cheese had to be a process beyond the ken of mere mortals.

Cheese would have arrived on the supper table when men learnt to be herdsmen. We know that a wild breed of Aurochs were raised for milking in Sumeria and ancient Egypt, and sheep were domesticated in Mesopotamia about 12,000 years ago. In the Old Testament there are many references to ewes' and cows' milk cheese. The discovery of cheese, so the story goes, happened when the ancient herdsmen tried to store milk. They discovered a strange phenomenon. The milk quickly soured and turned from its fresh liquid state to a semi-solid mixture of curds and whey. This natural acid-curdling produced a very sour product. However, fresh milk was often stored in pouches made from the stomachs of young goats or sheep, and on one occasion the pouch had not been properly cured and the fresh milk inside was soon curdled but, on this occasion, without turning sour.

Putting two and two together, it occurred to the herdsmen that sweet, solidified milk was also found in the stomachs of slaughtered unweaned animals. And, although, it would not be until recent years that the natural chemical process could be fully defined, the awareness that an animals' stomach lining could solidify the protein in the milk without turning it sour, as happened in the air, quickly led to many refinements and variations in both processing and end results. Of course, early human cultures would have evolved a cheesemaking process once animals for milking became a recognized food source. Many different animals were and still are used; sheep, cows, goats, buffalo, camels, yaks, mares and reindeer.

Classical Greek literature provides plenty of evidence to show that by that time cheesemaking was becoming quite advanced, and it was being made for both domestic use and for trade. There is evidence of a cheese market in Jerusalem and even a cheese factory in northern Israel, and by the 6th century BC the Romans were importing cheese and exchanging cheesemaking techniques from all over the empire.

Today there are well over 1,000 different cheeses being made and the cheese trade is big business. As people travel more than ever, there is an increasing demand for more unusual, native, cheeses of other countries, many of which are not available outside the country or even the region of origin. Some, especially fresh cheeses, do not travel well and may not be made in large enough quantities to export.

1

2

However, with ever increasing improvements in transport and storage operations, more and more cheeses from around the world are becoming available.

For as long as cheese has existed it has been prized not only as a staple food in an often frugal, peasant diet, but also as a delicacy. Today the more common native cheese is a valuable part of our diet, providing protein, energy, vitamins and minerals. It has a place in every meal and adds a great variety of textures and flavours to our cooking. The rarer and more expensive cheeses are cherished for their exquisite flavours and appearance and are often enjoyed best on their own.

But how often do we stick to the familiar favourites, little realizing that a great wealth of different cheeses are just along the cheese counter offering a whole new world of tastes and textures? Cheese can be robust or delicate, strong or soothing, an abundant meal in itself or a small and special part of it. This book will introduce you to cheese that will become a source of great pleasure, and ways of using them which will be fresh and exciting.

To keep cheese at its best, it should be stored in a cool place (45–50°F/ 7–10°C) and protected from moisture loss by wrapping in foil, plastic wrap or a damp cloth. Cheese should be served at room temperature so, if you store it in the bottom of the fridge, allow it to "warm up" for an hour before serving.

Experimenting with and discovering new cheeses is enormous fun and will bring great rewards.

1 Collecting sheep's milk for cheese in the Pyrenees, France.

2 Sheep's milk cheese draining – a shepherd's marker distinguishes his cheese from the rest.

3 Traditional cheese bearers in the Cheese Market at Alkmaar, Holland.

4 During the maturing process the cheeses are automatically turned daily to ensure that the air circulates and each individual cheese retains its correct shape.

The Processes of the Cheesemakers Art

Different types of cheese are produced using a variety of methods, and the simple milk-to-cheese formula has endless possibilities as the huge range of cheese listed in the next section illustrates. Even before man begins his part in the process, the nature of a cheese has already been partly determined by the animal, its pasture or feed, the climate and even the time of milking. These factors help to explain why it is so difficult to reproduce some cheeses outside their area of origin and how some experts can trace a cheese to the farm where it was made.

Cheddar cheese is the best known and most widely used of all hard cheeses. The method used for making traditional Farmhouse Cheddar cheese is, of course, peculiar to it, but it illustrates well many general principles of cheesemaking.

1

The worldwide reputation of Cheddar cheese has brought fame to the spectacular Cheddar Gorge in Somerset in England, where the cheese has been made since the early sixteenth century. Each cheesemaker has his or her own unique methods, so each farm has its own particular qualities of texture and flavour.

Early morning milking over (1), the fresh milk is poured into a huge oblong vat at the same time each day – 5am – on Mulberry Farm. A culture is then added to convert the milk sugar (lactose) into lactic acid. (The level of acidity is crucial to the success of the entire process.) The milk is kept at blood temperature and mechanical stirrers distribute rennet which causes the milk to coagulate (2). (Rennet is derived from the natural enzyme rennin.)

The coagulated "junket" is then steam heated and cut (3) to separate the curds from the whey which is drained off leaving the curd cooling on a tray, where it is cut into more manageable cakes.

It is here that the Farmhouse Cheddar process becomes unique to itself. The cubes of curd are "cheddared" – turning each one end to end by hand (4) to drive off the maximum amount of moisture. (Farmhouse Cheddar has a lower moisture content than other Cheddars.)

2

3

4

About mid-morning the cheese is ready for setting and milling. Salt is added to improve the flavour and control acidity and then the curds are "milled" (*5*) into small pieces and these are scooped into cylindrical moulds (*6*) where the individual cheeses are pressed for 24 hours; then after being bathed in hot water, greased with hot lard, and bandaged in soft cheesecloth, each one is returned to the press for a further 24 hours, and it is then the rind is formed.

The farm stores the cheeses for two months, at a steady 50°F/10°C turning them regularly each week to ensure even maturing, and then they are graded and moved to a central store. In the early '60s new central stores were built to ensure that quality control could be maintained by a constantly monitored and regulated environment for all Farmhouse Cheddars. Here they are stored for a minimum of nine months to two and sometimes three years – the shorter the maturing time, the milder the flavour. Expert sampling (*7*) ensures the cheeses leave the store at exactly the right maturity for the customer. Only the highest quality cheese is sold as English farmhouse, bearing the grader's stamp.

A-Z FRESH CHEESE

These are simple unripened or barely ripened cheeses. They may either be coagulated with rennet or with an acid culture (lactic fermentation). These two types are known respectively as rennet-curd and acid- or lactic-curd cheeses. Many fresh cheeses are made from skimmed milk or even whey. True double cream cheeses are not coagulated as their high fat content enables them to solidify and drain naturally. Fresh cheeses are largely unpressed, just lightly moulded after being salted. They generally have no rind. Most often they are very soft and are packed into tubs or crocks. Although intended to be eaten freshly made, these cheeses may be matured to sharpen their flavour and perhaps develop a bloom. Many of them are ideal for desserts and savoury dishes and are widely used in cooking.

Bakers (US)

Simple, unripened, fresh, low-fat cheese made from skimmed cows' milk and much used in the bakery trade to make cheesecake and pastries. Sloppier, smoother and rather more sour-tasting than Cottage Cheese, it is eaten fresh or may be deep-frozen and stored for several months. Occasionally made from skimmed milk powder. Best used for cooking.

Bibbelskäse (Fr)

Mild, fresh cows' milk cheese from Alsace, flavoured with horseradish and herbs.

Buttermilchquark (Ger)

Fresh lactic-curd cheese made with a mixture of buttermilk and skimmed milk.

Caboc (Scot)

The oldest recorded Scottish cheese. A fresh, soft white cheese with a crunchy coating of oatmeal. Revived in the 1960s on a farm in Ross-shire. Rich and creamy but a little bland.

Caillebotte (Fr)

Fresh, soft, rennet-curd cheese which can be made from any type of milk depending on the area. In the Basque country it will be ewes' milk, in Brittany cows' milk, in Poitou probably goats' milk. Farmhouse made, particularly in summer. Usually unsalted. Sold by weight or packed in earthenware jars or wicker baskets. The name comes from *caillé*, curdled milk. Also called Jonchée.

Caprini (It)

As the name suggests, (from *capra*, goat) these small delicate lactic-curd cheeses were once made with goats' milk. Goats' milk cheeses have however disappeared almost entirely in Italy and nowadays Caprini are produced almost exclusively from cows' milk. They are eaten fresh with sugar or with olive oil and seasoning. Caprini di Montevecchia are matured Caprini, distinguishable by a thin covering of brownish mould.

Colwick (Eng)

Recently revived soft fresh cows' milk cheese made to a traditional recipe. An agreeable, mildly sour flavour.

Cottage Cheese (Eng, US)

Cooked, skimmed cows' milk curds, drained, washed and coated with thin cream to produce a pure white, bland, low-fat granular cheese which is usually sold prepacked in tubs. It is eaten fresh or used in cooking, such as for cheesecake. It is very popular in America where many different kinds are available. The standard Sweet Curd type is a rennet-curd cheese coated with salt cream and many have large, small or flaked curds. Country Style uses sour cream. Whipped Cream is coated with whipped cream and has a higher fat content than usual, about 8 per cent. Any of the types may be flavoured with fruit or herbs or spices. It can be an acceptable culinary substitute for Italian Ricotta.

Cream Cheese (Eng)

Small unripened rennet-curd cows' milk cheese made from single or double cream. Eaten fresh or used in cooking.

Crema (LA)

Fresh soft cream cheese from Argentina ripened for about a week.

Cremet (Fr)

Unsalted fresh cows' milk cheese eaten with sugar or salted with chopped herbs. The best is said to come from Anjou.

Creole (US)

Fresh cows' milk cheese from Louisiana. Traditionally sold as one large curd bathed in thick cream. Particularly popular in New Orleans where homemade versions were once sold on the streets.

Crowdie (Scot)

Fresh, rather sour-tasting, unpressed cheese made from unpasteurized skimmed cows' milk curdled with rennet, enriched with cream and eaten as soon as possible after making. Once called Cruddy (curdy) Butter, it is traditionally eaten on Scottish farms for breakfast. Goats' milk Crowdie was also made at one time. In the Highlands these cheeses were enriched with butter rather than cream and were sometimes matured for several months. Crowdie is now made on farms all over Scotland. Sometimes cream is added, or herbs or wild garlic leaves. Hramsa is Crowdie with wild garlic *and* cream.

Curd Cheese (Eng)

Acid-curd unripened cows' milk cheese available with low or medium fat content. Also known as lactic-curd cheese.

Demi-Sel (Fr)

Originating in the Pays de Bray in 1872, a smooth, white, factory-made, fresh rennet-curd cheese from pasteurized milk.

Farmer (US)

A North American fresh white cheese similar to Cottage Cheese.

Fontainebleau (Fr)

Very light, factory-made, unsalted fresh cheese. White and fluffy, it uses whole pasteurized milk mixed with whipped cream. Served for dessert with sugar, fruit or fruit purée.

Formaggelle (It)

Small, soft cheeses made from ewes', goats' or cows' milk in the mountains of northern Italy, particularly around Brianza. Usually eaten fresh, but sometimes salted and kept longer.

Frischkäase (Ger)

German generic term for fresh unripened cheeses made from pasteurized milk and coagulated with or without rennet. See *Quark, Rahmfrischkäse, Schichtkäse*

Fromage Blanc (Fr)

Fresh rennet-curd cheese made from skimmed or whole cows' milk and with varying fat content. Used a great deal in cooking (the low fat variety is a favourite ingredient in the *nouvelle cuisine*). It can also be eaten as it is with sugar or seasoned with spices and herbs.

Fromage à la Crème (Fr)

Fromage Blanc coated with cream.

Fromage à la Pie (Fr)

Fresh cheese made from skimmed or partly skimmed cows' milk. In the Île de France a term for an unripened Brie or Coulommiers.

Fromage Frais (Fr)

Fresh (i.e. unripened) white acid- or rennet-curd cheese with varying fat content. Some are light, very soft, with almost a pouring consistency and are the basis for many dishes. This type is usually sold in tubs under a variety of brand names of which Jockey and Bon Blanc are perhaps the best known. Firmer fattier types are Demi-Sel and Petit-Suisse. There are also double- and triple-cream fresh cheeses which must have a minimum fat content of 60 to 75 per cent respectively. They should all be eaten as soon as possible after buying.

Howgate (Scot)

An unpasteurized cows' milk cream cheese rolled in oatmeal and similar to Caboc. The same dairy in Midlothian also makes a small peat-smoked soft cheese, a type of Camembert, Brie and Gouda, as well as Cottage Cheese and Crowdie all from unpasteurized milk.

Impérial Frischkäse (Aus)

A fresh, white, faintly salty cows' milk cheese.

Juustoleipä (Scan)

Rectangular or wheel-shaped fresh cheese made mostly on farms. After coagulating the milk, the cheesemaker drains and presses the curds by hand on to a special wooden plate and then roasts the cheese in front of an open fire. A speciality of central Finland and Lapland, especially Kajaani and Ostrobothnia. The name means 'cheese bread'. Often served for dessert, baked with cream and covered with cloudberries (*lakka*). May be used in coffee instead of milk. Also called Leipäjuusto.

Kwark (Hol)

Soft, white, lightly drained fresh curd cheese from The Netherlands. Used, in particular, in desserts combined with fruit. The most popular Kwark (Magere Kwark) is made from skimmed milk and the fat content is practically nil.

Labfrischkäse, Labquark (Ger)

Fresh curd cheese coagulated with rennet (from *Lab*, renner). Sometimes used as the basis for Sauermilchkäse. See *Quark*

Macquée (Belg)

Soft fresh cows milk cheese made from partly skimmed milk. Usually brick-shaped. Also called Fromage Mou.

Mascarpone, Mascherpone (It)

Delectable, virtually solidified cream, mildly acidulated by lactic fermentation and whipped up into a luscious velvety consistency. Originally produced in Lombardy only in the cool of autumn and winter but now available all year round. Sold in muslin bags and served fresh with candied or fresh fruit or flavoured with sugar, cinnamon, powdered chocolate or coffee and liqueurs.

Mollington (Eng)

Fresh mild soft cheese made in Cheshire from unpasteurized cows' milk and coloured with annatto.

Morón (Sp)

Fresh cheese made of a mixture of cows' and ewes' milk, or sometimes of goats' milk alone.

Cottage Cheese

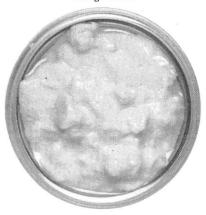

Fromage blanc

Mascarpone

Scottish crowdie

Ricotta

Petit Suisse

From the town of Morón de la Frontera in the province of Seville. After ripening for 24 hours, it is creamy, white and soft with a clean lactic aroma and mild flavour. May be further aged in a vat of olive oil, after which it is rubbed with paprika. It is then firmer and spicier.

Munajuusto (Scan)
Literally 'egg cheese'. A farmhouse cheese from the south and south-west of Finland, made in an unusual way. One or two eggs are added to about six litres of milk, which is then coagulated by heating. After the whey is drained off, the curds are lightly pressed in a wicker basket. The egg yolks give the cheese a wonderful golden colour. There is also a factory version sold under brand names, the best known being Ilves. Like Juustoleipä the fresh cheese can be roasted in front of a fire or grilled. The surface of the cheese becomes speckled with brown and will keep longer than the usual few days.

Petit-Suisse (Fr)
Fresh double-cream cheese made with pasteurized milk. Unsalted, very bland, with a moist, almost watery consistency. Made all over France. Invented in the mid 19th century by a Mme Heroult who was Swiss, hence the name. There is also a triple-cream version.

Philadelphia (US)
Brand name of America's best known cream cheese which originated in New York State in the late 19th century. Probably the biggest-selling packaged cheese in the world. Cream cheese and jelly (jam) and sandwiches are one of the nation's favourite foods.

Plattekaas (Belg)
Fresh curd cheese with a 20 to 40 per cent fat content.

Poustagnac (Fr)
Fresh cheese made from cows', ewes, or goats' milk and flavoured with peppercorns or pimento. From Les Landes.

Provatura (It)
Small, fresh, spun-curd cheese like Mozzarella, once made from buffalo milk, now from cows' milk. *Crostini di provatura* are circles of bread covered with cheese and anchovies and baked.

Pultost (Scan)
Made all over Norway with numerous local variations. A tangy cows' milk acid-curd cheese ripened for three weeks. Buttermilk, cream and spices (usually caraway seeds) may be added. Also called Knaost or Ramost depending on the particular area.

Quark (Ger)
A fresh unripened curd cheese that can be made from skimmed milk, whole milk, buttermilk or any of these mixed with added cream. The fat content varies from 10 to 60 per cent. Quark accounts for almost half the German cheese production and is eaten in vast quantities and in innumerable ways. One way and another the Germans each manage to eat about 5kg (11lb) per annum, nearly half their total consumption of all types of cheese. The name, incidentally, simply means 'curds'. See *Buttermilchquark*, *Labquark*, *Speisequark*

Queijo Fresco (Port)
Fresh, moist, creamy cheese made from any type of milk.

Rabaçal (Port)
Fresh white curd cheese made from ewes' and goats' milk in the province of Coimbra. Occasionally ripened for a month or so, when it becomes firmer and stronger. Often eaten for breakfast and at the beginning of meals.

Rahmfrischkäse (Ger)
Fresh unripened cream cheese usually sold in small foil-wrapped cubes. Made by adding more cream to Speisequark. For Doppelrahmfrischkäse (double-cream cheese) even more cream is added, bringing the fat content up to 60 per cent.

Ricotta (It)
Traditionally a whey cheese, but nowadays whole or skimmed milk is sometimes added, giving a much richer product. It is white and mild with a fine, granular consistency and is usually shaped like an upturned basin with basketwork marks on the outside. Ricotta Romana, Toscana, Sarda and Sicilanna are made from ewes' milk whey (left over from making Pecorino). Ricotta Piemontese is made from cows' milk whey and is smoother and slightly more bland. There are three types: the most familiar *tipo dolce* is bland, very soft, unripened and unsalted: *tipo moliterno* is salted and dried; *tipo forte* is matured to a dry hard consistency and used mostly for grating. Fresh Ricotta is used a great deal in Italian cooking: it can be mixed with spinach and made into *gnocchi* or used as a filling for *ravioli* and *cannelloni*; it makes a delicious base for cheesecake and is also often eaten fresh, sprinkled with powdered coffee or chocolate, or with sugar and fresh fruit. Ricotta laced with brandy or rum is called in Tuscany *Ricotta ubriaca* (drunken Ricotta). Ricotta can also be called Brocotte.

Schichtkäse (Ger)
A fresh unripened curd cheese combining layers (hence the name 'layer cheese') of skimmed milk and whole milk curds.

Semussac (Fr)
Small rich, creamy fresh cows' milk cheese from Aquitaine.

Sérac (Sw)
Fresh whey cheese similar to Italian Ricotta. Occasionally ripened or smoked or seasoned with herbs and spices. Fat content is usually at least 15 per cent.

Séré (Sw)
Fresh cheese made from whole or skimmed pasteurized milk. There are three types: *maigre* (0–15 per cent fat), *gras* (40 per cent fat), *à la crème* (50 per cent fat).

Speisequark (Ger)
Quark made from skimmed milk curds mixed with some of the skimmed fats, graded according to the proportion of fat replaced.

Texel (Hol)
Rare, fresh ewes' milk cheese from the island of Texel in The Netherlands. Rumour has it that the particular flavour of this cheese is, or at least was, a result of steeping sheep's droppings in the milk before coagulation.

Toma, Tumá (It)
Fresh, white, bland cheese, usually eaten after a meal, dressed with olive oil, pepper and salt. From Piedmont.

Topfen (Aus)
A fresh cheese used in many Austrian dishes.

Tvaroh (Cz), **Twaróg** (Pol)
White compact fresh curd cheese made of cows' or ewes' milk. In Czechoslovakia it is available in two forms: Mekky is soft and crumbly, eaten both as a spread and in salads and is also used to make cheesecake (*twarohový koláč*); Tvrdy is the cheese ripened until it is dry and hard, when it is used for grating. It is one of the main ingredients in the pastry for fruit dumplings. In Poland the aged type (*zgliwiaty ser*) is often fried with eggs.

Witte Meikaas (Hol)
Fresh white curd cheese with a high moisture content, made from whole milk and rather acid in flavour. The name means 'White May'. Made only by a few farms in The Netherlands all year round, but especially in spring.

Into this group come many of the very well known cheeses. The term "hard" means that during their manufacture they are pressed in moulds. The curds are cut into small pieces so that the maximum amount of whey is given off: the pressure in the mould helps extract even more. After that the cheese is allowed to mature and a rind develops. The rind is often formed by the curds at the edges of the cheese drying out. They may be brushed or bandaged to make them coarse and grainy or oiled to become smooth and shiny. Generally there are two main sub-groups. The Grana cheeses are very hard and gritty – eaten sliced when young and grated when older. Parmesan is the famous example. They are slowly aged and with their low moisture content they keep for up to several years. The Cheddar-type cheeses have a slightly higher moisture content and so are less firm. They are well matured to develop full flavour.

American (US)

A term loosely used to mean American-made Cheddar. American cheese is virtually synonymous with Cheddar. It represents over 70 per cent of America's gigantic production, was the first cheese brought to America (by the Pilgrim Fathers), the first to be made there and the first to be industrialized. Early farm-made cheeses were much praised by travellers, but factory production has now taken over entirely. American Cheddars, graded AA and A by the Department of Agriculture, come in all shapes and sizes and range from bland to medium strong. They are often heavily dyed with annatto and waxed black, red or orange. The various names under which the cheese is sold such as Barrel, Mammoth, Daisy, Picnic, Twin, Longhorn, Young American, refer usually to the size of the whole cheese, but there are also regional variants with different flavours, aromas and textures. See *Camosun, Coon, Pineapple, Vermont*.

Asiago (It)

Originally a ewes' milk cheese from the wild and rocky pine-clad plateau of Asiago in the foothills of the Dolomites, this cheese is now made from cows' milk throughout the province of Vicenza. Skimmed evening milk is added to whole morning milk. After coagulation the curds are scalded, pressed and ripened, producing a very firm cheese with a granular, yellowy buff paste with small, evenly scattered holes and a smooth, hard, golden rind. The ripening period varies between two and six months for a pleasantly sharp table cheese (Asiago di taglio or Asiago grasso di monte) to a year or more for an extra strong grating cheese (Asiago da allievo).

Beaufort (Fr)

'The prince of Gruyères' according to Brillat-Savarin—a hard-pressed cooked cheese, moulded into huge golden cartwheels and ripened for about six months in cool caves. It has been made in the high mountains of Beaufort in Savoie for centuries and probably dates back to Roman times. Higher in fat than the other Gruyères, Comté and Emmental, it has a marvellously fruity aroma, rich flavour and a smooth, creamy, buttery paste with very few, if any, holes or cracks. The best is Beaufort de Montagne or Beaufort Haute Montagne, a description legally restricted to cheese made from summer milk in Beaufort, Haute Tarentaise and the Col de la Madeleine-en-Maurienne and at their best between September and May. There is also a Beaufort Laitier or Beaufort d'Hiver, which is made in small dairies during the winter. Protected by an *appellation d'origine*. See *Gruyère*.

Bergkäse (Ger)

'Mountain cheese'; a hard-pressed cooked cheese with small round eyes, similar to Emmental but smaller in size, with a darker rind and a stronger, more aromatic flavour. Made in the Allgau in West Germany. Also called Alpenkäse.

Bethmale (Fr)

Firm, spicy cheese made in the foothills of the Pyrenees in summer and in lowland villages around Foix in winter. Aged for about three months, it is best in spring and summer. Sometimes ewes' milk may be used, either alone or mixed with cows'. Local variations include Aulus, Ercé, Oust, Saint-Lizier.

Bitto (It)

Originally from Friuli, now made throughout Lombardy on an irregular basis, this simple rustic cheese is made from skimmed cows' milk or a mixture of cows' and goats', or ewes' and goats' milk. It is a scalded, pressed, firm cheese with small eyes, ripened for a month or so for use as a table cheese or longer for grating. Similar to Fontina.

Bocconi Giganti (It)

Meaning 'giant mouthfuls', small smoked Provolone-type cheese.

Bündner Alpkäse (Sw)

Thick, wheel-shaped, hard cows' milk cheese with many cherry-sized holes. Made in Grisons.

Caciocavallo (It)

Type of cheese prevalent throughout the eastern Mediterranean and the Balkans and known under a variety of similar names. Light straw-coloured and close-textured with, occasionally, a few holes scattered through the paste, and a smooth, thin, golden yellow or brownish rind. These spun-curd cheeses are moulded by hand into fat skittle shapes and ripened for three months or so for a table cheese (sweet and delicate) and longer for grating. The ripening method, whereby the cheeses are hung in pairs over poles as if on horseback (*a cavallo*) accounts for one theory as to the origin of the curious name. Another suggests that the cheese was originally made with mares' milk. If true, this would make Caciocavallo the oldest Italian cheese, dating back to the nomadic era when mares' milk was an occasional food (though whether there was ever a surplus that could be used in cheese-making seems most unlikely). In any case, it was almost certainly known in Roman times. Columella in his classic treatise on agriculture *De Rustica* (AD 35–45) described precisely the method for making it.

Camosun (US)

Softish, crumbly, mild type of Cheddar invented in Washington State in 1932. Ripened for one to three months.

English Farmhouse Cheddar

Double Gloucester

Casigliolo (It)

Caciocavallo-type cheese made in Sicily. Also called Panedda and Pera di Vacca.

Chascöl d'Alp (Sw)

Made in Grisons, a hard wheel-shaped cheese made from cows' milk. Chascöl da Chascharia is a skimmed milk version of the same cheese. Chascöl Chevra is made from goats' milk.

Cheddar (Eng)

Golden yellow, close-textured cheese ranging in flavour from sweet and mild when young to mellow and nutty when mature. Cheddar is a much-maligned cheese, known irreverently to many as 'mousetrap'.

Things were not always so: in Queen Elizabeth I's time one observer wrote of Cheddars being so prized that they were 'bespoke before they were made'. But the making of Cheddar, which began near the Somerset village of that name, has spread throughout the world, not only to ex-British colonies. Egypt, Japan and Czechoslovakia among many other countries produce Cheddar: it is the most widely made cheese in the world. Unfortunately the quality has suffered. Of the millions of people who eat Cheddar daily, only a few will have tasted the real farmhouse product, the 'excellent prodigious cheeses . . . of delicate taste' that William Camden enthused about. There are now only 26 farms left in the West Country of England still producing Cheddar by traditional methods. These farmhouse Cheddars rank among the finest cheeses in the world. The distinctive process is the 'cheddaring' (see Glossary), which takes place after the curds have been cut into tiny pea-sized pieces, scalded in the whey, pitched and cut into blocks. This slow, persistent draining of as much moisture as possible and the subsequent heavy pressing give the cheese its smooth hard texture that, ideally, never crumbles when cut.

Cheddars are sold at various stages in their maturity. The 'mild' Cheddar marketed by the creameries is between three and five months old while 'mature' is over five and up to nine months or possibly more. Some good farmhouse cheese is kept longer—up to 18 months or even two years. Cheddar is a fine eating cheese and is also excellent for cooking, especially when good matured farmhouse Cheddar is used.

Cheddars can also be bought with added flavourings of chives (Cheviot), dried fruit, hazel nuts and cider (Nutwood), garlic, beer and parsley (Rutland), elderberry wine (Windsor Red), paprika and smoky flavouring (Applewood and Charnwood) and beer and garlic (Ilchester).

Comté (Fr)

One of the French Gruyère family, a hard-pressed cooked cheese with a smooth golden paste lightly scattered with medium-sized round holes. A good Comté can be judged almost entirely by the size, shape and condition of these holes or 'eyes'. They should not be too numerous or too close together. They should be perfectly round, no bigger than the size of a small marble and just moist and glistening. Comté has a dark, tough, brushed rind and is stronger than Emmental with a rich fruitier flavour. Made in Franche Comté since ancient times, it developed out of the need for isolated farm communities, with distant markets, to make a cheese that would keep in good condition for as long as possible. Since such cheeses also required more milk than could possibly be yielded by small herds it also necessitated pooling the milk from several herds and making the cheeses co-operatively. Farmers transported their milk to these local co-operatives (*fruitières*) each day and the cheeses were made by specialist, often itinerant, cheese-makers. This economic structure is documented back to the 13th century and is original to Gruyère country. Most usually sold in France as Gruyère de Comté. Protected by an *appellation d'origine*.

Coon (US)

One of the strongest American Cheddars with a fully matured tangy flavour although in fact it is only ripened for two to three months. It has a dry, crumbly very pale paste and a dark brown rind. A very rare cheese from New York State.

Double Gloucester (Eng)

Bright orange, waxy cheese with a strong mellow flavour. Originally Gloucesters were coloured artificially (first with carrot juice or saffron and later with annatto) only for the London market, where buyers thought the magnificent colour indicated a richer, creamier cheese. The locals had no need to be deceived into buying it: they knew only too well how good it was. Most Double Gloucester is now creamery made and coloured although there are a few farms making both white and coloured versions. One farm at Dymock still uses the unpasteurized milk of the original breed of Gloucester cattle and this is creamier even than Guernsey milk. Evening and morning milk are mixed before renneting; at one time they were skimmed and the cream added separately at a different temperature. The best Double Gloucester is that made from summer milk and aged for at least four months. It is also available layered with Stilton (Huntsman), and flavoured with chives (Cotswold) or cider vinegar and chopped nuts (Forest Cheese) or pickle (Sherwood). See *Single Gloucester*.

Dunlop (Scot)

Often described as Scottish Cheddar, which it closely resembles except that it is lighter in colour and texture and lacks the characteristic Cheddar 'bite'. As with many famous cheeses, a woman is credited with its invention. In this case it was Barbara Gilmour, who is said to have brought the recipe from Ireland at the time of Charles II. Previously only skimmed-milk cheeses were known in Scotland. The name derives from the village in Ayrshire where it was first made. It was also the name of the Ayrshire cows that originally provided the milk and, by a happy coincidence, the name of Barbara Gilmour's subsequent husband. Dunlop is now mostly creamery-made. Traditional cheeses are hard to find.

Emiliano (It)

Pale yellow Grana-type cheese from Emilia with a dark brownish-black oiled rind. Ripened between one and two years.

Emmental(er) (Sw)

Commonly known throughout the world as 'Swiss' cheese and imitated in many other countries, Emmental accounts for over half of Swiss cheese production. Genuine Swiss Emmental (stamped 'Switzerland' all over the rind) is made only from unpasteurized milk in both farms and factories. It is a pressed cooked cheese instantly recognizable by the round walnut-sized holes evenly distributed throughout the firm dense golden paste. The name comes from the Emmen valley near Bern where it originated. It takes about 1,000 litres of milk (the average daily yield of 80 cows) to make one 80kg (176) cheese. Evening and morning milk are mixed and coagulated with rennet. At the same time a culture of propionic acid producing bacteria is added to the milk. The curds are cut with a cheese harp, shredded into minute pieces, then 'cooked' in the whey for about half an hour. The mass of curd is then wrapped in a cheesecloth and lifted into a wooden hoop to drain. It is turned and pressed several times, soaked in a brine bath for one or two days and then taken to special cellars for ripening. It is during this ripening period of between four and ten months that the famous holes are formed. A secondary fermentation takes place after the curds have firmed and bubbles of gas become trapped in the mass. The number, size and shape of the holes depend on a host of factors: the scalding temperature of the curds, the level of salting, the temperature and humidity of the ripening store, the length of ripening, the number of times the cheese is turned during the ripening and so forth. The precise level of all these factors is itself determined by the way each batch of curds is 'working'—something that can only be judged by expert cheesemakers with years of experience. It is not surprising therefore that Emmental is generally considered to be one of the most difficult cheeses to make successfully, nor that the Swiss, with their centuries of experience, remain unimpressed by their innumerable would-be competitors elsewhere. 'Anyone can make the holes,' they say, 'but only the Swiss can make the cheese.'

Emmental Français (Fr)

More Emmental is made in France than in any other country, including Switzerland, yet little is exported. Production of Emmental in France was begun in the 19th century by Swiss cheesemakers. It is now made, mostly in factories, in Franche Comté and Savoie from raw and pasteurized milk. Aged between two and six months. The best is the mature cheese from mountain areas.

Friulana (It)

An exceptionally piquant, hard, close-textured cheese made from cows' milk in the countryside around Venice.

Grana (It)

The generic name Grana describes all those finely grained hard cheeses that originated in the Po valley and can be documented as far back as the 11th century. The most famous member of the group is undoubtedly Parmigiano Reggiano (Parmesan). All Grana cheese is made from partly skimmed milk and is matured in its distinctive drum shapes for at least a year. It is usually used as a grating cheese but when younger is also a delicious dessert cheese. Grana cheese should never be stored in the refrigerator; it keeps best covered with a cloth or greased paper in a cool cupboard or larder. For grating, buy a fair-sized chunk and grate it as and when you need it: this way it will release much more flavour and is ultimately more economical than the small packets of ready-grated cheese. In Italian cooking there is really no substitute for Grana. Practically every *primo piatto* (first course) whether it be soup or *pasta* owes it success to a sprinkling of some sort of Grana on top. See *Emiliano, Grana Padano, Lodigiano, Parmigiano Reggiano*

Grana Padano (It)

For centuries the cheese-producing centres of the Po valley wrangled over whose name should be associated with the excellent Grana they produced. Piacenza, long famed for its cheese 'il piacentino' and considered the most deserving contender, finally lost the battle when a compromise solution was reached in 1955. The name Grana Padano and Parmigiano Reggiano were given legal protection and the characteristics and area of production (*zona tipica*) of each cheese were precisely delineated. The qualifying provinces for Grana Padano were Alessandria, Asti, Cuneao, Novara, Turin, Vercelli, Bergamo, Brescia, Como, Cremona, Mantua (on the left bank of the Po), Milan, Pavia, Sondrio, Varese, Trento, Padua, Rovigo, Treviso, Venice, Verona, Vicenza, Bologna (on the right bank of the Remo), Ferrara, Forli, Piacenza and Ravenna. Grana Padano is made all the year round and matures more rapidly but, apart from that, its characteristics are basically the same as those of Parmigiano Reggiano. It is a pressed cooked cheese made from partly skimmed milk of two milkings. The ripening period varies from one to two years and the cheeses are sold at varying stages of their maturity. The paste is a pale straw colour darkening with age. The rind is thick, oily and very hard and can be black or yello-ochre in colour. See *Grana, Parmigiano Reggiano*

Graviera (Gk)

The second most popular cheese in Greece after Feta, this Greek version of Gruyère is yellowish in colour, with holes and an exceptionally hard rind. It is a rich, creamy cheese, eaten as an hors d'oeuvre, after a meal or even during the main course, sliced as a side dish. The Cretan version, made with ewes' milk, is much sought after.

Gruyère (Sw, Fr)

Like Emmental, a pressed cooked cheese, although Gryuère wheels are much smaller and have straight rather than convex sides. The holes are also smaller, roughly pea-sized, and much more sparsely scattered through the paste. The rind is a coarse reddish brown stamped all over with the word 'Switzerland' to indicate a genuine Swiss product. For Gruyère the curds are cut less finely, scalded at a higher temperature, pressed harder and longer and ripened at a lower temperature but for the same period (four to ten months), producing a drier, firmer cheese with a more

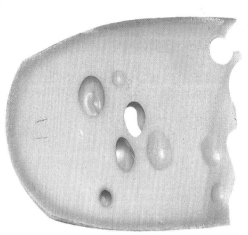

Emmental

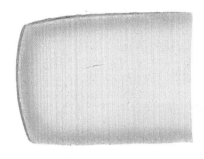

Gruyère

Leicester

Leyden

Parmigiano Reggiano

Provolone

pronounced sweetish flavour and a typically nutty aroma. A particularly fine cheese is marked by a slight dampness in the eyes and fine slits just beneath the rind. Gruyère is an excellent cooking cheese (even better than Emmental). Sauce Mornay is based on it, as is *fondue*, a hot cheese dip flavoured with garlic, pepper, white wine, kirsch and lemon juice, traditionally accompanied by more kirsch or a glass of hot tea. Gruyère, which originated in the town and the same name in the 12th century, should be kept wrapped in a cloth dampened with salt water. In France Gruyère is not one cheese but three—Emmental, Beaufort and Comté—of which Beaufort is perhaps closest in appearance and flavour to the authentic Swiss Gruyère. See *Beaufort, Comté, Emmental*

Hartkäse (Ger)
German genetic term for hard cheeses such as Emmental.

Herrgärdsost (Scan)
Literally 'manor cheese' or 'home cheese', once produced on small farms. Originally from West Gotland, it is now factory-made all over Sweden. Basically a Swiss-type, slightly softer than Gruyère with a sparse scattering of small holes, it is a pressed cooked cheese ripened for four to seven months. The rind is usually waxed yellow. The full-fat type (45 per cent, labelled Elite) is made from whole milk. There is also a low-fat version (30 per cent) made from partly skimmed milk and ripened for about four months only.

Ilha (Port)
Made in the Azores on the islands of Sao Miguel, Terceira and Pico (*ilha*, island). A firm-bodied pale yellow cheese with a hard natural crust almost certainly introduced to the islands by English immigrants. The flavour ranges from mild to mellow and nutty depending on age. Ripened between one and three months and eaten up to six months old. Both pasteurized and unpasteurized versions are available.

Kefalograviera (Gk)
A combination of Kefalotiri (a ewe's milk cheese) and Graviera eaten almost exclusively as a table cheese. The taste is nearer to Graviera but a little more salty, and the cheese is usually slightly smaller, although all these cheeses do tend to vary in size. Generally speaking, the larger the whole cheese, the better the flavour.

Lapparnas Renost (Scan)
Hard smoked cheese from Lapland made with reindeer milk. Extremely rare since reindeers produce very little milk, and seemingly liked only by Lapps, who dunk it in coffee to make it palatable.

Leicester (Eng)
Sometimes unnecessarily called Red Leicester (there is no other kind), this is a hard-pressed grainy cheese with a faint lemony bite. The colour, ranging from bright russet-gold to tomato-red, makes the huge wheels the most visually striking of all British cheeses. It is quick-ripening and sold between ten and twelve weeks old. A farmhouse version is

made on a single farm in Somerset and this is matured for a little longer. Leicester makes a good melting cheese.

Leiden (Hol)
Pressed, uncooked, crumbly, rather salty Dutch cheese made from partly skimmed milk and buttermilk and flavoured with cumin seeds. Modern cheesemaking hygiene forbids the traditional practice of treading the cumin into the curds: feet have been replaced by machines. Leiden is ripened for at least three months. Factory-made cheeses have natural yellow rinds but farmhouse Leidens have their rinds rubbed with annatto (at one time a mixture of vegetable dye and beestings was used), making them a deep, glowing orange-red. Farmhouse Leiden (stamped with the words *Boeren Leidse* and a pair of crossed keys, the arms of the city of Leiden) has a legal minimum fat content of 30 per cent (although usually higher in practice) and is drier and sharper than the factory version, which has a fat content of 40 or, occasionally, 20 per cent.

Lodigiano (It)
A Grana cheese produced around Lodi near Milan. The paste, typically hard and granular although more crumbly than Parmesan, is characterized by a slight greenish tinge. It is matured even longer than Parmesan, up to five years in some cases, and is extremely strong, even bitter to taste. It is also prohibitively expensive.

Mecklenburger Magerkäse (Ger)
Hard-pressed, skimmed milk cheese, coloured with saffron.

Moravský Bochnik (Cz)
A pressed cooked cheese with holes, modelled on Emmental.

Nieheimer Hopfenkäse (Ger)
Similar but not identical to Hopfenkäse. Both are made from sour milk curds partially ripened then broken up, remoulded, and allowed to ripen for a further period packed in boxes between layers of hops. In both, the curds are mixed with caraway seeds, but the Hopfenkäse curds, after the initial ripening, are mixed with fresh curds whereas for Nieheimer Hopfenkäse they are mixed with full milk or, occasionally, beet before being remoulded by hand into small cakes. Dry cheese good for grating.

Orkney (Scot)
A type of Dunlop made in the Orkney Islands. Available plain, coloured with annatto or smoked. The original Orkney cheese was well-known in Scotland before Dunlop and was in particular demand, apparently, for funeral feasts. A hard cheese made from skimmed milk, it's said to have been matured in barrels of oatmeal.

Parmigiano Reggiano (It)
The heavyweight champion of the cheese world, better known as Parmesan, yet now many people have tasted this wonderful cheese only as a commercialized, prepacked powder. The whole cheese is a truly magnificent sight: an enormous shiny brown drum with its name stamped vertically all over the

sides. When split open (among the natural grain of the cheese using a special leaf-shaped knife), it reveals a beautiful straw-yellow grainy paste, brittle and crumbly with a superb fruity flavour that should never be bitter. It has been lauded by name for at least 700 years, but the Grana family of cheeses to which it belongs has a much more ancient provenance.

The making of Parmigiano Reggiano is strictly controlled. It has to be made between 1 April and 11 November with milk from the *zona tipica* (the provinces of Parma, Reggio Emilia, Modena, Mantua on the right bank of the Po and Bologna on the left bank of the Remo). Unpasteurized evening and morning milk are partly skimmed and then mixed together in huge copper cauldrons. The starter is added and the milk brought gradually up to a temperature of 33°C (91°F) when the rennet is added to coagulate the milk over a period of about 15 minutes. The curds are then broken up with a sharp rod (*spino*) into tiny grains, which are then cooked in the whey at 55°C (131°F), left to settle on the bottom of the vat, scooped out in a cheese cloth and pressed in a special mould (*fascera*). The cheeses are left in these moulds for several days and then salted in brine for about three weeks before storing for at least one and no more than four years. Parmigiano is at the peak of perfection when it is *con gocciola*, which means that when the cheese is split open you can just see tiny tears of moisture glistening on the surface. It is a superb desert cheese when young and as it gets older it is grated and sprinkled on *pasta asciutta, risotto* and innumerable other dishes. See *Grana*

Passé l'An (Fr)

A French imitation of Italian Grana cheese. Made from pasteurized skimmed milk and developed during World War II when imports of Italian cheese were proscribed. The name derives from the fact that the cheeses must be aged for at least a year.

Piacentino (It)

Once a Grana cheese made in Piacenza. Now refers to a small long-ripened Sicilian Pecorino used for grating.

Pineapple (US)

Cheddar, hung to ripen in a net, which produces pineapple shapes and markings. First made in Litchfield, Connecticut in the 1840s. The paste is dry and grainy with a sharp tang. The surface is often treated with shellac making it brown and shiny and even more like a pineapple.

Provolone (It)

An uncooked, smooth, close-textured *pasta filata* cheese made from whole cows' milk coagulated with calf's rennet (Provolone Dolce) or kid's rennet (Provolone Piccante). Originated in southern Italy, but production has now spread to the Po valley and with it the increasingly pervasive trend (much deprecated by connoisseurs) towards the mild (*dolce*) rather than the piquant (*piccante*) varieties. The former, aged for two to three months, is softer, mild and smooth with a thing waxed rind. The latter, aged from six months to two years, is darker in colour with

small eyes, a tough hard rind and a stronger spicier flavour. Hand-moulded into multifarious shapes, and sold under a diversity of names, such as Ercolini, Silanetti, Sorrentini (the smaller ones) and Pancette, Pancetoni, Salami, Giganti, Gigantoli (their big brothers). The larger cheeses are sometimes smoked and are usually bound with raffia or string and hung up in pairs on poles while waiting to be sold. The best come from Campania and Puglia.

Romano (It)

Italians always distinguish between Pecorino Romano (made with ewes' milk), Caprino Romano (made with goats' milk) and Vacchino Romano (made with cows' milk). Outside Italy, Romano refers to cows' milk cheese. Like Pecorino Romano it is hard and sharp and eaten both young and matured.

Saanen (Sw)

Made in the Saanen valley in the Bernese Oberland since the 16th century. A very hard cheese similar to an Italian Grana, it has a deep yellow brittle paste with many tiny pinpoint holes and is used mostly for grating. Generally ripened for two to three years but will keep idefinitely.

Saint-Lizier (Fr)

A type of Bethmale made in Ariège. Also called Saint-Girons.

Sao Jorge (Port)

Made on the island of Sao Jorge in the Azores from unpasteurized milk. Crumbly with a strong piquant flavour. Ripened for two to three months. Similar to English Cheddar.

Sapsago (Sw)

A cheese with many names and few uses: Glarnerkäse, Grüner Käse, Grüner Kräuterkäse, Kräuterkäse, Schabziger, or simply 'Green Cheese', Whatever the name, it is a rock hard, pale green cheese, shaped like a cylinder tapering slightly at the top, strong and spicy to taste. Made of skimmed milk or whey, sometimes mixed with buttermilk, heated with lactic acid or vinegar to precipitate the proteins. The solids are then heavily pressed, ground up and mixed with powdered herbs and pressed again into special moulds to produce the characteristic shape known as 'Stöckli'. It was introduced into the canton of Glarus by monks at least 500 years ago. The curious flavour comes from blue meliot (*Melilotis coerulea*), a herb brought back from Asia Minor by crusaders and still only found in the area in which the cheese is made. Sapsago is a condiment cheese, used only for grating. It is sprinkled on bread or on local dishes. Sold wrapped in foil or powdered in cartons.

Sbrinz (Sw)

Probably the cheese that Poliny knew as *caseus helveticus*, 'Swiss cheese'. Sbrinz is the most ancient of Swiss cheeses and there has been a vigorous Italian market in it for many centuries. It is generally related to Italian Grana cheese, being a long-ripened, extra-hard, pressed, cooked cheese used mostly for grating and very spicy and piquant in flavour. Similarly, it is said to be easily digestible and has some reputation as a medicament. Made

only from unpasteurized milk and only in Central Switzerland: in Lucerne, Unterwalden, Schwyz and Zug. The name derives from the village of Brienz in the Bernese Oberland. It is ripened (stored, unusually, on edge) for 18 months to three years. Young sliceable Sbrinz is sold as Spalen or Spalen Schnittkäse. It is an excellent grating cheese and also melts making it ideal for cooking. It is frequently also eaten as an appetizer, shaved into paperthin curly slivers (*rebibes*). In this form it (and other hard cheeses similarly treated) is sometimes referred to as Hobelkäse (from *Hobel*, a carpenter's plane). Sbrinz is the best known (and the best) of a large family of extra-hard cows' milk cheeses. Other reputable members include Etivaz, Gessenay, Justistal and Splügen.

Schwyzer (Cz)

Hard cows' milk cheese made in Central Switzerland either in the mountains (*fromage d'alpage*) or the valleys (*fromage de campagne*).

Vermont (US)

Among the best of the American Cheddars. It has a smooth, white sharp paste and a shiny black-waxed rind. Occasionally spaced with caraway or flavoured with sage, which may be real chopped sage or chlorophyll juice extracted from green maize.

Vezzena (It)

Rare Grana-type cheese related to Asiago though very much sharper and without the holes. The grainy paste ranges from white (winter-made cheeses) to yellow (summermade). Eaten after six months as a table cheese and after a year or more for grating. Also called Veneto, Venezza.

Sapsago

Sbrinz

A-Z
SEMI-HARD CHEESE

This group encompasses the semi-hard and semi-soft cheese types. They range from the young, springy Gouda-type consistency to that of Port Salut, Chaumes and Bel Paese. Some, at the harder extreme are firm and elastic, others are soft and tender. Some, like Gouda, which are eaten at various stages of their development may pass from the softer end of this group to the firmer extreme as they mature. Included in this group are some cheeses made using the pasta filata or spun curd method of cheesemaking. The curd is immersed in hot water or whey and kneaded until it becomes elastic and malleable. It is moulded into shape and is typical of many Italian semi-hard cheeses like Caciotta. Other semi-hard cheeses are made by scalding the curds and are known as pressed uncooked cheeses. Caerphilly and Lancashire are good examples.

Abondance (Fr)

Firm smooth pressed farmhouse cheese made in Savoie from partly skimmed milk of the Abondance breed of cattle. It has a dry, grey rind and a mild, fruity flavour and is ripened for up to three months. Also called Tomme d'Abondance. Quite a different cheese may be sold either under the same name or as Vacherin d'Abondance. This small washed-rind cheese is also made in Savoie from milk of the same breed and encircled by a strip of spruce bark.

Appenzell(er) (Sw)

Delicate cheese with a fine, fruity flavour, made from unpasteurized milk. The paste is smooth and dense, scattered with a few pea-sized, perfectly round holes. The rind, washed with spices and white wine or cider, is hard and thick. Ripened for four to six months. Originated in the canton of Appenzell in the 8th or 9th century. See *Rasskäse*

Backsteiner (Ger)

'Brick' cheese; a washed-rind, surface-ripened, Limburger-type cheese made from partly skimmed milk.

Balaton (Hu)

Firm, hard-pressed, golden cheese with irregular holes and a thin rather greasy rind. The flavour is mildly acidulous. Ripened for five to six weeks. Named after Lake Balaton.

Barac (Scot)

Named from an Old Scottish word for milkmaid, an unpasteurized ewes' milk cheese made in Dumfrieshire. Very pale with a light tangy flavour. Ripened for 3 months.

Beaumont (Fr)

Mild, creamy, factory-made cheese with a smooth, pliant, pinkish-brown rind, similar in many ways to Reblochon. Invented in 1881 in Beaumont, Haute-Savoie. An unpasteurized version is also available on a small scale.

Bel Paese (It)

This sweet, buttery cheese, pale yellow with a smooth springy texture and a shiny golden rind, is a spectacularly successful 20th century invention, created by Egidio Galbani in 1906 and made in Melzo, Lombardy. It is an uncooked, pressed and quick-ripening cheese. The name (meaning 'beautiful country') derives from the book written by Abbot Antonio Stoppani, a friend of the Galbani family. His portrait, imposed on a map of Italy, appears on the foil wrapping in which the cheese is sold.

Bonbel (Fr)

Brand name for a factory-made Saint-Paulin. Baby Bel is a small French-made Edam from the same company, Bel.

Botton (Eng)

Unpasteurized semi-hard cows' milk cheese from Danby in Yorkshire. A recent cheese but made to a traditional Dales recipe and using vegetarian rennet.

Bratkäse (Sw)

Grilling cheese similar to Raclette but usually eaten with bread. Made from pasteurized or unpasteurized milk, it has a rich buttery yellow paste with many variously sized holes and a bright orange, firm, dry rind. Ripened between six and ten weeks. These cheeses were traditionally roasted on the end of a stick over an open fire. The best are said to be those from Nidwalden and Obwalden.

Brick (US)

Truly original, a lightly pungent sweetish cheese with numerous holes in a very pale supple paste. Many think of it as a cross between Limburger and Cheddar, but it is really much more like Tilsit than anything else. It was invented in the 1870s by a Swiss cheesemaker in Wisconsin, where most of it is still made. The name derives from its shape or, some say, from the traditional practice of pressing it with bricks. The rind is smeared with a culture of *Bacterium linens* and regularly wiped with a cloth dipped in brine during the three-month ripening. The resulting aroma is distinctly spicy but not overpowering compared to other washed-rind cheeses. The reddish natural rind is sometimes removed and the cheeses waxed before they are sold.

Bricquebec (Fr)

Saint-Paulin type made in Normandy at the abbey of the same name and sold under the brand name Providence.

Bruder Basil (Ger)

Smooth, firm, yellow cheese with a dark mahogany-coloured rind, made in Bavaria. Creamy with a pleasantly smoky flavour, it is a superior version of the Bavarian smoked processed cheese one finds almost everywhere. There is also a variation flavoured with chopped ham.

Brusselsekaas (Belg)

Smooth, salty, low-fat cheese made from pasteurized skimmed milk. Regularly washed with tepid water during the three-month ripening period. It has virtually no rind and is moulded into small irregular shaped cakes and packed in cellophane for sale. Fairly strong and tangy with a light spicy aroma. Also called Fromage de Bruxelles, Hettekees.

Burrini (It)

A speciality of southern Italy, Puglia and Calabria in particular. Small, pear-shaped, *pasta filata* cheeses, hand moulded around a pat of sweet butter, with a mild taste and a faint tang rather like Provolone dolce. They are ripened for a few weeks only and eaten with bread spread with the buttery heart of the cheese. For longer keeping, especially for export, the cheeses are dipped in wax. Also known as Butirri, Burielli and occasionally Provole.

Butterkäse (Ger)

A smooth, bland and, as the name suggests, buttery cheese made all over the country. The paste is a clear, pale yellow, with or without irregular holes, and the rind is golden to reddish in colour. It comes either in a loaf or in a wheel shape weighing 2kg (4lb) and 1kg (2lb) respectively. It is extremely delicate, odourless and quite inoffensive. Also called Damenkäse (ladies' cheese).

Cacetti (It)

Small pear-shaped, spun-curd cheeses. After moulding, the cheeses are dipped in wax and hung up by a loop of raffia attached at the narrow end to mature for about ten days.

Caciotta (It)

Deliciously creamy, softish small cheese ranging in colour from white to golden yellow and in flavour from sweet to mild to lightly piquant. The factory-made version is made from pasteurized cows' milk and tends to be rather bland. Otherwise, Caciotta can be made from any type of milk, since the term is less descriptive of a particular cheese type than an indication that this is a small cheese made from local milk by artisans and farmers in the traditional manner. These farmhouse versions show innumerable regional variations in flavour and shape. Some have smooth, firm, oiled rinds, others have the basketwork imprint typical of some Pecorinos. They are usually aged for about ten days. The best are said to be Caciotta di Urbino and Caciotta Toscana (traditionally eaten with fresh young broad beans).

Caerphilly (W)

Moist, crumbly, lemon yellow cheese with a salty, slightly sour buttermilk flavour, Caerphilly dates back only to the early 1800s. It was originally made not only in Caerphilly itself but also in dairy farms throughout the Vale of Glamorgan and in Gwent west of the River Usk, from the milk of Hereford cattle. For years it was known in Wales simply as 'new cheese' (a reference to its quick-ripening properties rather than its recent origins) and most of it was consumed locally both because relatively little was made and also because it did not travel well. Two batches were made daily, one from morning milk and one from evening milk, throughout the summer months. They were ready for sale within a week to ten days. This factor made them a tempting proposition for the Cheddar-makers on the other side of the Bristol Channel. Caerphilly could provide a quick turnover during the long months of waiting for Cheddars to mature and by the beginning of this century it was being made in large quantities in Somerset. In World War II the making of Caerphilly was banned completely and Welsh cheesemakers, without Cheddar to fall back on, never recovered from this blow. Nowadays Caerphilly is made entirely in England.

There are one or two farms in Somerset still making Caerphilly in the old way from unpasteurized milk. The cheese is rapidly drained and lightly pressed. Its rind is formed by soaking the cheese in brine for 24 hours after pressing and then whitened with rice flour. Farmhouse Caerphilly is best eaten a few days after making. The creamery version is matured for up to two weeks. Caerphilly is so mild and digestible that it can happily be eaten in large quantities. The Welsh crumble it on a slice of bread, add a few drops of vinegar and, of course, toast it.

Cantal (Fr)

Probably the oldest French cheese (*c.* 2,000 years), made in the Auvergne from the milk of Salers or Aubrac cows and protected by an appellation d'origine. Unfortunately, good Cantal is rarely found outside France. Often thought of as the French Cheddar, it has a smooth, close-textured, yellow paste with a pleasant rather nutty flavour. The rind is dry, grey and powdery. It is a pressed uncooked cheese, ripened between three and six months. There are two types: Cantal Laiter, a pasteurized version made all year round in creameries, and Cantal Fermier, made in summer during the period of transhumance in mountain huts (*burons*) or *fruitières*. Cantal Fermier is especially prized and is usually matured for longer than the creamery type. It also tends to be heavier. The biggest ones are made near Salers. Cantal Laitier rarely weighs more than 35kg (77lb). There is also a 'baby' farmhouse Cantal, known as Cantalet of Cantalon, weighing about 10kg (22lb), which is made towards the end of summer when the milk supply is drying up and so is particularly rich and high in fat content. These cheeses are usually consumed on special occasions. Cantal is used a great deal in regional dishes. Also called Salers, Fourme de Cantal, Fourme de Salers.

Caramkäse (Ger)

Smooth, bland, elastic cheese, occasionally smoked.

Cebrero (Sp)

Oddly shaped—a drum with an overhanging rum, like a thick-stalked mushroom—this pressed firm cheese has a creamy close-textured paste and a fairly sharp rustic flavour. The rind is firm and crusty with white streaks radiating from the centre of the 'lid'. It is ripened for three to four days. Cebrero is made in Lugo in the Cebrero mountains near the Portuguese border and sometimes sold under its Portuguese name Queixo do Cebreiro.

Chanco (LA)

Named after a small coastal town south of Santiago, Chile. Smooth, mild buttery cheese with a golden-brown rind made mostly from pasteurized milk. Also called Mantecoso.

Chantelle (US)

Full-fat, mild sliceable cows' milk cheese with a springy yellow paste similar to Italian Bel Paese. Coated in red wax.

Caerphilly

Cantal

Cheshire

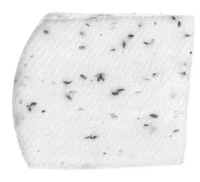

Danbo

Chaumes (Fr)
From the Dordogne, a cheese with a rich golden creamy paste and a tough yellowy brown rind. Made from pasteurized milk, it has a springy, rather elastic consistency and a full, nutty flavour. Watch out for hardening beneath the rind and avoid any cheese which looks murky or dull.

Chaux d'Abel (Sw)
Smooth, sweetish, pale yellow cheese with a few irregular holes and an orange, firm, dry rind. Made near Neuchâtel in Switzerland.

Cheshire (Eng)
Moist, friable, slightly salty cheese, mild when young but acquiring a more pronounced tang with age. The paste is 'white' (pale yellow) or 'red' (annatto-dyed to a deep peach colour). Red Cheshire tends to be more popular in the Midlands and the South of England and White Cheshire in the North, but there is no difference in the flavour.

Cheshire is the oldest British cheese. It was mentioned in the Domesday Book in 1086, but the evidence of folklore suggests that it is much older, going back, perhaps, even earlier than the Roman occupation. One story tells how the Romans hanged a cheesemaker at Chester Cross for refusing to divulge the recipe. The Romans were wasting their time: Cheshire can only be made from the milk of cattle grazed on the salty pastures of the Cheshire Plain, either in Shropshire or Cheshire. The Chester produced in France and many other European countries is related to English Cheshire in name only.

Most Cheshire nowadays is creamery-made, but there are still about 20 farms producing farmhouse cheeses. The cheese takes only about two to three hours to make. Evening and morning milk are mixed and after coagulation the curds are scalded in the whey for about 40 minutes. Then the whey is drained off very quickly while the cheesemaker cuts the curd and then tears it into small pieces. It is then salted, milled, put into moulds and pressed for between 24 and 48 hours. Some farmhouse Cheshires are still bandaged in the traditional way with cheese cloths dipped in lard. Others are dipped in wax. The cheeses are usually ripened for between four and eight weeks, but sometimes a particularly fine one will be selected for longer ripening, which may be anything up to 15 months.

Cheshire is a very even-tempered cheese. It is almost always good and often superb. Choose a farmhouse cheese if possible, even though Cheshire suffers less from factory methods than do most other cheeses. There is no hidden pitfalls in buying Cheshire: if it looks bright and fresh, buy it; if it is dry and cracked or sweating inside a vacuum pack, leave it alone. It is an excellent all-purpose cheese. Its flavour makes it especially delicious in omelettes and soufflés. See *Blue Cheshire*

Colby (US)
From Colby, Wisconsin, a Cheddar variant first made in 1882 by Ambrose and J.H. Steinwand. The curd is not 'cheddared', which makes the paste more open and granular than an ordinary Cheddar. It is dyed deep orange yellow and waved or vacuum packed in variously sized blocks or rounds. The flavour is mild and rather sweet. A popular everyday cheese.

Cornhusker (US)
A rare, softer, milder springy Cheddar with holes, developed by the Nebraska Agricultural Experiment Station in 1940, and named after the local football team.

Cotherstone (Eng)
Blue-veined and white cheeses made from unpasteurized milk on two farms near Cotherstone, Yorkshire, between May and December. Open-textured with a soft crust and a sharp flavour and ripened for up to three months.

Danablu (Scan)
Invented in Denmark in the early 20th century as a substitute for Roquefort and a huge commercial success. Quite different from Roquefort but excellent value and widely available. It can be rather dry and is often very sharp and salty. The paste should be clear and white.

Danbo (Scan)
A member of the Samsø family, rather bland with a springy pale yellow paste scattered with a few small round holes. The natural rind is firm and butter-coloured but is normally coated with yellow or bright red wax. Usually ripened for about five months and occasionally spiced with caraway seeds from Denmark.

Derby (Eng)
Mild, primrose yellow cheese with a close rather flaky texture. Neither a particularly interesting nor a popular cheese possibly because it is almost always sold far too young at between four and six weeks old. Ideally it should be ripened for around six months, but such mature Derbys are rare even in specialist shops. Derby cheese has the distinction of having been industrialized earlier than any other English cheeses, for the first cheese factory opened near Derby in 1870. Farmhouse production has now ceased entirely. Traditionally, Derby is eaten with soft bread rolls and a mixture of sliced onions steeped overnight in sugar-sweetened vinegar. See *Sage Derby*

Devon Garland (Eng)
Moist rich crumbly cheese with a layer of mixed fresh herbs in the middle, Made from unpasteurized Jersey milk near Barnstaple in Devon to a traditional Dales recipe but using vegetarian rennet. Named after a local village.

Dietkaas (Hol)
Similar to Gouda and produced especially for those on low-salt diets. Fat content ranges between 20 and 48 per cent and it is distinguished by a 'D' on the control stamp.

Edam (Edammer) (Hol)
Its shiny bright red coating of paraffin wax makes Edam the most immediately recognizable cheese in the world (although in the Netherlands itself the cheeses are sold with the natural gold rind uncovered). Its equally dis-

tinctive perfect spherical shape occurs because the cheese forms quickly before the interior has time to settle. Edam is smooth and supple with a slightly acidulous aftertaste, sold young, at about three or four months old, or after a year or so, when it becomes stronger, drier and saltier. It is entirely factory-made and may sometimes be flavoured with cumin seeds.

Edam originated in the town of Edam at least 600 years ago and has always been highly successful commercially. By the late 17th century about 454,000 kg (1,000,000 lb) of cheese was being exported every year, much of it to the Dutch colonies. Some of these countries have used it to produce wonderfully exotic dishes, such as *keshy yena* from the Dutch Antilles—a cheese stuffed with fish or meat and vegetables and baked whole. Edam's excellent keeping properties make it particularly suitable for warmer climates, and not only, it seems, for eating. One story insists that the Uruguayans once defeated the Argentinians in a naval battle by substituting aged Edams for cannonballs. Such old hard cheeses are now rarely found, but Edam is sold in several different versions to suit contemporary tastes. The normal size weighs around 1.7 kg (3½ lb). There is also a small Baby Edam, a stronger double-sized Commissiekaas (sold as Mimolette in France and coloured deep orange with annatto), and Middelbaar, a heavyweight at 6.5 kg (14 lb).

Elbo (Scan)
A member of the Samsø family, bland, inoffensive and faintly aromatic. Usually coated in red wax. From Denmark.

Entrammes (Fr)
Pressed, uncooked, monastery-made cheese from the Abbaye de'Entrammes, Maine, whose cheeses were once sold as 'Port-Salut' until the monks sold the name to a commercial enterprise. See *Port-du-Salut*

Esrom (Scan)
Washed-rind cheese once known as the Danish Port-Salut but actually closer in character to Tilsit. The paste is pale and creamy with lots of irregular holes and slits. It has a sweet, rich flavour and a definite spicy aroma when fully aged. Esrom lovers always insist that the rind should definitely be eaten with the cheese.

Fjordland (Scan)
Norwegian factory-made block using partly skimmed cows' milk. It has a pale smooth paste with unevenly distributed large round holes. Full nutty flavour faintly reminiscent of Emmental.

Fondu au Raisin (Fr)
Processed cheese made mostly from Emmental and impressed on the surface with toasted grape pips. Also called Fondu au Marc, Tomme au Raisin.

Fontal (It)
Cheese similar to Fontina which was, in fact, called Fontina until the Stresa Convention of 1951 protected the exclusive claims of the Val d'Aosta. It is produced on an industrial scale throughout Piedmont and Lombardy but unlike genuine Fontina it is made largely from pasteurized milk, and has fewer eyes and a slightly darker rind.

Fontina (It)
One of the best of the many excellent Italian cheeses, genuine Fontina comes only from the Val d'Aosta high up in the Alps near the borders with France and Switzerland. Made from whole unpasteurized milk of one milking, it is a pressed, cooked, medium-ripened cheese with a smooth, slightly elastic, straw-coloured paste that has sparse small round holes. The rind is an uneven light brown, thin and lightly oiled. Fontina has a delicate, nutty, almost honeyed flavour, somewhat like Swiss Gruyère but sweeter and more buttery. The best is made in mountain chalets between May and September when the herds pasture on the alpine meadows. In the winter months the milk is processed in small cheese factories in the valleys. Like Gruyère in *fondue*, Fontina is the most important ingredient in the Piedmontese version, *fonduta*, which boasts the additional speciality of white truffles.

Friese Nagelkaas (Hol)
Surprisingly, the Dutch homeland of the ubiquitous black and white Friesian cattle has not produced many original cheese types. Nagelkaas (literally 'nail cheese') is a rather coarse, hard-pressed, long-ripening cheese made from whole milk sometimes mixed with buttermilk and studded with cloves and cumin seeds. Sometimes sold as Friesian Clove. The paste is grey-white, dry and extremely spicy and piquant after a minimum of six months' ageing. The rind is tough and hard, especially in well-matured cheeses. Friese Kanterkaas is the same cheese without spices.

Fromage de Trappiste (Bel)
Semi-hard cheese factory-made from pasteurized milk and inspired by Port-Salut and other French monastery cheeses. There are numerous types variously shaped into flat wheels or loaves and with smooth springy rinds ranging from light golden yellow to black. Often sold as 'Saint-Paulin' or under brand names such as Echte Loo, Vieille Abbaye, Perrette, Nouvelle Abbaye, Abbaye de la Vallée, Père Joseph and Paterskop. Mild and sometimes spiced.

Fynbo (Scan)
A member of the Samsø family, first made on the island of Fyn, Denmark. Mild, buttery, smooth-textured with a few round holes, usually coated in yellow or red wax. Trope-fynbo is smaller, firmer and darker in colour.

Gammelost (Scan)
'Old cheese'; an ancient type, from Norway, and as intimidating in appearance as the Vikings who reputedly enjoyed it. It is an excellent keeping cheese (ideal, perhaps, for long sea voyages) and was traditionally made in summer for winter use. The pitted hard brown crust makes it look at least a century old but in fact the entire making and ripening process takes only a month. Skimmed milk is coagulated with lactic bacteria and heated. The curds are heavily pressed, moulded and

Edam

Baby Edam

Mimolette

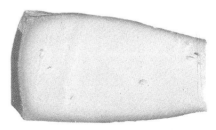

Fontina

Gouda

Jarlsberg

Lancashire

Monterey Jack

then boiled in whey for several hours. The cheeses are left to dry for a day or so and then pierced with *Penicillium*-coated needles or broken up, kneaded with *Penicillium* spores, remoulded and re-pressed. During the ripening period another mould, *Mucor*, grows on the surface, producing a long soft fuzz that is regularly worked back into the cheese by hand. This growth is now artificially induced, although in the past it developed spontaneously from minute traces either left in the moulds from the previous batch of cheese or impregnated in the walls of the dairy. Traditionally the cheeses were stored in straw scented with juniper berries. The result of all this, not surprisingly, is an extremely potent cheese, sharp, strong and aromatic with some blue-green veining in a brownish-yellow paste, quite unique—but an effective antidote for the rigours of a northern winter. Virtually inedible unless sliced very thinly.

Gaperon (Gapron) (Fr)
Shaped like an upturned basin, lightly pressed cheese made from skimmed milk or buttermilk. Flavoured with garlic or sometimes peppercorns. Made in farms and small factories in the Auvergne. Ripened for about two months. These cheeses used to be hung to ripen from the beams of the farmhouse kitchen, enabling visitors to gauge the family wealth by a stealthy glance at the number of Gaperons.

Geheimratskäse (Ger)
Small loaf- or wheel-shaped Edam-type cheese with a few small round holes in the pale close-textured paste. Coated in wax.

Glynhynod (W)
A new cheese made in Dyfed from unpasteurized cows' milk. Semi-hard and golden with round pea-sized holes, an elastic Gouda-like texture and superb creamy taste. Made with vegetarian rennet. Also available flavoured with chives, cumin, pepper and chilli or garlic.

Gold'nRich (US)
Semi-soft buttery Brick-type cheese from Mid-West America. First made in Elgin, Illinois in the 1930s.

Gouda (Goudsche) (Hol)
The most important Dutch cheese, accounting for over two-thirds of the total production, which originated in Gouda in the 13th century, Made from full milk, it is a pressed uncooked cheese with a firm straw-coloured paste scattered with small irregular holes or a few large ones depending on the type of starter culture that has been used. The young cheeses, aged for one to four months, are very mild and buttery, but mature Goudas, sometimes ripened for as long as a year, are darker in colour and much tangier, with a fuller, richer flavour and a more pronounced spicy aroma. These mature Goudas can also be farmhouse cheeses made from unpasteurized milk, in which case they will have the word *Boeren* (*boer*, farmer) stamped on the rind. There are still about 1,000 farms in Zuid-Holland and Utrecht making Gouda by traditional methods, even though most is now factory-made. In earlier days farmers brought their cheeses every Thursday morning to the

cheese market at Gouda outside the 17th-century cheese weigh-house (*Kaaswag*) and, after a ritual bargaining over price, the deals were customarily sealed with a slapping of hands (*handje-klap*). Nowadays a version of this ceremony is presented for tourists.

Gouda is produced in various sizes. The smallest, Baby Gouda or Lunchkaas, is usually eaten young, after four weeks' ripening, and is factory- and farmhouse-made. Amsterdammer, ripened for four to eight weeks, is a small, softer, creamier Gouda with a higher moisture content than usual and a distinctive shiny orange rind. There is also a version flavoured with cumin seeds. Gouda is an excellent cooking cheese at all stages of its maturity: it is used as a melting cheese when young, especially in the *kaasdoop*, the Dutch version of fondue, and as a grating cheese when older. Traditionally eaten with brown bread and boiled potatoes.

Grevéost (Scan)
The Swedish version of Emmental, but softer, paler and with huge round eyes. Ripened for about ten months.

Güssing (Aus)
Mild sweetish cheese with a springy consistency and a golden buttery paste made from partly skimmed milk.

Havarti (Scan)
Named after the farm owned by Hanne Nielsen, pioneering 19th-century cheesemaker who scoured Europe in search of new techniques and, almost single-handed, revitalized the then moribund Danish cheese industry. Her greatest success was Havarti, once known as Danish Tilsit. It is a supple, creamy, washed-rind cheese with innumerable irregular holes throughout the paste. Fairly full-flavoured at about three months old, it becomes stronger and more pungent with age. The higher-fat version (60 per cent) is richer, slightly softer and may be flavoured with caraway seeds. It has no rind and is usually vacuum-packed in blocks or drums.

Herefordshire (Eng)
Made from May to October from the unpasteurized milk of Welsh Black or Jersey cattle. Sold at various stages from semi-soft to hard. Occasionally blued naturally.

Hertog van Brabant (Belg)
Creamy cows' milk cheese similar to Saint-Bernard.

Hushaållsost (Scan)
'Household cheese', one of Sweden's oldest types, smooth, mild and creamy with a faintly acidic edge. The paste is straw-coloured, either with small, round, regular holes or with irregular holes and slits. Sometimes spiced with cumin and cloves. Ripened for one to three months.

Jarlsberg (Scan)
Based on an old Norwegian type but re-invented in the 1950s and now extremely popular. A good all-purpose cheese with a mellow, slightly sweet flavour and an elastic texture rather similar to Dutch Gouda. The paste is golden yellow with variously sized

round holes. Factory-made from pasteurized milk and ripened for six months. A great deal is exported, particularly to the United States.

Kaggost (Scan)

Semi-hard, mild cows' milk cheese from Sweden with a springy creamy yellow paste sometimes spiced with cumin seeds and cloves. Wheel-shaped, ripened for one to three months and mild apart from the spices.

Kampanjebrood op stro (Belg)

Literally 'country loaf on straw' in Belgian. A semi-hard cows' milk cheese, mellow-flavoured, sold on a straw mat.

Kesti (Scan)

Type of Tilsit flavoured with caraway seeds. From Finland.

Lajta (Hu)

Piquant pale yellow cheese with numerous elliptical holes and a deep orange, moist, washed rind. Ripened for four weeks.

Lancashire (Eng)

White, slightly salty, crumbly cheese with a rich, full-bodied flavour. Lancashire is underrated even in England, probably because most people know only the creamery type. An infinitely superior farmhouse version is made from unpasteurized milk on five farms in the Preston area. Making Lancashire in the traditional way is a laborious and time-consuming process. The curd made on one day is added to the previous day's curd, which has already been drained, salted and partly pressed. Both curds are then milled, placed in moulds, pressed for 24 hours, bandaged, waxed and ripened for (at best) two months. Lancashire is the softest of the English pressed cheeses. It is an excellent melting cheese and is therefore ideal for cooking. See *Sage Lancashire*

Llangloffan (W)

A creamy cheese made from unpasteurized Jersey milk near Haverfordwest. Mild, matured or flavoured with chives and garlic.

Maasdam (Hol)

A factory-made, recently developed cheese similar to Swiss Emmental, It has a firm, plump, golden body with many large holes caused by the action of propionic acid bacteria added to the curds. Ripened for at least four weeks. The flavour is sweetish and mildly nutty. Maasdam is commonly sold under trade names such as Westberg and Leerdammer.

Mahón (Sp)

Made in the Balearic islands, particularly in Menorca. It has a white, creamy, soft paste becoming harder and darker with age. The rind is yellowy brown and hard with darker patches. The cheeses are moulded in cloths, salted in brine and ripened for 20 days or longer, and coated in olive oil.

Mamirolle (Fr)

Made in Franche Comté from pasteurized milk, a recently invented, lightly pressed, washed-rind cheese. Reminiscent of German Limburger but gentler in every respect.

Manteca, Manteche (It)

Cheeses similar to Burrini but larger, with a lump of butter encased in a coating of *pasta filata*, either Mozzarella, Provolone of Cacio-cavallo. The butter is usually whey butter made as a by-product of the two latter cheeses. Made in a variety of shapes (loaf, pear, ball, etc.) and sometimes smoked. The cheese jacket preserves the butter—a useful device in a hot climate before refrigeration was common. Originally from Basilicata.

Maredsous (Belg)

Type of Saint-Paulin, rectangular with a white powdery rind.

Maribo (Scan)

Fuller in flavour than Samsø-type cheeses, Maribo has a firmer, drier paste scattered with numerous irregular holes. Ripened for about four months. Usually coated in yellow wax. From Denmark.

Mesost *(Scan)*

'Whey cheese' made in Sweden by heating whey (a proportion of whole milk, cream or buttermilk is usually added nowadays) to precipitate the residual protein matter. For a whey cheese like Italian Ricotta the process stops at this point. For Mesost the boiling continues until the liquid is reduced considerably and the solids condense into a sticky brown mass caused by caramelization of the milk suger (lactose). This is then poured into moulds, cooled, cut up into blocks and packed in foil or boxes. Extra sugar and spices are sometimes added. Whey cheese with cream added may be soft and spreadable, but more usually it is firm and close textured, light tan in colour with a bitter-sweet flavour.

Mischlingkäse (Aus)

A dark golden cheese with an orangey dry rind. It has a pleasantly spicy aroma and a full-bodied sharpish flavour. The paste is scattered with a few irregular holes. Made in the mountains of western Austria.

Molbo (Scan)

Although Danish, in flavour and appearance almost identical to the red-waxed exported Dutch Edam.

Mondseer (Aus)

Firm, moist, butter cheese with a few irregular eyes and a soft dry rind. Also called Mondseer Schachtelkäse.

Monterey Jack (US)

Distantly related to Cheddar and first made in Monterey, California in the 1840s. There are two kinds: High Moisture Jack is made from whole milk, ripened for up to six weeks and rather bland and buttery; Dry Jack is a hard tangy grating cheese made from skimmed or partly skimmed milk and ripened for six months or more. Dry Jack is also sold as Grating-Type Monterey. Both cheeses are moulded in various shapes and sizes and sold waxed or vacuum-packed. Dry Jack is often oiled black.

Montségur (Monségur) (Fr)

Factory-made, fairly tasteless pressed cheese from Ariège in the foothills of the Pyrenees. It

has a thin washed rind, artificially blackened. Sometimes pepper flavoured.

Morbier (Fr)

An odd-looking cheese made in mountain chalets in the Juras during the winter. The pale yellow smooth paste is divided horizontally by a band of blue-black soot or powdered charcoal. Traditionally the cheese was made partly from morning milk and partly from evening milk coagulated separately. The layer of soot protected the morning curds until the evening curds were placed on top. A mellow cheese, virtually odourless, with a light grey dry rind.

Mutschli (Sw)

Originally a mountain cheese now made all over Switzerland from pasteurized and unpasteurized milk. Fragrant, sweet-tasting with irregular holes and a warm, slightly rough, golden crust.

Nantais (Fr)

The most important Breton cheese, invented in the last century by a priest from the Vendée. A pressed, uncooked cheese with a full flavour and pronounced smell. Golden, light brown rubbery rind. Usually made from pasteurized milk. Also called Curé, Fromage du Curé.

Nøkkelost (Scan)

A milder copy of Dutch Leiden. *Nøkkel* means 'keys' in Norwegian, recalling the crossed keys emblem of Leiden cheese.

Óvár, Ovari (Hu)

A pressed Tilsit-type made from pasteurized milk.

Pantallyn (W)

Caerphilly-type cheese made from unpasteurized Jersey milk with vegetarian rennet. The cows are raised organically.

Patagras (LA)

Springy, mild, firm cheese with a red waxed rind similar to Gouda. Made from whole or partly skimmed pasteurized milk in Cuba.

Pavé d'Auge (Fr)

Washed-rind cheese which looks like a much larger Pont l'Evêque. Fairly firm yellow paste with lots of small elliptical holes. Strong-tasting, almost bitter. The rind is thick, resilient, ridged, dull orange in colour and smeared with powdery white moulds. Ripened for two to four months. Made in the Pays d'Auge. (*Pavé*, 'slab' or 'paving stone'). Also called Pavé de Moyaux, Carré de Bonneville.

Pinzgauer Bierkäse (Aus)

A piquant washed-rind cheese made in Salzburg.

Poivre d'Auvergne (Fr)

Recently invented cheese with a smooth, dense, pale yellow paste and a hard, black, shiny, artificial rind. Creamy, mild and flavoured with crushed black peppercorns.

Pompadour (Hol)

Trade name for a new, smooth, creamy cheese made in several versions: Naturel (mild with a white rind), Rouge (mild, coloured red with annatto, white rind), Pikant (sharp, ripened for 12 weeks. brown rind), Alt (very strong, ripened for 24 weeks, black rind). Also flavoured with caraway seeds (yellow rind) or herbs (green rind).

Port-Salut, Port-du-Salut (Fr)

The archetypal monastery cheese, lightly pressed with a tawny washed rind and smooth, springy, semi-soft paste. The flavour is full and mellow with a slight edge but not so tangy as other washed-rind cheeses. Port-du-Salut originated in the early 19th century at the abbey of Entrammes near Laval in the *département* of Mayenne. The abbey was the home of a community of Cistercian monks from 1233 until the Revolution, when it and many other similar establishments were forced to close and their occupants flee the country. In 1915 a group of Trappists, returning from exile in Switzerland, were allowed to make use of the abbey, which they renamed L'Abbaye de Notre Dame de Port-du-Salut. Their cheeses, influenced by Swiss techniques, became well-known in Parisian markets under the description *façon Port-du-Salut*. Such was the demand for these cheeses that they were widely imitated and the monks took steps to protect their product. Finally in 1938 the name Port-Salut was legally defined as the trade mark of Port-du-Salut cheeses and cheeses with either name are the same. This mark was sold after World War II to a commercial enterprise but the monks continued making their own cheeses, which are now sold under the name of the abbey, Entremmes. See *Entrammes, Saint-Paulin.*

Prästost (Scan)

'Priest's cheese', made in Sweden for 200 years. Now mostly factory-made, often from a mixture of pasteurized and unpasteurized milk. Also called Prestost, Saaland Pfarr.

Pressato (It)

Firm, yellow, cooked cheese with many uneven holes spread throughout the paste, made from partly skimmed milk. It was first developed in Vicenza as a variant of Asiago. Pressato is a more even-tempered cheese than Asiago and, at least locally, is now more popular. Unlike Asiago, it is salted partly before and partly after being pressed, it ripens in a much shorter time—about 40 days maximum—and is eaten only as a dessert cheese. The flavour is pleasantly sweet and fragrant.

Pyrénées (Fr)

Two types of cheese are sold in France under this designation. One is a factory-made cows' milk cheese, with a shiny black thin rind and a firm springy yellow paste punctuated by many small holes. The flavour is mild and rather indifferent. The other is a ewes' milk cheese with a firm golden orange rind, a very smooth dense paste with few holes and a tangy flavour. Related to the classic Pyrenean ewes' milk cheeses such as Ardi-Gasna, Esbareich, Ossau-Iraty-Brebis and Laruns.

Raclette (Sw)

Literally 'scraper', the name given to a family of semi-hard cheeses mostly from the canton of Valais. A firm, buttery cheese made from

unpasteurized milk, it has a golden paste with a few small holes and a rough grey-brown rind deeply impressed with the name of the cheese. The flavour is full and fruity and similar to Gruyère. Eaten as it is or particularly suitable for use in the traditional Swiss dish also called *raclette*. To make raclette a whole cheese is sliced in half and the cut surface placed before an open fire. As the cheese melts it is scraped on to a dish and eaten immediately with potatoes boiled in their skins, pickled onions and gherkins. There are many types of Raclette cheese. Among those officially recognized as the best are Anniviers, Bagnes, Binn, Conches, Gomser, Haudères, Heida, Illiez, Orsières, Simplon and Walliser.

Ragusano (It)

From Ragusa, Sicily, whose flowery meadows produce fine-quality milk with a high fat content and give this *pasta filata* cows' milk cheese its particular flavour and aroma. It can either be steeped in brine and aged for up to six months as a table cheese, or ripened longer, when the rind is rubbed with olive oil, to produce a grating cheese with a strong, spicy flavour.

Rasskäse (Sw)

A type of Appenzell made with skimmed milk, giving it a very low fat content of around 16 per cent. Much darker, sharper and more pungent than ordinary Appenzell.

Reblochon (Fr)

One of the magnificent cheeses from the mountains of Haute-Savoie, in particular the Aravis Massif centring on Thônes. Reblochon uses the pasteurized or unpasteurized milk of Tarentaise cattle and is made by farms, *fruitières* and large dairies. It is a lightly pressed, scalded cheese with a supple creamy paste and firm pinkish-brown washed rind. The flavour is mild, fruity and absolutely delicious. It gets rather bitter as it ages. Usually ripened for about five weeks. Sold between two paper-thin wooden discs. The name comes from a dialect word for second milking which refers not to the second milking of the day but to the particularly rich milk that is left in the cow towards the end of a milking. This was very often appropriated by the cowherds themselves. It would be left in the cow until the farm proprietor had safely departed from checking the milk yield and then used to make their own cheese, namely Reblochon. Protected by an *appellation d'origine.*

Ridder (Scan)

A Norwegian variety similar to Saint-Paulin with an orange, lightly washed rind and a rich buttery paste.

Royalp (Sw)

Introduced in the 19th century by German cheesemakers and known as Tilsit in Switzerland and Royalp abroad. More like Appenzell than German Tilsit, it is firmer with far fewer more regularly shaped holes. It has a rather mild flavour with a spicy, piquant aftertaste. The unpasteurized version, made only in eastern Switzerland where the cheese originated, is marked with a red label. The pasteurized version, made all over the country, has a green label.

Sage Derby (Eng)

Derby with green marbling produced by soaking sage leaves in chlorophyll and adding the juice to the curds. This process produces a more subtle flavour than the chopped leaves used in Sage Lancashire. Spinach juice was once used. See *Derby*

Sage Lancashire (Eng)

Farmhouse Lancashire with chopped sage added to the curds. The flavour of sage is overpowering for some tastes. Sage cheeses were traditionally made for festive occasions such as Christmas and harvest festivals. See *Lancashire*

Saint-Bernard (Belg)

Similar to Dutch Gouda. Lightly salty with a tough black rind and a creamy yellow smooth paste.

Saint-Nectaire (Fr)

From the Dore mountain in the Auvergne, an ancient cheese made twice a day from morning and evening milk separately. Pressed for 24 hours and ripened on rye straw for two months. The natural crust shows patches of red, yellow and white moulds. It has a firm, golden paste with a gentle mellow flavour. The *fermier* type has an oval plaque on the crust. The factory version has a rectangular plaque. A good melting cheese and a good keeping one. Protected by an *appellation d'origine*

Saint-Paulin (Fr)

A factory-made descendant of Port-du-Salut made from pasteurized milk throughout the year all over France. It has a smooth, bright orange rind and a buttery yellow interior. A pressed uncooked cheese, it is ripened for about two months and has a mild, bland flavour. Also made in other countries.

Saint-Rémy (Fr)

Lightly pressed washed-rind cheese similar to Gérômé. It has a mid-brown rind, springy pale yellow paste, pronounced smell and a tangy flavour. From Franche Comté and Lorraine.

Samsø (Scan)

The everyday all-purpose Danish cheese, supposedly inspired by Emmental; it has the holes, though not so many nor so large, but the consistency of the paste is more reminiscent of Cheddar. Like Cheddar it is sold fairly young (about eight to ten weeks old), when it is mild and sweet, or it is aged for several months more to become stronger and more pungent. Named after the island of Samsø and the direct ancestor of many Danish cheese types. See *Danbo, Elbo, Fynbo, Tybo.*

San Simón (Sp)

Smoked pear-shaped cheese from Lugo in Spain with a creamy paste, a glossy chestnut-coloured rind and a mildly acid flavour.

Single Gloucester (Eng)

White, open-textured cheese which is softer and milder than Double Gloucester but is also made from the milk of Gloucester cows on a single farm in Gloucestershire. The processing is conducted at a lower temperature and a lower acidity level than that of Double Gloucester. The curds are cut more finely and the cheese ripened for only about two months, Also available flavoured with herbs or nettles.

Sirene (Bulg)
The most popular and widely produced Bulgarian cheese. Basically similar to Brinza, this white brined cheese is made either from ewes' or cows' milk. Crumbly, sharp and salty although the cows' milk type is milder.

Sno-belle (US)
Pale soft creamy cheese with white rind flora made from a mixture of whole and skimmed milk. Similar to Camembert but firmer and more buttery with a slight mushroomy flavour.

Spycher (Sw)
Low fat, semi-hard, drum-shaped smooth yellow cows' milk cheese with a soft brown rind. Also called Fromage de Chalet.

Steinbuscherkäse (W.Ger, Ger)
A yellowy brown cube-shaped washed-rind cheese with a smooth, firm pale straw-coloured paste, mildly piquant in flavour and fairly strong smelling. First produced in the mid 19th century in Steinbusch (now Choszczno, in Poland). Ripened for between two and three months.

Steppenkäse (W.Ger)
Rich buttery greyish-yellow cheese with a pronounced full-bodied flavour. Originally made in the USSR by German immigrants from whole milk coloured with annatto and cured in cool humid conditions for about three months.

Sveciaost (Scan)
'Swedish cheese', the everyday cheese eaten in vast quantities and available in many forms and varying fat contents, spiced or unspiced, young and mild or mature and extremely piquant. These factors are endlessly permutated to produce an extended family of cheese suiting virtually all tastes.

Swaledale (Eng)
A semi-soft creamy coloured mild cheese made in Swaledale itself from unpasteurized Jersey milk. Like Wensleydale, and Cotherstone it is a legacy of William I's monastic companions, and was also once a blue ewes' milk cheese.

Tête de Moine (Sw)
A monastic cheese made only from summer milk and available in winter. The season lasts from September until March (traditionally the cheeses go on sale each year when the first leaves of autumn begin to fall). It is a delicate, creamy, pressed, uncooked cheese ripened for four to six months in cool cellars. The paste is straw yellow and the rind rough and rather greasy to touch. It was invented by Monks at Bellelay Abbey who later taught the method to local farmers. The name (meaning 'monk's head') derives, some say, from a tax levied by the abbey whereby the farmers would provide one cheese for each monk during the season. Others say it refers to the tonsured appearance of the cheese when it is served in the traditional way: with the top sliced off and the rind cut away to a depth of about 2cm (¼in) all round. The cheese is usually sliced into thin curls with a special knife and eaten sprinkled with pepper and powdered cumin. Also called Bellclay.

Tilsit(er) (Ger)
Named after the town of Tilsit (now Soviet Sovetsk), where it was first made by Dutch immigrants in the mid 19th century. It has a lovely buttery yellow paste with many small elliptical holes. The consistency is springy and elastic yet rather moist and creamy and the flavour is mild and delicate with spicy undertones. Made from whole or skimmed milk and the skimmed milk type is sometimes flavoured with caraway seeds. The curds are lightly scalded in the whey before being moulded in stainless steel hoops and, in some places, very lightly pressed. The initial ripening period lasts for about a month, during which time the cheeses are regularly washed with brine. Afterwards they are stored for about five months before being sold. The traditional shape for Tilsit is a large wheel but the loaf shape tailored to the demands of slicing machines is becoming increasingly common. (Known as Tollenser in the German Democratic Republic).

Toggenburger Ploderkäse (Sw)
Made in the Alps north of the Walensee, a cube-chaped white-pasted cheese made from skimmed milk coagulated by lactic fermentation. It is Switzerland's only sour milk cheese. The milk is usually soured naturally, then heated and the curds allowed to drain in the moulds without pressing. During the six month ripening period the cheeses become covered with a fat layer (*Speckschicht*) – not actually fat but a thick bacterial smear which is often removed before the cheeses are sold.

Tomme au Fenouil (Fr)
A Tomme de Savoie flavoured with fennel.

Tomme Fraicher (Fr)
An unripened or partly ripened Cantal or Laguiole. Used a lot in local Auvergne cuisine. Also called Tomme d'Aligot.

Tomme de Savoie (Fr)
Generic term for the countless semi-hard, pressed cows' milk cheeses made in Savoie from whole or partly skimmed milk by farms, *fruitières* and creameries. They are firm, smooth cheeses with a yellowy paste and a dry, hard powdery rind varying in colour from greyish-white to pinky brown. The flavour is usually fairly mild and nutty and the fat content may be between 20 to 40 per cent.

Torta (San) Gaudenzio (It)
One of several trade names for Gorgonzola con Mascarpone: alternate layers of these two cheeses pressed together like a gâteau. The mixture of Gorgonzola and Mascarpone is a traditional one, originating in the Trieste area, where it may also be flavoured with anchovy and caraway seeds.

Turunmaa (Scan)
Originating in the 1500s from the south-west of Finland, a rich, slightly sharp cheese, deli-

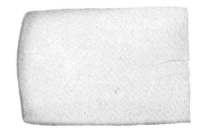

Port-Salut

Reblochon

Sage Derby

Tilsit

Tybo

Wensleydale

cously creamy and smooth-textured. Almost entirely factory-made. Ripened for two months. Usually eaten for breakfast. The name means 'Turkuland' and derives from Finland's oldest city. Often sold under brand names such as Korsholm and Mazurka.

Tybo (Scan)
Smaller and with more holes but virtually identical to Elbo. A caraway-flavoured version is also available from Denmark.

Ulloa (Sp)
A mild cheese with a white paste and a springy yellow rind. The curds are scooped into cheese cloths, moulded and lightly pressed before being ripened. Made in the Spanish provinces of La Coruna, Lugo and Pontevedra. Also called Gallego and Patela.

Vachard (Fr)
Cheese similar to Saint-Nectaire made on farms in Puy-de-Dôme. Tangy with a smooth grey crust.

Vacheloo (Belg)
A cows' milk Saint-Paulin type: plain (yellow rind), spiced (back rind) or with peppercorns (red rind).

Vacherin Fribourgeois (Sw)
Quite a different cheese from Vacherin Mont d'Or but often confused with it. This is mountain cheese, one of the oldest in Switzerland, dating back to the 15th century. Made only in the canton of Fribourg from pasteurized or unpasterurized milk. Smaller and softer than Gruyère, it has a dull yellow paste with many small holes and slits. The rind is pinkish brown and rather coarse. There are two kinds: Vacherin à Foundue is winter-made from a mixture of whole or skimmed milk and is used mainly in *fondue fribourgeoise* or *foundue moitié-moitié*, mixed half and half with Gruyère; Vacherin à la Main is softer, maturing after about three months.

Västerbottenost (Scan)
'West Bothnian cheese', invented in the mid-19th century and still exclusively made in West Bothnia, Sweden. A strong-tasting friable cheese ripened for about a year.

Weisslackerkäse (Ger)
The shiny white surface of this Bavarian cuboid cheese is presumably responsible for the name, which means 'white lacquer'. It is a surface-ripened cheese, developed about 100 years ago, and is extremely pungent with a powerfully piquant flavour, becoming even more pronounced with age. Made from a mixture of skimmed evening and whole morning milk, it is salted, dry or in brine, for two to three days before being placed in conditions of high humidity for a few more days, the cheeses just touching, for the surface flora to develop. They are then separated and ripened for up to seven months. Also called Weisslacker Bierkäse.

Wensleydale (Eng)
Until the 1920s, Wensleydale meant the blue-veined cheese we know as Blue Wensleydale. Now, however, the white, unveined version is much more common and is what you will get if you ask for Wensleydale. It is a lightly pressed, smooth-textured cheese with a subtle, milky flavour which is clean and refreshing. Generally eaten young, at about a month old. It is not a cheese that improves with age, though a prize specimen may be matured for a few months longer. Traditionally eaten with apple pie, gingerbread or fruitcake.

White Wensleydale is often unfairly compared with Blue on the grounds that it is not 'the real thing'. Yet nor is the Blue. The original Wensleydale was a ewes' milk, soft, blue-veined cheese which must have been somewhat similar to Roquefort. This and other cheeses, such as Swaledale, Gotherstone and Coverdale (now extinct) were introduced into England by monastic orders who settled in the Yorkshire Dales after the Norman Conquest in 1066. The Wensleydale recipe was the property of the Cistercian monks of Jervaulx Abbey but other monasteries also made cheeses, usually, it seems, from ewes' milk. Some time after the Dissolution of the Monasteries in the 16th century, Wensleydale and other cheeses began to be made from cows' milk and production moved first to farmhouses and then later to small dairies. See *Blue Wensleydale*

White Stilton (Eng)
Bland, close-textured white cheese made in the same way as Blue Stilton except that *Penicillium roquefortii* is not added to the milk and the cheese is sold at about eight weeks old. If left, a White Stilton will blue naturally and this produces a slightly milder flavour than the 'normal' blue. See *Blue Stilton*

Wilstermarschkäse (Ger)
An ivory-coloured slightly sour-tasting cheese from Wilster in Schleswig Holstein and, like Tilst, said to have been invented by Dutch immigrants. It can be made from whole or partly skimmed milk and is ripened for about four weeks. Also called Holsteinermarschkäse, Marschkäse.

SOFT CHEESE

During the making of soft cheeses the curd is treated very gently. It is either never cut at all except when layered into moulds or it is lightly broken up and stirred before being moulded. It is very rarely pressed, and the whey drains naturally. Soft paste cheeses with a bloomy, unwashed rind are matured for about a month, and a white furry mould is allowed to develop which may be eaten. They are creamy, mild and buttery and should never be eaten when there is even a hint of ammonia. Examples are Brie and Camembert. Soft cheeses with washed rinds such as Pont L'Eveque and Munster are slightly less moist and may have a pungent aroma but are often rather sweet tasting. These washed rinds are rarely eaten.

Baguette (Fr)
Recently invented cheese from Laon. A type of Maroilles with a rich creamy yellow paste, a soft brown washed rind and the typical aroma of this family of cheeses. Factory-made and ripened in humid conditions for three or four months. Best from summer to the end of the year. Usually sold boxed. A smaller, rather milder version is known as Demi-Baguette. Also called Baguette Laonnaise, Baguette de Thierache.

Belle Bressane (Fr)
Modern, soft, blue-veined cheese shaped like a ring and made from pasteurized milk. Fairly mild, rich and creamy.

Bonchester (Scot)
Made from March to December near Hawick from unpasteurized Jersey cows' milk by a variation of the Camembert method. Eaten young and mild or ripened for up to five weeks.

Bondaroy au Foin (Fr)
Small soft tangy cheese with a smooth, greyish rind covered with wisps of hay. Ripened in hay for about five weeks, hence the name (*foin*, hay). Also called Pithiviers au Foin.

Bondon (Fr)
Originally a farmhouse cheese produced almost entirely for domestic consumption but now increasingly made in small dairies and factories on a commercial basis. It is a fresh or barely ripened soft cheese, with a light covering of white rind flora and comes from the Pays de Bray in Normandy, noted for its cider. The name Bondon reflects the shape of the cheese, which is similar to the *bonde* or bung of a cider barrel. Also called Bonde, Bondard, Bondart or, when flavoured with garlic, Bondail. There are several sizes and the ripening period varies from a few days for small cheeses (Bondons) to a few weeks for the largest ones (Bondards). Some very large ones were at one time ripened for several months and eaten on festive occasions by which time they were very piquant and the white rind had darkened to a brownish red. The name is also used for other similar cheeses moulded in the same shape, such as Bondon Neufchâtel. Cheeses like this have been made for at least 1,000 years.

Bouille, La (Fr)
Full-flavoured double-cream cheese from Normandy. Ripened for between two and three months. Covered with a thin downy white mould tinged with pink. Fairly strong fruity smell.

Boulette (Belg)
There are various local types of Boulette (those from Namur, Huy, Charleroi and Romedenne are the best known and most widely available). All are small, soft, surface-ripened farmhouse cheeses moulded into cylinders, drums, rolls and balls and variously flavoured with herbs, rolled in crushed spices or wrapped in leaves. Fairly strident in flavour and aroma. Generically related to the Boulette of French Flanders.

Boulette d'Avesnes (Fr)
There are two versions of this cheese. The authentic farmhouse type is made by heating buttermilk and draining and seasoning the resultant solids with herbs and spices. This mixture is then kneaded to a smooth paste, hand-moulded into small cones and ripened for at least three months in a humid environment, during which time the cheeses are regularly washed, usually with beer. The commercial type is ripened in the same way but uses unripened maroilles curds rather than buttermilk solids as a base. both cheeses are very tangy and strong-smelling with bright red rinds, which are natural in the case of farmhouse cheeses but often tinted in factory products. From Flanders.

Bouquet des Moines (Belg)
A type of Boulett, small, shaped like a tall drum and with a light covering of white rind flora.

Boursault (Fr)
Small factory-made, triple-cream cheese, using pasteurized milk. Very rich and creamy with a soft, bloomy rind tinged with pink. Mildly aromatic and just mellow in flavour. Avoid it if at all red or runny. Named after its inventor and made in Normandy and the Île de France. A herb-flavoured version is also available. Sometimes called Lucullus.

Boursin (Fr)
Small, factory-made, triple-cream cheese using pasteurized milk. Available plain or flavoured with garlic and herbs, or crushed peppercorns. Should be eaten fresh.

Braided Cheese (US)
Of Armenian origin, strips of fresh *pasta filata* cheese plaited or twisted together. Very white, rubbery and quite tasteless unless flavoured with caraway or nigella seeds (Nigella damascena, better known as Love-in-a-mist). Not usually eaten raw but often melted and used in cooking. Also called String Cheese.

Brie (Fr)
After Camembert, the most famous and most imitated of all French cheeses. It is, in fact, a much older cheese than Camembert and can be documented by name at least as far back as the 13th century. It boasts a string of illustrious admirers including, it seems, virtually

Brie de Meaux

Camembert

Coeur de Bray

Fongéru

Limburger

all the kings and queens of France. Even Louis XVI, before his execution, asked for '*du vin rouge et du Brie*'. Its supremacy was finally confirmed at the Congress of Vienna in 1814. A cheese contest, organized by Talleyrand to relieve the boredom of the assembled throng of diplomats and princes, resulted in the unanimous proclamation of Brie as '*le roi des fromages*'. The Brie in question was Brie de Meaux. The term Brie covers a small family of cheeses, nowadays much depleted, but all of which at one time carried the name of the particular place where they were made. All are soft, unpressed, naturally drained cows' milk cheeses with white rind flora, moulded into large flat discs and ripened for three to four weeks. Nowadays Brie is made all over France and in many other countries as well. There are numerous modern variations on the traditional cheese, such as herb- and pepper-flavoured Bries and versions with blue and/or white internal moulds. The classic farm-made Bries of Brie itself are regrettably becoming overshadowed by their more glamorous descendants.

All Bries should be full-flavoured, fruity and mildly tangy. Ideally, the paste is rich, glossy and straw-coloured. It should be plump and smooth but not runny. Avoid cheeses with a hard, chalky centre and any that are liquefying. The rind should be firm but tender, not hard or sticky. The smell should be clean and pleasantly mouldy. Cheeses that smell of ammonia are dangerously overripe and should not be eaten. Always buy Brie cut from a whole cheese.

Brie Laitier (Fr)
The commercial version of Brie made from pasteurized milk, both throughout France and in other countries as well. The rind flora should be perfectly white with possibly some browning at the edges. The interior is generally paler in colour than most farmhouse cheeses. Ripened for about three weeks. Often sold pre-packed in wedge-shaped boxes. See *Brie*

Brie de Meaux (Fr)
Brie *fermier* made in the Île de France from unpasteurized milk. The rind is darker with more red-brown coloration than is acceptable in Brie Laitier. Very fruity. Ripened for five to six weeks. Protected by an *appellation d'origine*. See *Brie*

Brie de Melun Affiné (Fr)
Brie *fermier* made in the Île de France from unpasteurized milk. Very dark rind with traces of white. Fairly firm, golden paste, strong smelling and tangy, ripened for about seven weeks. The mould *Penicillium candidum*, develops naturally on the surface. The strongest of the Bries, it is the original from which all the others have descended. Protected by an *appellation d'origine*. See *Brie*

Brillat-Savarin (Fr)
Soft, triple-cream cheese made in Forges-les-Eaux, Normandy. Mild with a rich buttery paste and a light bloomy rind.

Cambridge (Eng)
One of the few traditional soft cheeses still occasionaly available—a delectable mixture of plain and annatto-coloured curds made from raw or pasteurized cows' milk curdled with rennet. Sold fresh or ripened for a few weeks.

Camembert (Fr)
One of the three great Normandy cheeses, Camembert, in name at least, is relatively young in cheesemaking terms—a mere 280 years old. As a type it is certainly much older. The Pays d'Auge, still the best source of good Camembert, was known for its cheese as far back as the 11th century. ('*Fromage d'angelons*', ancestors of Pont L'Evêque, were mentioned in the *Roman de la Rose* [1236].) In 1702, 90 years before Mme Harel is credited with the 'invention' of Camembert, it was mentioned, along with Livarot, as being sold in the market at Vimoutiers. But Mme Harel did for Camembert what Mrs Paulet did for Stilton: she refined the recipe and launched it into the wider world. Like Mrs Paulet, she passed her secrets on to her daughter, whose husband, Victor Paynel, presented one of his wife's best cheeses to Napoleon III. With the royal seal of approval, the future of Camembert was assured. But two further developments were essential to its subsequent spectacular commercial success. One was the invention of the chipwood box in the 1890s. (Previously the cheeses were wrapped in sizes in paper and straw and rarely survived distances farther than Paris.) The second was the introduction in 1910 of *Penicillium candidum*, the snowy white mould which is sprinkled or sprayed on the surfaces of the cheeses. Previously, Camembert rinds were often blue.

Camembert is now made in enormous quantities in virtually every country in Europe and in the United States. In France it accounts for over 20 per cent of total cheese production. Most of this is factory-made from pasteurized milk and whatever the merits of these cheeses, they simply do not compare with the traditional hand-made Normandy cheeses using unpasteurized milk from local herds. These are in season from the end of spring through to the autumn. Check the label for the words *fromage fermier, lait cru* or *non pasteurisé* and the initials V.C.N.—*Véritable Camembert de Normandie*. If it also says Pays d'Auge, so much the better. The rind should be smooth and supple, the creamy white mould flecked with red, not cracked, crumpled or sticky. The paste should be plump and pale golden in colour with no chalky or greyish patches. It should not be runny or sunken in the middle. The smell should be clean and lightly fruity with no trace of ammonia.

Caprice des Dieux (Fr)
Factory-made, oval, double-cream cheese with white rind flora and a mild flavour. Sold boxed.

Carré de Bray (Fr)
From the Pays de Bray, Normandy, a small, Neufchâtel-type cheese made in small dairies in spring and summer.

Carré de l'Est (Fr)
Camembert type from Champagne and Lorraine. Mostly factory-made from pasteurized milk. Mild but slightly salty. The white

rind flora should be smooth with no red or grey streaks. The export version is usually smaller.

Cassette de Beaumont (Belg)

Smooth, pale, creamy cheese moulded into a rough rectangular shape. A type of Boulette flavoured with salt and pepper. Sometimes sold in small willow baskets.

Cendré (Fr)

Generic term for small soft cheeses ripened in wood ash for about two months. They are often strong and pungent. Beech, poplar, vine stems or any other suitable timber provide the ashes. Shaped into small discs, truncated cones or pyramids with greyish-black rinds. Traditionally prepared for consumption by farm workers during the harvest period particularly in Champagne.

Chaource (Fr)

Milky white smooth-pasted cheese with a dryish rather than creamy consistency. It has a thin covering of white rind flora closely covered with a paper wrapping. Named after a small village near Toyes, it has a pleasantly fruity lactic flavour. Made mostly in small dairies from whole unpasteurized milk. Best in summer and autumn. Protected by an *appellation d'origine*.

Cîteaux (Fr)

Pressed, washed-rind cheese made in the monastery of the same name in Burgundy. Made from unpasteurized milk, it has a clean, fairly tangy flavour. Lightly dotted with holes. Should not be too smelly.

Cœur d'Arras (Fr)

Heart-shaped, soft, washed-rind, cows milk cheese with a fairly strong flavour. Similar to Maroilles.

Cœur de Bray (Fr)

A kind of heart-shaped Neufchâtel. Fruity with a faint lactic edge. From the Pays de Bray in Normandy.

Cœurmandie (Fr)

Factory-made heart-shaped soft cheese with white rind flora.

Colommiers (Fr)

Sometimes called Petit Brie or Bri de Coulommiers and made, mostly in factories, in the same area as Brie. Much smaller in size and eaten younger, preferably as the surface mould is beginning to appear (after ripening for a month). At this stage the flavour is quite mild and delicate: allowed to ripen further it becomes increasingly reminiscent of Camembert. Slower ripening cheeses enriched with added cream can sometimes be found as can those made from unpasteurized milk. See *Fougéru*

Convive (Sw)

Small, soft, rich cows' milk cheese with white rind flora.

Délice de Saint-Cyr (Fr)

Rich, mild, triple-cream cheese with white rind flora. Ripened for three weeks. Factory-made in the Île de France.

Epoisses (Fr)

Smooth, pungent, washed-rind cheese made in Burgundy. Spicy, tangy and occasionally also flavoured with black pepper, cloves or fennel. It has a rich orange-red rind which is washed either in white wine or eau-de-vie-de-marc (a job which was at one time allocated to orphans or other children dependent on public welfare).

Excelsior (Fr)

Invented in 1890, a double-cream Normandy cheese with white rind flora, very smooth, mild and delicate.

Exmoor (Eng)

Semi-soft pale moist cheese with a fresh, clean flavour. Made from unpasteurized Jersey milk on the same Devon farm as Devon Garland and Satterleigh.

Explorateur (Fr)

Rich triple-cream cheese made in small dairies in the *département* of Seine-et-Marne. Virtually odourless with a light covering of snowy white mould. Mild flavour. Ripened for three weeks.

Fior di Latte (It)

The official designation for Mozzarella made with cows' milk, meaning 'the cream of the milk'.

Fougéru (Fr)

A type of Coulommiers ripened in fronds of bracken.

Fresa (It)

A Caciotta—mild, sweet, almost sugary—made from cows' or goats' milk in Sardinia.

Frühstückskäse (Ger)

'Breakfast cheese'. Cheese is an important ingredient of the German breakfast, especially the *Zweites Frühstück*, the 'second breakfast' taken mid-morning, which fills in the gaps left by the first one.

This cheese is a small version of the Limburger type made from whole or partly skimmed milk and eaten either fresh or after a short ripening period, when the surface becomes smeared with coryne moulds.

Gérôme (Fr)

Washed-rind cheese similar to Munster. Made in the Vosges mostly from pasteurized milk. Sometimes flavoured with cumin seeds and sold as Gérômé Anise.

Gournay (Fr)

A type of small Camembert from the Pays de Bray, ripened for no more than a week. The rind has a light down and the flavour is fairly mild. Strictly speaking this is Gournay Affiné.

Grand Rustique (Fr)

Soft cheese with white rind flora made from unpasteurized milk. The paste is buttery yellow and almost foamy in consistency with a delicate flavour. Looks like a small Brie and sometimes sold as a Camembert *non pasteurisé*.

Herve (Belg)

Generic term for a family of strong pungent cheeses, of which Remoudou is the best known, deriving from the town of Herve in northern Liège. It is a washed-rind cheese dating back at least to the mid-16th century. Its warm golden crust covers a rich velvety paste ranging from sweet to spicy depending on the length of the ripening period (two to three months). Traditional drinks with Herve cheese are coffee or port.

Kappeli (Scan)

From Finland, a strong, aromatic, washed-rind cheese similar to German Romadur.

Kernhem (Kernhemse) (Hol)

Washed-rind cheese reminiscent of traditional monastery cheeses but recently invented by the Netherlands Institute of Dairy Research. Made from slightly pasteurized milk with an augmented fat content. It is lightly pressed and ripened for about four weeks in cool humid conditions, during which time it is regularly turned and the rind washed with water. The paste is creamy and golden in colour, with a full, rich flavour. Kernhem is classed by the Dutch as a *meshanger* cheese—one that clings to the knife when cut.

Kühbacher (Ger)

Soft cheese made near Munich from a mixture of whole and partly skimmed milk.

Kümmelkäse (Ger)

A small, soft, washed-rind, low-fat cheese made from partly skimmed cows' milk and flavoured with caraway seeds.

Liederkrantz (US)

Soft, moist, washed-rind cheese invented by Emil Frey at Monroe, New York in 1892, and now made by the Borden Cheese Company in Van Wert, Ohio. Frey was apparently trying to duplicate the popular Bismarck Schlosskäse then being imported from Germany but which arrived in poor condition after the long Atlantic crossing. The new cheese turned out to be a considerably milder, less pungent form of Limburger. It has a rich velvety golden paste and a very pale brown bacterial crust. It should not be eaten overripe and goes well with beer. The name, meaning 'wreath of song', was that of a singing group to which Frey belonged. It was the Liederkrantz workers in Ohio who raised a subscription for the repair of Mme Harel's statue in Vimoutiers, France, after it had been destroyed by Allied bombardment in 1944.

Limburger (Ger)

Strictly speaking, of Belgian origin, but adopted by Alligäuer dairymen in the 19th century. A washed-rind, surface-ripened cheese with a slightly moist, typically reddish-brown skin and a creamy rich yellow paste. After moulding and draining, the cheeses are salted in brine for seven to 24 hours depending on the size of the cheese and then washed at intervals with coryne bacteria. After about a month the yellowy mould begins to develop on the surface, becoming darker and firmer during a further ripening period of eight weeks or so. Despite the many jokes surrounding the notorious ferocity of Limburger it should not, at least in appearance, be in the least menacing. As far as flavour goes, its decidedly aromatic bark is considerably worse

Livarot

Maroilles

Mozzarella

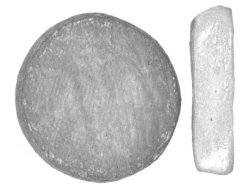

Munster

than its bite. If the paste is runny or the rind slimy it means that the cheese is overripe and well past its best. It is available in various grades according to fat content. The lower the fat the firmer the cheese.

Livarot (Fr)

One of the great Normandy cheeses and one of the oldest. Farmhouse production has now been almost entirely superseded by factory-made cheese. A washed-rind cheese with an assertive flavour and a smell to match, made from a mixture of skimmed evening and whole morning milk. Ripened in a warm, humid, unventilated environment for about three months. The rind should be a smooth, shiny brown and just moist, neither too dry nor too sticky. The paste should be golden and fairly springy. Avoid cheeses that are runny or sunken in the middle. The traditional drink with Livarot is the local cider or Calvados. Protected by an *appellation d'origine*.

Magnum (Fr)

Triple-cream cheese from the Pays de Bray. Aged about three weeks. Similar to Brillat-Savarin, Excelsior.

Mainauerkäse (Ger)

A Münster type named after an island in Lake Constance.

Mano (LA)

Pasta filata cows' milk cheese wrapped in banana leaves from Venezuela.

Mantecoso (LA)

In Peru a popular farm-made soft cheese. In Chile a semi-hard cheese similar to European monastery types.

Marienhofer (Aus)

This is a Limburger type cheese made from partly skimmed evening milk mixed with whole morning milk.

Maroilles (Fr)

The *pater familias* of flemish washed-rind cheeses. Certainly one of the most ancient cheeses, invented in the 10th century by one of the monks at the abbey of Maroilles. Since then it has acquired a string of admirers and as many variations and imitations. The rind is reddish with a light damp sheen and should not be too sticky or too dry. The paste is a smooth pale yellow and, while certainly tangy, is rather more subtle in flavour than other similar cheeses. It should not be bitter or chalky in texture. The smell is strong and full but not ammoniacal. The ripening period lasts about four months. Most Maroilles are still farmhouse-made. Smaller versions are sold under the names Maroilles-Sorbais, -Mignon and -Quart. Eaten as a dessert cheese. Protected by an *appellation d'origine*.

Minas (LA)

Bland, slightly sour acid-curd cheese made in small factories in Minas Gerais, Brazil, from whole pasteurized milk. Sold either fresh (*frescal*) or pressed and partly ripened (*prensado*). Used in cooking and eaten for breakfast and as a dessert with candied fruit or preserves.

Mon Chou (Hol)

Rich, creamy, factory-made cheese with a mild, faintly acid flavour. Sold wrapped in foil; of recent origin.

Monsieur Fromage (Fr)

Rich, delicate double-cream cheese from Normandy. It has a thick bloomy white rind and a creamy velvety yellow paste with a superb fruity flavour. Eaten fresh after six weeks' ripening or aged a little more so that the rind becomes slightly spotted with reddish patches. Invented in the last century by the appropriately named Monsieur Fromage. Also called Fromage de Monsieur.

Mozzarella (It)

The colonization of half the world by pizza chains has made Mozzarella the best-known Italian cheese after Parmesan and Gorgonzola. Melted on top of pizza it becomes quite palatable and is wonderfully stringy. In other respects, however, its flavour is one of the least interesting, especially if judged by the insipid factory product (often not Italian-made) available in most supermarkets. Choose Italian Mozzarella whenever possible and, for the best results, eat it the Italian way, dressed with olive oil, salt and freshly ground pepper and accompanied by tomatoes, olives, chillis, anchovies or even a sharp citrus fruit. Better still, if you can find it, is the original Mozzarella di Bufala (made from the milk of water buffaloes usually mixed with cows' milk) which is still made in parts of the south.

Mozzarella, which dates back to the 16th century, is a fresh *pasta filata* cheese, hand-moulded into creamy white balls and, in Italy, sold swimming in a bowl of whey. Elsewhere the cheese is wrapped in parchment or grease-proof paper or sealed into plastic bags with a little whey. Ideally it should be eaten as soon as possible after buying, but it will keep for a day or two if it is moistened with a little fresh milk and put in the refrigerator. Although Mozzarella is now made all over Italy (and in Denmark, England, and the United States among other places) the best is reputedly that from Capua, Cardito, Aversa and the Sele valley. A lightly smoked version called Mozzarella Affumicata is also available.

Apart from pizza, Mozzarella is used in the making of many dishes including *lasagne, suppli* (rice balls – with cheese in the middle) and the ubiquitous *mozzarella in carrozza* (a sandwich of bread and cheese dipped in beaten egg and milk and fried until golden brown and crunchy, while the cheese melts inside).

Munster (Fr, Ger)

An ancient cheese from Alsace and the Vosges, supposedly first made by Irish monks who settled in the area in the 7th century. The cheese is red-skinned and very spicy and tangy with an emphatic aroma like all washed-rind cheeses. The paste is buttery yellow and very rich and creamy. In Alsace itself it is often eaten when younger and milder. The farmhouse type (Munster Fermier) is made in summer in the *hautes chaumes* (literally 'high stubble') of the Vosges mountains, and in winter on farms lower down the slopes. Munster Laitier is made all year round from pasteurized milk. The ripening period is one to three months depending on the size of the cheese. Best between November and May especially, according to enthusiasts, with hot baked jacket potatoes. Protected by an *appellation d'origine* Munster (without an umlaut) is French; Münster (with an umlaut) is German. Münster has a smooth, softish, yellow paste with a thin brown skin and a mildly piquant flavour.

Neufchâtel (Fr)

Famous rich creamy cheese eaten fresh or ripened from the Pays de Bray, Normandy. The curds are finely milled, making the consistency particularly smooth and homogeneous. Nowadays mostly factory-made although farmhouse versions can still be found. Fresh Neufchâtel is white with a faint sourish lactic flavour and a bloomy white rind. Neufchâtel Affiné is darker, more golden in colour, the find shows traces of red-brown pigmentation and the flavour becomes much more pronounced and rather salty. It is moulded in a variety of shapes—heart, roll, loaf, square—known as Cœur, Bondon, Briquette and Carré. The ripened type goes particularly well with strong, full-bodied wines. Protected by an *appellation d'origine*.

Nidelchäs (Sw)

Soft creamy cows' milk cheese with a white bloomy rind. Shaped like a thick disc.

Old Heidelberg (US)

Delicate washed rind cheese similar to Liederkrantz and made in Lena, Illinois.

Olivet Bleu (Fr)

A light, almost sweet-flavoured cheese reminiscent of Coulommiers. The white rind flora has a blue tinge and arises naturally during the one-month ripening period. Sold wrapped in leaves. There is also an Olivet Centré, which is cured for three months in the ashes of vine stems and has a much stronger flavour. Olivet au Foin is ripened in hay.

Ovoli (It)

Egg-shaped Mozzarella cheeses.

Pagliarini (It)

Small, medium-ripened, softish cheeses from Piedmont, usually somewhat sour-tasting. Sold on little straw mats (*paglia*, straw), they are often eaten dressed with oil and seasoned.

Parfait (Fr)

Brand name for a triple-cream cheese made near Forges-les-Eaux. Much like Excelsior but ripened a little longer.

Passito (It)

A Stracchino made from summer milk. The paste is less moist and more compact with a rather acid taste compared to the traditional winter-made stracchino.

Pivny Sýr (Cz)

Salty 'beer cheese' similar to West German Weisslacker. Straw-coloured with a smeary yellow rind and strong sharp flavour. Ripened for four to six months. Foil-wrapped.

Plateau (Belg)

Larger, milder, firmer member of the Herve family.

Pont l'Evêque (Fr)

Probably the oldest of the Normandy cheeses, known to the author of the *Roman de la Rose* as Angelot. Since the 1600s it has been called Pont l'Evêque after the market town in Calvados which became the principal distribution point. Still made mostly on farms from unpasteurized milk, although factory production is being to gather momentum. It is a soft, rich, golden-yellow cheese with a rind that is yellowy gold or light tan depending on the finishing. During the two-month ripening period the rind may be brine-washed or simply brushed. The milk should be coagulated as soon as possible after milking. (Traditionally two batches of cheeses were made, one from morning and one from evening milk.) The curds are divided into large blocks (one per cheese) rather than cut, and these blocks are then lightly drained for ten minutes before being placed in square moulds. The smell should be moderately strong but not offensive and the flavour rich and tangy without being sharp or bitter. Larger versions (Pavé de Moyaux, Pavé d'Auge) are ripened for four to six months and are considerably stronger. Avoid cheeses where the rind is brittle or cracked. Protected by an *appellation d'origine*.

Prato (LA)

The name, meaning 'plate', derives from the original shape of the cheese. One of the most popular Brazilian types. Made from cows' milk, it is a mild, soft, pressed cheese with a deep golden waxed rind. Ripened for six to seven weeks.

Prince Jean (Belg)

Type of Boulette available in several versions: unripened (*vers*), ripened with white surface moulds (*geaffineerd*), or rolled in crushed black peppercorns (*met peper*).

Provola, Provole (It)

Can be either unripened Provolone moulded into small balls or longer ripened Mozzarella. The cheese is soft, sweet and mild with a hard wax coating. Burrini are somtimes sold under this name and Provola is sometimes sold under a brand name (e.g. Ciccillo). To add to the confusion, a variety of other diminutives may be used (such as Provolette or Provolini), but they are all basically the same (literally, tiny Provoloni). Also available smoked (*affumicata*).

Radolfzeller Rahmkäse (Ger)

Surface-ripened cheese similar to Mainauer Käse, drained on straw mats, dry salted and ripened for about a month.

Remoudou (Belg)

Belgium's famous 'stinking cheese', a particularly strong type of Herve which originated in Battice in the reign of the Emperor Charles V (1519–58). Usually larger and ripened for longer than the normal Herve, it has a darker, brownish-orange rind. The name is derived from *remoud*, a Walloon word for the exceptionally rich milk provided towards the end of the lactation period. Nowadays mostly factory-made.

Rigotte (Fr)

Very small round cheese made in Lyonnais and the Auvergne from cows' milk or a mixture of cows' and goats' milk. Usually ripened for no more than a couple of weeks. Fairly mild to tangy in flavour depending on the milk and the finishing. Some are ripened naturally, some steeped in white wine or oil. Some are artificially coloured. The name is probably a corruption of *recuite*, meaning 'recooked', or of the name Ricotta, meaning the same in Italian. Both words indicate that the cheeses are, or at least were, whey cheeses, though nowadays full milk is used. Rigotte de Condrieu, Rigotte des Alpes and Rigotte de Pélussin are the best known.

Neufchâtel

Pont-l'Evêque

Taleggio

Vacherin

Rocamadour (Fr)

Tiny cheeses made in Aquitaine from ewes' or goats' milk and ripened for one week. The same cheeses wrapped in leaves and aged for a further period in stoneware pots become extremely strong and are then known as Picadou.

Rollot (Fr)

Round or heart-shaped washed-rind cheese from Picardy. Soft and supple with a smooth, moist, orange-red surface, it is strong-smelling and has a pronounced tang. Ripened for two months. Similar to Maroilles.

Romadur (Ger)

Similar to Limburger but softer and milder. Also a washed-rind, surface-ripened cheese with a yellowish-brown skin and a rich golden paste which has a scattering of irregular holes. Made either from whole or partly skimmed milk and in various grades of fat content. The brining and ripening periods are shorter than those for Limburger, about four hours and two weeks respectively, and the flavour and aroma are consequently less assertive. It should be kept quite cool and not allowed to become overripe. Like Limburger, it originated in Belgium, where a similar cheese is known as Remoudou.

Rotschmierkäse (Ger)

Generic term for cheeses like Limburger, Romadur and Münster which have reddish skins produced by the action of coryne bacteria on the surface of the cheese during ripening.

Royal Brabant (Belg)

Small washed-rind cheese similar to Limburger.

Saint-Florentin (Fr)

Washed-rind cheese from Burgundy similar to Epoisses. It has a rich, ruddy colour, a strong smell and a spicy tang.

Saint-Gildas (Fr)

Triple-cream cheese from Brittany made with pasteurized milk. Mild and creamy, with a smooth white, bloomy rind.

Saint-Marcellin (Fr)

Used to be made with goats' milk but now a cows' milk cheese from Dauphiné. Fairly mild and unpressed. The rind is thin and covered with a light blue mould. Sometimes wrapped in chestnut leaves. It is *à point* when the paste just clings to the blade of the knife. Best between April and September.

Scamorza (It)

From Abruzzi, Italy, a type of cows' milk Mozzarella. The word means 'dunce' in southern dialect.

Schlosskäse (Aus)

Rather mild washed-rind cheese made in northern Austria.

Sharpham (Eng)

Soft Camembert-type cheese made from unpasteurized Jersey milk with vegetarian rennet. Mild and creamy.

Stracchino (It)

Stracchino is a generic term for a type of cheese that was at one time made in the autumn and winter from the milk of cows that had come down from their summer alpine pastures to be wintered on the plains. The milk of these 'tired' cows (*stracche* in the Lombardy dialect) imparted a distinctive flavour to the cheese (as a result of the change of grazing). They were also quick-ripening cheeses that in the days before refrigeration could be made only in the winter. Nowadays these cheeses are made all year round and many different types come under the same etymological umbrella. Gorgonzola is a Stracchino. So are Taleggio and some Robiola cheeses. Frequently they are sold under brand names such as Certosa, Certosino, Stracchinella, Invernizzina, Pannerino, etc. A typical representative of this group of cheeses, Stracchino-Crescenza is square-shaped, rindless, white and lusciously creamy with a rather gentle luxurious flavour. It is ripened for a maximum of ten days and should be eaten as soon as possible after that. The best Crescenza comes from around Milan and Pavia.

Subenhara (Hol)

Rich, soft, new factory-made cheese flavoured with garlic and herbs.

Taleggio (It)

Named after a small town near Bergamo, this is an unpressed uncooked cheese of the Stracchino type. The paste is white and supple with a thin pinkish-grey rind that should never be cracked or broken. The cheese ripens in about 40 days, when the flavour is mild and fruity. Under perfect conditions some cheeses can be ripened for twice as long: the flavour deepens, the cheese becomes plumper, more aromatic and the paste a deeper yellow. Taleggio made with unpasteurized milk is prized.

Teasajt (Hu)

'Tea cheese' (in Hungarian), recently invented. It has a creamy yellow paste with small round holes and a smeary rind. Rather sour. Ripened for two weeks.

Tetilla (Sp)

A flattish pear-shaped cheese with a pleasantly clean, slightly sourish, salty flavour. Made in Pontevedra, La Coruna and Lugo. Also called Perilla.

Tomme Vaudoise (Sw)

From the canton of Vaud, north of Lake Geneva, small quick-ripened cheeses made mostly in small dairies from pasteurized or unpasteurized milk. The paste is rich yellow and supple with a lightly crumpled covering of white mould which becomes streaked with red as the cheeses mature. Very mild, faintly spicy and sometimes flavoured with cumin. Ripened for about a week.

Trecce, Treccia (It)

Plaited type of Mozzarella.

Vacherin des Beauges (Fr)

Soft washed-rind cheese made in Savoie in autumn and winter. An old type suited to small farmhouse production. Ripened for three months, it has a pale pinkish-brown crust and a delicate, lightly spicy flavour. Bound with a strip of spruce bark and boxed. Also called Vacherin d'Aillons.

Vacherin Mont-d'Or (Fr)

A superb cheese made in Franche Comté, similar to Vacherin des Beauges. The larger cheeses are generally superior to the smaller ones.

Vacherin Mont d'Or (Sw)

Justly famous, a marvellous cheese when at its best, it has a rich velvety texture and a faintly resinous flavour. Made in the Vallée de Joux near the French border from unpasteurized milk and virtually identical to the French cheese of the same name. It is a winter cheese, bound with a strip of pine bark and sold in wooden boxes (in which it is also customarily served). The paste is a dull, almost greeny yellow and has the consistency of thick clotted cream. The crust, pale reddish brown rather like lightly baked bread, becomes gently crumpled when the cheese is *à point*. Served traditionally, this crust is removed in one piece and the inside scooped out with a spoon. If the cheese is sliced, the cut surfaces should be protected with a small sheet of glass or wood to prevent the paste flowing out of the crust. A whole Vacherin Mont d'Or makes a wonderfully luxurious dessert cheese. Locally it is also eaten sprinkled with cumin seeds and accompanied by plain boiled potatoes.

Weinkäse (Ger)

A small, round, creamy, mild cheese whose name derives from its particular affinity with wine. Has a superb glossy paste and a thin, smooth, pinkish skin.

A-Z
BLUE CHEESE

Blue-vein cheeses may be wholly natural but many are encouraged to blue during manufacture. The type of cheese varies from soft to hard but generally they are scalded and lightly pressed. Blue or green moulds develop in the minute spaces between the curds. Many blue cheese are pierced with fine stainless steel needles to innoculate and aerate the paste and so help the veins to spread. Other cheeses are injected with a culture of mould such as *penicillium roqueforti*. The colour of the paste of a blue cheese may range from the white of Danish Blue or Danablu to the creamy yellow of Blue Cheshire, but whatever the cheese, it should never be brown.

American Blue (US)

Based on Roquefort, but made from pasteurized cows' milk, to which *Penicillium roquefortii* has been added. Ripened for three to four months. Among the better brands are Maytag, Nauvoo and Oregon Blue.

Bavaria Blu (Ger)

A recently invented hybrid cheese with a pale creamy paste showing splodges rather than veins of blue mould. It also has the white rind flora characteristic of Camembert types. Made from pasteurized cows' milk with additional cream.

Beenleigh Blue (Eng)

Semi-hard blue-veined cheese made in Devon from the unpasteurized milk of Friesland ewes.

Blå Castello (Scan)

Recently invented, a Danish cheese with sharply defined dark blue internal veining and a downy white surface mould. Rich and fairly mild, similar to West Germany's Bavaria Blu.

Bleu d'Auvergne (Fr)

From the Massif Central, particularly the *départements* of Cantal and Puy-de-Dôme and the mountains of Cantal and Aurillac. Since each Bleu takes very much less milk to make than Cantal—the other great cheese of the area— it was more suited to the smaller farmer. The cheeses used to be brought down the mountain twice a week on donkeys or mules and sold to co-operative *affineurs* for ripening. The best Bleu d'Auvergne is still made on mountain farms by traditional methods, but a great deal is now also made in commercial dairies from pasteurized milk. It is a lightly piquant creamy cheese which has a very pale paste with sharply defined dark blue

veining throughout the body of the cheese. The mould, *Penicillium glaucum*, is added either at the renneting stage or sprinkled in powder form on to the moulded curds. The cheese is ripened in cool cellars for an initial period of two months, when it is regularly turned and pierced with steel needles to distribute the mould. Then it is wrapped in foil to mature slowly for another month or so. The label should show that it is a legally protected cheese.

Bleu de Bresse (Fr)

Mildly spicy blue-veined cheese with a rather undignified history. It is a variation on an imitation. Restrictions on the import of Gorgonzola during World War II led to the development of a French imitation known as Saingorlon. Bleu de Bresse, invented in 1950, is a smaller, more easily marketable version of the same cheese. It comes in three sizes, *mini, moyen and maxi*—weighing between 100 and 500g (3½–18oz). A factory-made product using pasteurized milk.

Bleu des Causses (Fr)

Similar to Bleu d'Auvergne but saltier. From Rouergue in the midst of the stark limestone country known as Les Causses which provides the natural caves used for ripening the cheeses. The name is legally protected.

Bleu de Corse (Fr)

Most of the ewes milk cheese made in Corsica is sent 'white' to the Roquefort caves to be blued. Bleu de Corse is the name for cheese that is ripened in Corsica itself. Since most people prefer Roquefort this cheese is fast dying out.

Bleu de Gex (Fr)

A naturally blued cheese, first made about 100 years ago. The rind is powdery dry and rather

crusty with yellowish or reddish tinges. The paste is smooth white, marbled with deep blue. Lightly pressed, it has a full flavour with a mildly sharp edge. The best is made in Saint Germain-de-Joux in summer and autumn.

Bleu du Haut-Jura (Fr)

The legal term for the much sought-after Bleu de Gex and Bleu de Septmoncel. Protected by an *appellation d'origine*.

Bleu de Laqueuille (Fr)

A lightly piquant blue from the Auvergne, invented in 1850. Factory-made and milder than Bleu d'Auvergne, it is ripened for about three months at relatively high temperatures.

Bleu du Quercy (Fr)

From Aquitaine, a blue cheese similar to Bleu d'Auvergne.

Bleu de Sassenage (Fr)

Lightly pressed blue cheese similar to Bleu de Gex made in the area of Villard-de-lans and Vallonnais in the province of Dauphiné. Uses partly skimmed milk and is ripened for about three months. Once made from cows', goats' and ewes' milk or a mixture of any two, but now exclusively from cows' milk.

Bleu de Septmoncel (Fr)

Has slightly smoother rind but otherwise virtually identical to Bleu de Gex. See *Bleu du Haut-Jura*

Bleu de Thiézac

A variation of Bleu d'Auvergne produced exclusively on mountain farms and much prized, especially from Thiézac itself.

Blue Cheshire (Eng)

A blue-veined cheese made in Shropshire and Cheshire. At one time Cheshires blued natur-

Stilton

Blue Wensleydale

ally but so rarely and unpredictably that it was more a matter of luck than judgement. This still happens occasionally and the resulting cheese is called Green Fade. Nowadays science has taken a hand and a degree of artifice is employed in the veining: *Penicillium roquefortii* is added to the milk before renneting. The cheese is pressed less than ordinary Cheshire and is aerated with steel needles during ripening. Only red farmhouse Cheshires are 'blued' and the maturation period is a little longer than usual—about three months. Blue Cheshire is still fairly hard to find and it is correspondingly expensive. Its flavour is exceedingly rich since the natural saltiness of mature Cheshire combines with the additional sharpness of the mould. According to Cheshiremen, should be eaten with plain chocolate biscuits. See *Cheshire*

Blue Stilton (Eng)

Velvety, close-textured unpressed cheese with a smooth, creamy white to pale ivory paste, grading to amber at the edges and marbled with a network of greenish-blue veins. The rind is dry, crusty, greyish brown and slightly wrinkled with white powdery patches. The flavour ranges from mild with a sharp edge when young, to rich and tangy when mature. Stilton, known everywhere as the 'King of English cheeses' is one of the few with any reputation in other countries. It already existed in 1727, when Daniel Defoe mentioned 'Stilton, a town famous for cheese'. In fact, Stilton was never made at Stilton, although it was sold there from the Bell Inn to coach travellers on the Great North Road. Its actual origins are somewhat hazy. We do know that the landlord of the Bell Inn was married in the early 18th century to one of the daughters of Elizabeth Scarbrow, housekeeper at Quenby Hall near Leicester. Mrs Scarbrow, housekeeper at Quenby Hall near Leicester. Mrs Scarbrow was famous for her cheeses, which were known first as Lady Beaumont's cheese and later as Quenby cheese. A second daughter married Farmer Paulet of Wymondham and continued to make cheese according to her mother's recipe. This cheese was supplied to the Bell Inn and became known as Stilton. Whether it was the original Stilton, nobody knows.

Nowadays Stilton is made in 12 dairies scattered around Leicestershire, Nottinghamshire and Derbyshire and protected by a certificated trade mark. One of the dairies still uses unpasteurized milk, but otherwise milk is collected from neighbouring farms and pasteurized at the dairy. A culture of *Penicillium roquefortii* is added to the milk with the starter and rennet is added a short time later. After renneting the curds are cut by hand into small cubes and allowed to settle on the bottom of the vat. They may then either be ladeled into draining troughs or run off together with the whey into coolers. In both cases they are left to drain until the following morning, when they are milled, salted and placed in plastic or stainless steel hoops for three days to a week. During this time each cheese is turned daily to drain further. Once removed from the hoops each cheese is rubbed down by hand to smooth out creases and seal the edges. The cheeses are then stored in precise conditions of temperature and humidity for an average of three to four months, when the characteristic crust will develop. During the first month the cheeses are turned every day and at eight weeks they are pierced with steel needles to promote veining.

The best Stilton (in the shops from September onwards) is made from summer milk and is distinguishable by a slightly yellower paste than usual. The age at which it should be eaten is largely a question of personal taste. Obviously as the cheese ages the mould spreads and the flavour deepens. When buying Stilton look for one where the veins are evenly distributed throughout the paste and where there is a good contrast between the creamy yellow paste and the blue streaks. Avoid a cheese where the paste is dry, cracked or brownish (except at the edges). Stilton is an excellent dessert cheese and is traditionally accompanied by port. At one time it was fashionable to pour the port into the middle of a fat whole cheese (producing what Ambrose Health called 'a purplish kind of mash of cheese and whine of the most disgusting smell and appearance') and then scoop it out with a spoon. This practice is now universally frowned upon. Stilton, like other cheeses, has recently been the subject of various marketing experiments. Layered with Double Gloucester, it becomes Huntsman. Mixed with Cheddar and chopped walnuts and coated with more walnuts, it becomes Walton. See *White Stilton*

Blue Vinney (Eng)

Does Blue Vinney actually exist any more? It certainly *has* existed for there are still people who can claim to have eaten it in the past. It was made only in Dorset from partly skimmed cows' milk and was an extremely hard, white, blue-veined cheese. One of the many tall tales surrounding Blue Vinney (sometimes called Dorset Blue) insists that veining was encouraged by steeping old leather harnesses and even boots in the milk. Perhaps this explains its apparently sudden demise. Something labelled Blue Vinney can occasionally be found in shops selling cheese, but such a cheese is almost certainly second-grade Stilton.

Blue Wensleydale (Eng)

An exquisite close-textured blue-veined cheese. The paste is white with the barest hint of cream and has a delicate, almost honeyed flavour. It is made in the same way as Wensleydale except that *Penicillium roquefortii* is added to the milk. The cheese is pressed for only 24 hours before being transferred to the cheese store, where it is turned regularly, pierced to help the mould develop and matured for at least six weeks. It is, if anything, more temperamental than Stilton and more trouble to make. Perhaps because of this it is now made by only one dairy in the Dove Valley, Derbyshire. See *Wensleydale*

Bolina (Scan)

Like a very mild Gorgonzola with a white, crumbly paste and sparse blue veining from Denmark.

Cabrales (Sp)

Spain's major veined cheese is made mostly with cows' milk, sometimes mixed with ewes' or goats' milk, on mountain farms in Asturias, mainly around Cabrales and Penamellera Alta. It is a strong-smelling cheese with a powerful flavour. The paste is an uneven dull white with yellow-brown patches and irregular blue-brown veining. The rind is greyish-red and crusty, sometimes wrapped in sycamore leaves. Ripened in natural limestone caverns for about six months. The term Cabrales can apply generically to goats' milk cheese. Also known as Cabraliego.

Castelmagno (It)
Blue-veined cows' milk cheese similar to Gorgonzola. named after a mountain village near Dronero, Piedmont.

Dolcelatte (It)
Smooth, creamy, blue-veined cheese, deliciously mild and delicate (the name, a registered trade mark, means 'sweet milk'). It is a factory-made, more easily digestible version of Gorgonzola. Sometimes labelled Gorgonzola Dolcelatte.

Dolceverde (It)
Factory-made cheese similar to Dolcelatte.

Edelpilzkäse (Ger)
A fine blue-veined cheese with a pale ivory paste and very dark veins travelling vertically through the cheese. It has a strong fruity flavour. An excellent dessert cheese. The name, appropriately, means 'glorious mould cheese' and it is something marketed outside Germany as 'German Blue'. It can be drum- or loaf-shaped.

Fourme d'Ambert (Fr)
Looks like a tall baby Stilton and has a similar rough brown-grey crust. A lightly pressed creamy white cheese marbled with dark blue-green veining. The paste should be smooth and fairly moist, tasting quite rich and tangy but not too bitter. Best in summer and autumn at about four to five months old. It is a cheese that, like Stilton, should be cut horizontally. It has also been similarly much abused in the past by the practice of pouring alcohol (eau-de-vie or port) into the centre of the cheese to moisten it. Made in the Livradois, Auvergne. Protected by an *appellation d'origine*.

Fourme de Forez. Fourme de Montbrison, Fourme de Pierre-sur Haute (Fr)
All similar in most respects to Fourme d'Ambert. Fourme de Forez can be used as a generic term covering these and other related cheeses.

Gorgonzola (It)
Italy's principal blue-veined cheese has enjoyed a deservedly high international reputation for generations. Originally a winter-made cheese, a Stracchino, it has the mild creamy paste typical of that wonderfully fertile family of Lombardy cheeses. Its greenish-blue mould gives Gorgonzola the sharp, almost spicy flavour which contrasts so agreeably with the delicacy of the paste. The naturally formed rind is coarse and reddish-grey in colour with powdery patches. Many decidedly apocryphal tales have arisen to explain its origins well over 1,000 years ago.

One that seems plausible tells how migrating herdsmen travelling south to winter pastures stoped over at the village of Gorgonzola near Milan and, embarrassed by the innkeepers' bills, paid in kind with freshly made cheeses. Having no use for this unexpected windfall, the innkeepers stored them in their cellars, which provided ideal conditions for natural mould formation (The caves at Valsassina and Lodi were later to fulfil the same purpose.) With the typically Italian genius for improvisation in matters of food, the innkeepers served these 'mouldy' cheeses to their guests, apparently to their considerable satisfaction.

Nowadays Gorgonzola is still made in Lombardy, but all the year round and no longer at Gorgonzola itself. *Penicillium glaucum* is added to whole pasteurized milk of two milkings. After coagulation the curds are cut into small pieces and placed in wooden hoops to drain naturally, with the warm morning curds in the middle and the cool evening curds on the outside. The curds are salted and turned at regular intervals over a period of about two weeks, then ripened in a cool, humid environment for three to four months (a process that formerly took at least a year). The cheeses are usually sold wrapped in foil. Avoid any cheeses that are brownish or hard or that have a sour, bitter smell. Contrary to popular imagination, Gorgonzola should have a sharp, clean smell but not be overly pungent. Usually eaten as a dessert cheese with bread (and no butter), but there are some local culinary specialities, notably the Milanese *pere ripiene*, a delicious combination of pears stuffed with Gorgonzola. Also an ingredient of *pasta ai quattro formaggi*: pasta coated in a rich mixture of four cheeses and flavoured with sage and garlic. See *Dolcelatte and Stracchino, Torta Gaudenzio*

Lymeswold (Eng)
Newly invented white rind soft cheese with blue veining. Made in Somerset from pasteurized cows' milk.

Montecenisio (It)
Rare blue-veined cheese made from cows' or goats' milk on the Italian-French border.

Mycella (Scan)
Once known as Danish Gorgonzola, the veins are greenish-blue and the paste creamy yellow. Mild for a blue cheese.

Niva (Cz)
Crumbly piquant blue-vein cheese made from pasteurized milk. Ripened for two to three months and wrapped in foil.

Paglia (Sw)
Creamy blue-veined cheese similar to Gorgonzola. Ripened on beds of straw. Made in Ticino.

Pierre-sur-Haute (Fr)
Blue-veined cheese similar to Fourme d'Ambert and also made in the Auvergne.

Pipo Crem' (Fr)
Semi-soft long-shaped blue-veined cheese similar to Bleu de Bresse.

Dolcelatte

Gorgonzola

Mycella

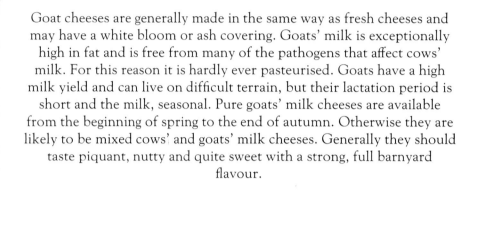

Goat cheeses are generally made in the same way as fresh cheeses and may have a white bloom or ash covering. Goats' milk is exceptionally high in fat and is free from many of the pathogens that affect cows' milk. For this reason it is hardly ever pasteurised. Goats have a high milk yield and can live on difficult terrain, but their lactation period is short and the milk, seasonal. Pure goats' milk cheeses are available from the beginning of spring to the end of autumn. Otherwise they are likely to be mixed cows' and goats' milk cheeses. Generally they should taste piquant, nutty and quite sweet with a strong, full barnyard flavour.

Banon

Bouton-de-Culotte

Charolais

Autun (Fr)

Burgundian soft cheese made entirely from goats' milk or from a mixture of goats' and cows'. The fat content varies with the type of milk used, but should be at least 35 per cent.

Avers (Sw)

Soft white goats' milk cheese with a lightly bloomy skin.

Banon (Fr)

Delicious small cheese from Provence. The authentic farmhouse version is made either from goats' or ewes' milk, depending on the time of year. The dairy variety is usually a cows' milk cheese with a mild, slightly sour flavour, or a *michèvre*. Instantly recognizable by its chestnut leaf wrapping and raffia ties. The leaves are previously soaked in eau-de-vie and grape marc and the parcels are left to ferment in terracotta jars for anything from two weeks to two months. The cows' milk types can be eaten all year round; the ewes' and goats' are best in spring and summer, and in summer and autumn respectively. Banon au Pèbre d'Ai (also known as Poivre d'Ane or La Sarriette) is a similar cheese, but after draining it is rolled in sprigs of savory. Sold in boxes lined with savory (*prèbre d'ai* in Provençal dialect). Banon can also be found with various flavourings.

Bifost (Scan)

Mild, white, fresh goats' milk cheese from Norway. Also called Hvit Gjetost.

Billy (Fr)

Small goats' milk cheese made near Selles-sur-Cher. Wrapped in plane leaves to ripen and packed in stoneware crocks.

Bougon (Fr)

Factory-made Poitevin cheese with a pale, creamy paste and white rind flora. Pleasantly mild goaty flavour.

Bouton-de-Culotte (Fr)

Literally 'trouser button'. A tiny goats' milk cheese from Burgundy, dried and stored for winter use. Extra sharp with a dark greyish-brown rind, often grated. Also called Chevre-ton de Mâcon.

Bozeat (Eng)

Fresh soft goats' milk cheese from Northamptonshire. Sold plain or flavoured with herbs or roasted poppy seeds.

Burgos (Sp)

A fresh rennet-curd cheese made in Burgos. The paste is white, smooth and very mild with just a hint of saltiness. It keeps for about two days after making. Fresh cheeses such as this are often eaten for dessert sprinkled with sugar and honey.

Cabécou (Fr)

The name, a diminutive of *chèvre*, applies to several tiny, flat, goats' milk cheeses made in Aquitaine. They are ripened for about a month and range from semi-soft to firm. The flavour is generally fairly pronounced. Occasionally made with ewes milk, or a mixture of cows' and goats' milk.

Cabreiro (Port)

Smooth white cheese made in Castelo Branco from mixed ewes' and goats' milk. Eaten fresh or ripened in brine.

Charolais, Charolles (Fr)

Small soft cheese made from goats' milk or a mixture of cows' and goats' milk near Charolles, Burgundy. Eaten fresh or ripened for a couple of weeks, when the rind becomes tough and grey-blue in colour and the flavour more pronounced.

Chèvre (Fr)

The generic term for goats' milk cheeses, of which there are innumerable local types and variations. By law, cheeses described as chèvre or *pur chèvre* must be made entirely of goats' milk and must contain at least 45 per cent fat. Cheeses using a minimum of 25 per cent goats' milk mixed with cows' milk are described as *mi-chèvre* and have a yellow band on the label.

Chevret (Fr)

Soft goats' milk cheese from Bugey in Franche Comté. Also called Tomme de Belley, Saint-Claude.

Chevreton (Fr)

The generic term for *chèvre* or *mi-chèvre* cheeses from Burgundy and the Auvergne.

Chevrette (Fr)

Fresh double-cream cheese flavoured with garlic and herbs.

Chevrotin des Aravis (Fr)

A mild-flavoured pressed cheese with a firm grey-brown rind made in Haute-Savoie. With Chevrette des Beauges and other similar medium-ripened, semi-hard goats' milk cheeses made in the area it is often sold simply as Tomme de Chèvre, or Tomme de Chèvre de Savoie.

Claquebitou (Fr)

Burgundian fresh goat cheese flavoured with herbs and garlic.

Crottins de Chavignol (Fr)

Tiny, hard, dry cheese with black or grey-brown mouldy rinds made for winter consumption on remote farms in Berry, France. Horribly sharp and salty when fully aged and somewhat intimidating to all but the most dedicated. The name is hardly inviting: it means 'horse-droppings'.

There is a milder, factory-made version which is rather more approachable. Protected by an *appellation d'Origine*.

Gjetost (Scan)

A Norwegian whey cheese made from a mixture of cows' and goats' milk or entirely from goats' milk. In the latter case it is marked *Ekte* (genuine) Gjetost.

Apart from the milk base the manufacturing process is virtually the same as for Swedish Mesost although the finished product is somewhat darker in colour. Eaten for breakfast, shaved into thin slices, and on spiced fruit cake at Christmas, the appropriate accompaniment is said to be hot coffee or chilled *akevitt*.

Lezay (Fr)

From Poitou, cheese with a smooth medium-flavoured white paste and a semi-hard creamy skin.

One of several fine goat cheeses made in a variety of shapes in the Poitevin town of the same name. It is ripened for a couple of weeks between layers of vine- or plane-tree leaves and has a fairly pronounced flavour and a downy white rind. Also called Fromage de la Mothe, Mothais, Chèvre à la Feuille.

Parthenay (Fr)

Soft, fresh goats' milk cheese from Poitou.

Pelardon (Fr)

Small, white, barely ripened cheese from Languedoc. Odourless, with a very agreeable nutty flavour and the typical goaty aftertaste. There are several variations, such as Pelardon d'Anduze, some flavoured with herbs. All are basically simple rustic cheeses and are still made almost entirely on local farms. According to an old wives' tale, Pelardon is an effective cure for jaundice.

Plasencia (Sp)

Semi-hard goats' milk cheese from Extremadura. Pale, creamy paste with a firm golden rind. Rather mellow in flavour. Ripened for a minimum of four months. There is also a smoked version.

Ramequin de Lagnieu (Fr)

Small cylindrical farmhouse goats' cheese made in Bugey, France. Eaten after two or three weeks' ripening, when it is firm and tangy, or aged further and used grated for *fondu bugiste*.

Saint-Gelais (Fr)

Farmhouse *chèvre* similar to Chabichou, from Poitou.

Sainte-Maure (Fr)

Both *fermirt* (farmhouse) and *laitier* (creamery) types are available. Made in Poitou and Touraine, a soft and creamy cheese with a full goaty flavour. Crusted with a downy white rind tinged with pink. Recognizable by the length of straw through the centre of the cheese (not always present in the factory-made variety). There is also a Sainte-Maure Centré.

Satterleigh (Eng)

Firm pressed cheese made from the milk of Anglo-Nubian and Toggenberg goats. Rich full flavour. From the same farm as Devon Garland and Exmoor.

Sedrun (Sw)

Semi-hard wheel-shaped goats' milk cheese with a thick dry greyish crust. Ripened for a maximum of five months. Dry matter fat content is 45 per cent.

Thiviers (Fr)

Small goats' cheese similar to Cabécou.

Tomme de Crest (Fr)

One of the many soft goats' milk *tommes* made in Dauphiné.

Valençay (Fr)

The *fermier* (farmhouse) type is made in Berry from the end of spring until autumn. A flat pyramid shape with a deep blue-grey surface covered with wood ash. Ripened for about five weeks, the paste is smooth and white with a delicate, by no means overpowering, goaty flavour. The commercial version, Valençay Laitier, is made all year round using frozen curds or powdered milk out of season. Ripened for a shorter time and coarser and stronger than the farmhouse type.

Chevrotin des Aravis

Crottins de Chavignol

Gjetost

Pelardon

Valençay

This group contains many famous cheeses such as the Italian Pecorinos and Greek Feta. Ewes' milk cheeses are also often blued. Sheep can thrive in harsh conditions and on thin pasture that would be unsuitable for cattle. The lactation period is short and the yield low, but the use of ewes' milk enables cheesemaking to take place in areas where it would not otherwise be possible. Unlike cows' milk, the availability is highly seasonal. In France for example, the season lasts from about January to mid-May. The availability of ewes' milk cheeses depends also therefore, on the length of the ripening period.

Ewes' milk cheeses are almost always sharper in flavour than cows' milk cheeses.

Amou (Fr)
Pressed uncooked farmhouse cheese made in Gascony on the edge of Les Landes. It has a thin, oiled, golden rind and a smooth firm paste with a mild, slightly tangy flavour. Ripened for a minimum of two months, when the cheese is faintly reminiscent of Saint-Paulin, and up to six months. The older, harder cheeses are grated and used in regional dishes.

Ardi-Gasna (Fr)
Made on mountain farms in the Basque country. A firm, smooth, pressed cheese with a pronounced sheepy aroma matched by a full mellow flavour. Best eaten after three months. Also called Arnéguy, Esterençuby.

Asco (Fr)
Small-round Corsican cheese made from ewes' milk or a mixture of ewes' and goats' milk. Eaten from early spring to late autumn.

Baccellone (It)
Ewes' milk cheese similar to Ricotta Siciliana, made in and around Livorno especially in spring. Eaten with fresh broad beans (*baccelli*).

Bijeni Sir (Yug)
Sharp white cheese made from cows' or ewes' milk and ripened in brined whey. From Macedonia. Factory and farm-made.

Brinza de Burduf (Rom)
Strong, pungent, spreadable cheese ripened in an animal skin bag (a *burduf*). Has a yellow paste and a grey rind spotted with mould. Traditionally eaten at the end of Lent.

Bruccio, Brucciu (Fr)
Fresh Corsican cheese once made from the whey by-product of Sartenais but which now increasingly uses a proportion of whole or skimmed milk. Made from ewes' milk (or occasionally goats') it looks and tastes very much like Italian Ricotta. It can also be dried and ripened for several months.

Brynza (Bulg), **Brinza** (Rom),
Bryndza (Hu, Cz, Pol)
Salty white brined cheese made in many parts of eastern Europe, particularly in the Carpathian mountains, usually from ewes' milk but occasionally from cows' or goats' milk. Available in several versions ranging from soft and spreadable to firm and crumbly. Sometimes also smoked. It is made in factories from partially ripened curds supplied by mountain shepherds. The curds are scraped of any rind, broken up, salted, milled and remoulded in blocks or packed into wooden barrels with yet more salt. Eaten raw, often cubed in salads or with olives, pickled vegetables and strong rye bread. It also features in a great many local dishes and can be used as a base for Liptauer, a savoury cheese spread. See *Liplói*

Cachat (Fr)
Fresh, white cheese from Provence made from the milk of animals grazed on the slopes of Mont Ventoux. Goats' milk may occasionally be used instead of ewes'. Very sweet and delicate when fresh. Also called Tomme de Mont Ventoux.

Camargue (Fr)
A cheese made in the Camargue in springtime. Flavoured with thyme and bay and eaten fresh. Also called Tomme Arlésienne or Tomme de Camargue.

Canestrato (It)
Traditionally a ewes' milk cheese from Sicily, pressed in a wicker mould (*canestro*) which leaves its imprint on the outside of the cheese. Made between October and June it has a dense, whitish-yellow paste with a few scattered holes. Also known as Incanestrato and sometimes as Pecorino Siciliano or Pecorino Canestrato (or Incanestrato) to distinguish it from the cows' milk version of the same cheese. When the feminine form of the word is used (Canestrata or Incanestrata) it denotes a hard, matured ewes' milk Ricotta made especially for grating.

Castelo Branco (Port)
Made from ewes' or mixed ewes' and goats' milk in Castelo Branco. The paste is white and smooth with a light scattering of small holes. Eaten after three or four weeks' ripening when strong and peppery, or fresh, when it is sold as Queijo Fresco de Castelo Branco.

Castelo de Vide (Port)
Serra-type cheese of limited production and variable quality.

Cotronese, Crotonese (It)
Ewes' (or ewes' and goats') milk cheese made in small dairies near Crotone, Calabria. Sometimes flavoured with peppercorns.

Esbareich (Fr)
Pressed, uncooked Béarnaise ewes' milk cheese, ripened for three months.

Évora (Port)
Very strong salty cheese made from ewes' milk, occasionally mixed with goats' milk. Yellowy white and crumbly with a darker hard crust. Ripened between six and 12 months and becoming harder with age.

Fet(t)a (Gk)
Sharp, salty, white cheese, either firm and crumbly or hard. The American, Australian,

German, Italian and Danish versions are made from pasteurized cows' milk while the original Greek Feta (like the Bulgarian) is still made mostly from ewes' milk, although it is currently available only in Greece because of the export ban. Ewes' milk Feta has a fat content between five and ten per cent higher than the cows' milk cheese. It has been made in Greece by more or less the same method for thousands of years. Fresh milk is curdled by lactic fermentation and the curds and whey are then reheated together causing the remaining fats and proteins in the whey to flocculate. The curds are scooped into cloths or ladled into moulds to drain and then turned and light pressed at regular intervals. When sufficiently firm they are cut into blocks and salted in brine for varying amounts of time. The longer the salting, the harder the cheese becomes. The saltier kinds are best soaked in a little milk or lukewarm water to temper the flavour.

Feta is eaten in vast quantities in Greece (so much so that it also has to be imported, mostly from Denmark). It can be eaten with crusty bread for breakfast or with olives and sliced raw tomatoes for a light lunch. It is crumbled or cubed into the typical Greek mixed salads and used in stuffings for aubergines, peppers and vineleaves. It may be crumbled on to stews or used to fill deliciously light Greek flaky pastries, such as *tiropitta* (tiny cheese puffs). In Greece, Feta is sold floating in a brine bath, but elsewhere it is generally found in vacuum packs.

Feta is also made in other Balkan countries, particularly Bulgaria. Exceptionally good Bulgarian ewes' milk Feta is occasionally exported to the West. If you find any, it is well worth trying. It is superb—creamier and more delicate than the more commonly available cows' milk types.

Foggiano (It)

Type of Pecorino (the ewes' milk is sometimes mixed with cows' or goats' milk) from Foggia, in Puglia.

Gomolya (Hu), Homoly, Hrudka (Cz)

White ewes' milk cheese made on mountain farms. Eaten partially ripened or sold to factories for making Bryndza. Sometimes used as a base for Liptauer. See *Liptói*

Haloumi (Gr)

Creamy white cheese with a somewhat fibrous texture, generally less salty than Feta even though it is also soaked in brine during processing. Firmer than Feta and less brittle, it can be sliced but not crumbled. In Cyprus the cheese is dipped in hot water, kneaded with chopped mint, rolled out like pastry and cut into bars. It is either eaten soon after making or ripened for about a month. About ten per cent of the Haloumi produced is made with cows' milk and this must be eaten within a month or it becomes impossibly hard. The ewes' milk type is used a great deal in cooking. It can be grated on top of *moussaka*, sliced in salads, or dipped into hot water and pulled out in strings to be eaten as a snack. Very often it is sliced and fried in oil and eaten for breakfast with fried eggs and raw tomatoes. It should be washed in lukewarm water or milk before using.

Idiazabal (Sp)

Firm, waxy, lightly smoked cheese with small sparse holes from the Basque country. The paste is creamy white and the rind a dark, smooth caramel colour. Ripened for about a month in mountain caves. Has a rather delicate, smoky, herby flavour. Also called Aralar, Urbia and Urbasa.

Kaseri (Gk)

Hard-pressed, strong white cheese with a scattering of tiny holes, which provides an example of a happy invention mothered by necessity. In thrifty rural economies (often near or just above subsistence level), nothing can be wasted; and yet cheesemaking, especially before the days of scientific agriculture, was often a hit or miss affair. So much could go wrong, and frequently did. However, rather than consign unsuccessful cheeses to the dustbin, in Greece they make them into Kaseri. The cheeses are dipped in hot water (like Italian *pasta filata*), then kneaded and shaped or moulded into large wheels, In fact, Kaseri is very similar to Provolone Dolce in texture and the Greeks prefer it to Mozzarella on pizza. It is also eaten sliced as a table cheese, or can be dipped in flour and fried in oil.

Kashkaval (Bulg)

Made throughout the Balkan lands since Roman times and based on Italian Caciocavallo. The best cheeses are made from ewes' milk, although mixed milk and sometimes only cows' milk types are found. Like Caciocavallo the processing involves a kneading stage where the curds are immersed in hot water to make them malleable before being finally moulded, brined and aged for about two months. The mature cheeses range from almost white to golden yellow depending on the milk and are generally rather hard and crumbly in consistency. The flavour is mild and faintly salty to strong and nutty according to age. Kashkaval is the Cheddar of the Balkans, eaten as a table cheese and also used in cooking. Often it is cubed and fried. Old hard cheeses are used for grating. One of the best types is the Bulgarian Balkanski Kâskaval.

Kefalotir (Yug)

Hard grating cheese with a smooth shiny rind, full flavour and pungent aroma. See *Kefalotiri*

Kefalotiri (Gk)

Close-textured, slightly oily cheese, pale biscuit-coloured with a thin, hard rind and a pronounced ewes' milk tang. Somewhat harder than Kaseri, Kefalotiri is used mainly in cooking.

The name 'head cheese' comes from its supposed resemblance to a Greek hat. Most of the Kefalotiri found outside Greece is Kefalograviera, since the original is too strong for foreign tastes.

Kopanisti (Gk)

A veined cheese from the Aegean Islands made from cows' or ewes' milk. The fresh curds are roughly cut, put into cloths to drain for a few hours, then hand moulded into balls and left to dry. After a while the surface of the cheese becomes covered with mould, and this

Asco

Feta

Ossau-Iraty-Brebis Pyrénées

Pecorino Romano

is worked back into the cheese with a quantity of salt. The cheeses are then left to ripen for a couple of months until they become soft, creamy and salty. Some of the best come from the island of Mykonos.

Liptói (Hu), and
Liptovská Bryndza (Cz)
Liptov in the Tatra mountains was reputedly the place where Bryndza was first made and its name is still used to denote particularly fine, white, creamy, soft ewes' milk cheeses made from whole unpasteurized milk. Such cheeses were the traditional base for a spread that is now widely known as Liptauer. The soft curd cheese is mixed with ingredients such as paprika, caraway seeds, onions or mustard or sometimes with anchovies and capers.

Logudoro (It)
Mild sweet factory-made dessert cheese from Lombardy. The paste is creamy white and there is no rind apart from wicker mould marks. Ripened for three to four weeks.

Manchego (Sp)
Spain's most famous cheese is made in the plain of La Mancha. The best Manchego is said to be that from around Ciudad Real, but Toledo, Albacete and Cuenca are also important centres. It is a beautiful cheese, with a firm, ivory to golden paste, sometimes dotted with a few small eyes, and a lovely creamy yellow rind impressed with plaited esparto marks along the sides. The top and bottom retain the elaborate patterns of the cheese press (where the cheese remains for six to seven hours). During the ripening period, the surfaces become covered with a greenish-black mould that is usually cleaned off before the cheeses are sold, but to satisfy some sections of the market, certain cheeses are sold with the mould coating intact. The taste, depending on the age of the cheese, remains unaltered.

Manchego is sold at various stages of its maturity: *fresco* (under three weeks old), *curado* (up to 13 weeks), *viejo* (over three months) and *en aceite* (in olive oil, when it is ripened for at least a year and has a rough blackish rind). Eaten for dessert or grated, when older. Sometimes cubed and fried in olive oil.

Mandur, Manur (Yug)
Dry grating cheese made from the whey by-product of Kashkaval and Kefalotir mixed with milk or buttermilk.

Manouri (Gk)
Fresh, whole ewes' milk cheese from Crete. It is white and creamy and slightly firmer than Mizithra, shaped into ovals and waxed or packaged in foil. Eaten with honey as a dessert.

Mizithra (Gk)
Whey cheese made from the by-products of Feta and Kefalotiri. Whole fresh ewes' or cows' milk is sometimes added to make it richer. Similar to Italian Ricotta, it is used in cooking in much the same way and is also eaten fresh, sometimes while still warm. It is occasionally preserved in salt and can also be dried and used for grating.

Nasal (Rom)
Low-fat washed-rind cheese made from cows', ewes' or water buffalo milk in the hills near Cluj.

Njeguski Sir (Yug)
Hard ewes' milk grating cheese from Montenegro.

Nuns de Caens (Eng)
Semi-soft, unpasteurized ewes' milk cheese with a very creamy fruity flavour. Made in Gloucestershire.

Ossau-Iraty-Brebis Pyrénées (Fr)
Made in Béarn and the Basque provinces in farms and small dairies by traditional methods. This is the original authentic Pyrenean ewes' milk cheese, now widely imitated. Lightly pressed, uncooked with a golden springy paste scattered with small irregular holes and openings. The rind is smooth orange-yellow to brown, the flavour delicate to full and mellow according to age. Ripened for at least three months. Older drier cheeses are used for grating. Protected by an *appellation d'origine*.

Parenyica (Cz, Hu)
Sometimes called 'ribbon cheese', long strips of spun-curd cheese rolled up and lightly smoked. Traditionally made with ewes' milk. In Eastern Europe. Now also factory-made from cows' milk.

Pecorino (It)
Generic name for ewes' milk cheeses (from *pecora*, sheep)—one of the most important Italian cheese families and particularly associated with central and southern Italy. A typical Pecorino is a hand-pressed, cooked, drum- or wheel-shaped cheese, made from whole or skimmed unpasteurized milk coagulated with sheep's rennet, and decidedly piquant in flavour. The farther south one goes, the more *piccante* the cheeses become. Any ewes' milk cheese can be called a Pecorino and there are many local variations and a bewildering prolixity of names and designations for what are basically similar cheeses. Over the centuries some have become more widely known and more important commercially than others, notably Pecorino Romano and Pecorino Siciliano.

Pecorino Pepato (It)
A Pecorino (usually Siciliano) flavoured with whole black peppercorns, sometimes simply called Pepato.

Pecorino Romano (It)
The most famous of the Pecorino cheeses and the legendary cheese made by Romulus, Pecorino Romano had its characteristics and *zona tipica* precisely laid down by the Stresa Convention of 1951. Made between November and June, the traditional area of production is Lazio, but this has now been extended to include Sardinia.

Pecorino Romano has always been a popular cheese both in Italy and overseas. Columella talks of it being exported in the 1st century AD and a considerable amount of the cheese produced today finds its way abroad, especially to the United States. It has a greyish-white close-textured paste and a dark brown or black very hard rind rubbed with oil and wood ash or wax or a yellow clay-based compound. It is ripened for a minimum of eight months, when the flavour is sharp and dry and goes particularly well with coarse country bread. Grated, it is an essential part of many regional dishes. It gives off a somewhat arid smell when sprinkled on hot food, but this should be tolerated in the interests of authencitiy; the flavour is not adversely affected. See *Pecorino, Pecorino Saro*

Pecorino Sardo (It)
The traditional Sardinian Pecorino, made with whole or skimmed ewes' milk. Its characteristics are basically the same as Pecorino Romano since the processing is identical. The slight variations in flavour are a result of inevitable local differences in the milk. True connoisseurs can tell the two cheeses apart, unlike most of the rest of us. If anything, they say, Sardo is drier and slightly more piccante than Romano.

Pecorino Senese (It)
A type of Pecorino Toscano made near Siena. The rind is rubbed with tomato paste or with olive oil and wood ash.

Podhalanski (Pol)
Lightly smoked cheese made from ewes' and cows' milk.

Queijo de Ovelha (Port)
Ewes' milk cheese made in Castelo Branco. Coarse and salty.

Raveggiolo (It)
A creamy white ewes' milk cheese with a slightly elastic texture. Eaten within a few weeks of making.

Roncal (Sp)
Piquant, slightly greenish cheese with a hard, leathery rind formed by salting, washing and smoking. Ripened for one to two months. Made in Roncal, Navarre. Good for grating.

Roquefort (Fr)
A cheese with champions as diverse as Pliny, Charlemagne and Casanova arouses formidable expectations. Its aphrodisiac qualities, predictably emphasized by Casanova, have yet to undergo properly conducted scientific experiments, but its gastronomic merit remains unchallenged to this day. Even people who do not like blue cheeses generally like Roquefort. At its best it is extraordinarily delicate and subtle with none of the harsh overtones which typify many other blues. It has been made in Les Causses for thousands of years and its makers have regularly ensured that their product is legally defined and protected. They were first granted a monopoly on its making in 1411 and this has been confirmed at frequent intervals ever since, culminating in the Stresa Convention of 1951. It is now protected by an *appellation d'origine*.

Roquefort is made from the milk of the Larzac breed of sheep and ripened in the caves of Combalou. Some cheeses made from Corsican milk are brought to the same caves over virtually a whole year. The caves, ventilated by currents of air known as *fleurines*, provide ideal conditions for the development of the mould, now defined as *Penicillium roquefortii*. This mould, which once grew naturally, is now partly induced by being sprinkled in powdered form on the curds as they are labelled into the moulds. The cheeses are then pierced with steel needles during three-month ripening period. For the final part of this time the cheeses are closely wrapped in tin foil so that the finished product has virtually no rind. The veining (more green than blue) should be evenly distributed throughout the cheese and the paste should be creamy white and rather buttery. The sheepish origins of the cheese should be easily detectable in both flavour and aroma.

Each cheese, foil-wrapped, carries a label depicting a sheep printed in red ink. Unfortunately many exported Roqueforts tend to be oversalted to improve their keeping qualities. Those sold in France are much the best. Roquefort is eaten as a dessert cheese and also used in spreads and salad dressings.

Scanno (It)
Table Pecorino from Abruzzi. Traditionally eaten with fresh fruit. Black on the outside and buttery yellow inside. The flavour has a mildly burnt tinge.

Schafmilchkäse (Ger)
Generic term for ewes' milk cheese. Only Schnittkäse can officially be made from ewes' milk in Germany. Two good cheeses are Abertamerkäse and Friesischer Schafkäse.

Serra (Port)
Portugal's most famous cheese is an ancient type, farm-made in the Serra da Estrêla and at Manteigas, Celorico da Beira, Gouveia, Seia and Guarda. It has a pale yellow buttery paste with sparse small holes and a soft, smooth, golden rind. The flavour is mildly lactic and rather refreshing. Coagulated with vegetable rennet and ripened for four to six weeks. Sometimes aged further (five months or more) and sold as Serra Velho. Best between December and April. A harder and inferior factory-made version is sold as Tipo Serra.

Somborski Sir (Yug)
From Sombor, Vojvodina. Soft, slightly bitter cheese made with ewes' milk or mixed ewes' and cows' milk diluted with a proportion of water. It has a strong-flavoured yellowish paste with medium holes and a thin rind. Ripened for three weeks stacked in wooden vessels during which time gases produced in the cheese expand causing it to rise like yeast dough.

Telemea (Rom)
White brined cheese similar to Feta. Made from ewes' or cows' milk, or from cows' milk mixed with buffalo milk.

Toscanello (It)
Tuscan cheese made either from ewes' milk or a mixture of ewes' and cows' milk. Small firm cheese with a pale golden paste and smooth rind. Eaten as a table cheese after a few months or aged for grating. Also called Caciotta Toscana when made with mixed milk, and Pecorino Toscano when made entirely with ewes' milk.

Travnicki Sir (Yug)
From the town of Travnik, Bosnia. Made from ewes' or mixed ewes, and cows' milk. It has a softish white paste scattered with holes. The flavour is sour and salty.

Venaco (Fr)
Salty ewes' or goats' milk Corsican cheese, Square with wickerwork impressions on the surface, it has a greyish, coarse paste and is ripened for three to four months.

Villalón (Sp)
Fresh, white, mild, slightly sour cheese, hand-pressed and steeped in brine for two to three hours, usually eaten immediately, but occasionally ripened for long periods. From Villalón de Campos, Valladolid. Also called Pata de Mulo.

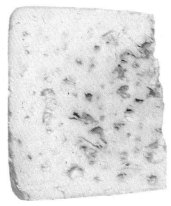

Roquefort

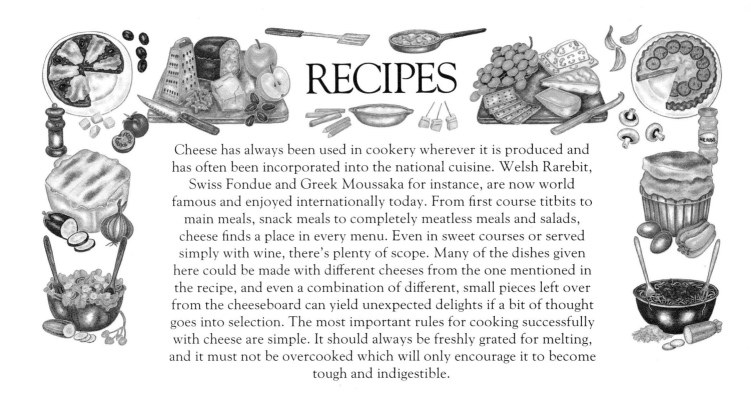

RECIPES

Cheese has always been used in cookery wherever it is produced and has often been incorporated into the national cuisine. Welsh Rarebit, Swiss Fondue and Greek Moussaka for instance, are now world famous and enjoyed internationally today. From first course titbits to main meals, snack meals to completely meatless meals and salads, cheese finds a place in every menu. Even in sweet courses or served simply with wine, there's plenty of scope. Many of the dishes given here could be made with different cheeses from the one mentioned in the recipe, and even a combination of different, small pieces left over from the cheeseboard can yield unexpected delights if a bit of thought goes into selection. The most important rules for cooking successfully with cheese are simple. It should always be freshly grated for melting, and it must not be overcooked which will only encourage it to become tough and indigestible.

Appetizers and Starters

CHEESE DATES

1⅓ **cups/225 g** fine smooth dates
2½ **cups/225 g** Cheddar cheese, grated
½ **tsp** made mustard
8 drops Angostura bitters
⅓ **cup/50 g** blanched almonds,
toasted

Makes about 30

1 Split the dates and remove the stones. Beat the cheese, mustard and Angostura bitters together into a smooth paste.

2 Count the dates and divide the cheese mixture into a similar number of equal portions. Form the portions of cheese into small rolls.

3 Stuff each of the dates with a roll of cheese and press an almond on top. Place the dates in small paper cups/cases and serve.

ASPARAGUS CHEESE TOASTIES

20 medium slices, white
bread
1¼ **cups/125 g** Cheddar cheese,
grated
dash Worcestershire sauce
pinch paprika
½ **tsp** made mustard
2 tbs/30 ml milk

2 tbs/25 g butter
10 oz/300 g can asparagus spears, drained
2 tbs/30 ml butter, melted
1 bunch chives

Makes 20

1 Remove the crusts from the bread. Using a rolling pin, roll each slice of bread out thinly. Cover the slices with a damp cloth while preparing the filling.

2 Mix the cheese with the Worcestershire sauce, paprika and mustard. Heat the milk and the 2 tablespoons of butter together over gentle heat until the butter melts – but do not boil. Pour this milk and butter into the cheese mixture and beat thoroughly until smooth.

3 Spread some of the cheese mixture over each slice of bread. Place an asparagus spear on top of each slice and roll up tightly, dampening the edges of the bread to seal if necessary. Secure the rolls with wooden cocktail sticks.

4 Place the rolls in a buttered baking tray, brush the melted butter over the tops and bake at 425°F/220°C/ Gas Mark 7 for about 10–15 minutes or until golden brown. Cool on a wire rack.

5 Meanwhile, place the chives in a dish and cover with boiling water, leave to stand for 1 minute then drain thoroughly.

6 Garnish the toasties by first removing the cocktail sticks, then tie a strand of blanched chive around each.

CURRIED CHEESE BALLS

1¼ **cups/125 g** Cheddar cheese, grated
4 **tbs/50 g** butter, softened
4 **tbs/50 g** fresh white bread crumbs
1 **tsp** curry powder
1 **cup/50 g** dessicated coconut

Makes about 20

1 Mix together the cheese, butter, bread crumbs and curry powder. Beat until thoroughly combined.

2 Divide into small balls about the size of a hazelnut and coat with the dessicated coconut.

3 Chill slightly, then serve on cocktail sticks.

CHEESE MOUSSE

2 **eggs**, separated
½ **cup/50 g** White Cheshire cheese, grated
1 **tsp** made mustard
pinch freshly grated nutmeg
⅔ **cup/150 ml** heavy/double cream, whipped
lemon slices
parsley

Serves 4

1 Beat the egg yolks with the cheese, add the mustard and nutmeg.

2 Fold in the cream. Whisk the egg whites until stiff and fold into the cheese mixture. Spoon into 4 small dishes and chill.

3 Garnish with lemon and parsley, and serve with brown bread.

CHEESE STARLETS

¾ **cup/175 g** butter
1½ **cups/150 g** Cheddar cheese, grated
1½ **cups/175 g** all-purpose/plain flour
1 **tsp** paprika
1 **tsp** salt
4 **tsp** sesame seeds

Makes 60–70

1 Cream together the butter and cheese until soft, pale and very creamy.

2 Sift the flour, paprika and salt together. Gradually beat these ingredients into the creamed mixture with half the sesame seeds.

3 Fit a large star nozzle into a piping bag. Using two-thirds of the mixture pipe small star cookies/biscuits on to ungreased baking trays.

4 Roll the reserved dough into tiny balls, then coat in the remaining sesame seeds. Top each of the piped cookies/biscuits with one of these balls, pressing it in to form a flower shape.

5 Bake at 350°F/180°C/Gas Mark 4 for 12–15 minutes, or until very lightly browned. Cool on a wire rack.

Cheese Mousse

Cânapés

CAERPHILLY CHEESE AND ANCHOVY ROLLS

3 tbsp/40 g butter, softened
1 cup/75 g Caerphilly cheese, finely grated
1 small can anchovy fillets, drained
1 small brown bread loaf
2 tbs/25 g butter, melted

Serves 6 as cânapés

1 Cream the butter and cheese. Split the anchovies lengthways. Slice the bread thinly and cut off crusts.

2 Roll the slices of bread even thinner with a rolling pin. Spread each slice generously with the cheese mixture and place an anchovy fillet at one end.

3 Roll up each slice like a cigar and cut in half. Place in a baking tin/pan, spoon over a little melted butter and bake until crisp at 375°F/190°C/Gas Mark 5. Turn the rolls from time to time. Serve warm.

LANCASHIRE STUFFED TOMATOES

1 lb/450 g cherry tomatoes
1¼ cups/125 g Lancashire cheese, finely crumbled
small rounds of brown bread and butter

Serves 6 as canapes

1 Skin the tomatoes. Cut a cap from the rounded end of each. Scoop out the seeds and some of the flesh with the handle of a teaspoon.

2 Season inside the tomatoes and fill with the crumbled cheese. Replace the caps on top.

3 Set each tomato on a round of brown bread and butter.

STUFFED CELERY

1 bunch/head celery
½ cup/125 g butter
1¼ cups/125 g Stilton cheese
rounds of brown bread
and butter
pimento, diced

Serves 6

1 Wash and dry the sticks of celery thoroughly. Soften the butter, cut any rind off the Stilton and discard. Cream the cheese and butter together.

2 Fill each celery stick with the cheese mixture and starting with the smallest pieces, reshape the celery bunch. Wrap in wax/greaseproof paper or foil: chill for 30 minutes.

3 Unwrap the celery and cut across into thin slices. Cut the buttered bread into rounds the same size as the celery slices. Place the celery on the bread and decorate with the pimento.

CÂNAPÉS

10 thin slices white bread
¼ cup/65 ml oil

Devilled Shrimp/Prawn Topping
1 cup/125 g peeled shrimp/prawns
salt
ground black pepper
cayenne pepper
2 tbs/30 ml tomato relish/chutney
1 tbsp/15 g butter

Mushroom Topping
2 tbsp/25 g butter
1 shallot or thick slice of
onion, finely chopped
6 flat mushrooms, finely
chopped
2 tsp chopped parsley and
thyme
2 tbs/1 oz fine fresh bread crumbs

Cheese Cream
2 tbs/25 g butter
2 tbs/25 g flour
1 cup/250 ml milk
salt
ground black pepper
1 pinch dry mustard powder
1 cup/75 g Cheddar cheese, grated

Serves 6

1 Cut the bread into 1½in/4cm rounds using a pastry or cookie/biscuit cutter. Heat the oil in a frying pan and fry the rounds until golden on both sides.

2 **Shrimp/Prawn Topping:** toss the shrimp/prawns over the heat with the other ingredients. When hot, divide between half the rounds of fried bread.

3 **Mushroom Topping:** melt the butter in a saucepan. Add the shallot or onion and after a minute the mushrooms, herbs and seasoning. Cook for 5 to 6 minutes until dry and then add the bread crumbs. Place a teaspoonful on top of each of the remaining fried bread rounds.

4 **Cheese Cream:** melt the butter in a small saucepan. Remove from the heat, add the flour then blend in the milk. Return to the heat and stir until boiling. Add seasonings, draw off the heat and stir in the grated cheese. Spoon over the shrimp/prawn and mushroom toppings on the bread rounds. Brown under a broiler. Serve hot.

SMOKED FISH PÂTÉ

1½ cups/175 g kipper fillet, cooked
2 tbs/30 ml lemon juice
1 cup/75 g Mozzarella cheese, grated
⅔ cup/150 ml heavy/double cream
3 tbs/45 ml mayonnaise
salt
cayenne pepper
lemon slices
fresh dill

Serves 4–6

1 Flake the cooked kipper into a bowl. Stir in the remaining ingredients except the lemon and dill.

2 Blend until smooth. Spoon into a dish and garnish with lemon slices and fresh dill. Serve with melba toast or crisp crackers/biscuits.

TARAMASALATA

1½ cups/350 g smoked cod's roe
4 slices white bread,
crusts removed
⅓ cup/90ml milk
2 cloves garlic, crushed
1¼ cups/125g cream or curd cheese
½ cup/125 ml olive oil
1 lemon, juice only
salt
ground black pepper

Serves 6–8

1 Using a teaspoon scoop the roe out of its skin into a bowl. Soak the bread in the milk. When the bread is soft, squeeze out any excess milk and add the bread to the roe.

2 Beat in the garlic and cheese. Add the oil and lemon juice a spoonful at a time, beating well between each addition.

3 Put the mixture into a liquidizer or processor a little at a time and blend until smooth. Season to taste and add more lemon juice if necessary.

4 Serve with black olives and toast or pitta bread.

DANISH CUCUMBER MOUSSE

1 cucumber
2½ **cups/225 g** Danish Blue Brie cheese
¼ **cup/65 ml** mayonnaise
1 **tsp** castor sugar
1 **tsp** lemon juice
salt
ground black pepper
1¼ **cups/300 ml** unflavoured/natural yogurt
1 **tbs/15 g** unflavoured gelatin/ gelatine
sliced cucumber
shrimp/prawns

Serves 8

1 Peel the cucumber, cut in half lengthways and remove the seeds with a teaspoon. Grate the flesh and reserve.

2 Sprinkle the gelatin over ⅔ cup/150 ml water in a small bowl. Stir and set over a small saucepan of hot water. Stir until dissolved. Cool.

3 Thinly remove the rind from the cheese and discard. Beat the cheese in a bowl until soft. Add the mayonnaise, sugar, lemon juice and seasoning. Beat together and mix in the yogurt.

4 Stir the cooled gelatin into the cheese mixture. Mix in the cucumber and pour into a lightly oiled 5 cup/1 litre ring mould. Chill until set.

5 Dip the mould briefly in hot water and turn out on to a serving plate. Garnish with slices of cucumber and fill the centre with shrimp/prawns.

DANISH BLUE CHEESE MOUSSE

1 **tbs/15 g** unflavoured gelatin/ gelatine
1¼ **cups/300 ml** heavy/double cream
1¼ **cups/125 g** Danish Blue cheese, grated
1¼ **cups/125 g** Samsoe cheese, grated
½ **cup/25 g** almonds, chopped and toasted
2 egg whites
pinch mustard powder
ground black pepper
Danish Blue cheese, sliced
tomatoes

Serves 8

1 Sprinkle the gelatin over 2 tbs/30 ml water in a small bowl. Stir and set the bowl over a pan of hot water. Stir until dissolved. Cool.

Danish Cucumber Mousse

2 Whip the cream and mix with the cheeses and toasted almonds. Stir in the cooled gelatin.

3 Whisk the egg whites until stiff and fold carefully into the cheese mixture. Add the mustard and pepper to taste.

4 Pour into a 2½ cup/600 ml lightly oiled mould or 8 individual dishes. Chill until set. Turn out and garnish with cheese, tomatoes and watercress.

CHICORY AND HAM MORNAY

8 heads curly endive/ chicory, trimmed
lemon juice
2 cups/500 ml milk
1 chicken stock cube
1 small onion, chopped
4 peppercorns
1 small bay leaf
8 slices ham
butter
4 tbs/50 g flour
⅔ **cup/150ml** light/single cream
5 tbs/50 g Parmesan cheese, grated
5 tbs/50 g Gruyère cheese, grated
1 egg yolk
ground black pepper
freshly grated nutmeg

Serves 8

1 Put the curly endive/chicory in a saucepan of salted water and add 2 tbs/30 ml lemon juice to each 2 cups/500 ml water and boil, for 15 minutes.

2 Pour the milk into a saucepan, add the stock cube, onion, peppercorns and bay leaf. Bring to the boil and dissolve the stock cube. Remove from the heat and allow to infuse for 15 minutes.

3 Drain the curly endive/chicory. Squeeze each head between the folds of a cloth to extract as much moisture as possible. Wrap each in a slice of ham. Pack them tightly, head to tail, in a buttered dish that holds them snugly.

4 Melt 3 tbs/40 g butter in a heavy saucepan. Blend in the flour and cook over a low heat for 2 to 3 minutes. Gradually strain in the milk, stirring continuously to make a smooth sauce. Stir in the cream.

5 Bring the sauce to simmering point and cook gently, stirring often for 15 minutes. Remove the pan from the heat. Beat in most of the cheese and the egg yolk. Season to taste with salt, pepper, nutmeg and a few drops of lemon juice.

6 Spoon the sauce over the curly endive/chicory and sprinkle with the remaining cheese. Bake at 400°F/200°C/Gas Mark 6 for 25 minutes or until the sauce is golden on top.

CHEESE AND SEAFOOD SCALLOPS

Cheese and Seafood Scallops

¾ **lb/350 g** cod fillet, skinned and boned
½ onion, chopped
3 tbs/40 g butter
½ **tbs/15 g** cornstarch/cornflour
¾ **cup/175 ml** milk
2 tbs/50 g ground almonds
½ **tsp** ground mace
1 cup/125 g peeled shrimp/prawns
salt
ground black pepper
½ **cup/50 g** Leicester cheese, grated
2 tbs/25 g bread crumbs
lemon slices
4 shrimp/prawns on the shell
fresh chopped parsley

Serves 4

1 Cut the fish into small cubes. Gently fry the onion in 1 tablespoon of the butter until softened. Add the cornstarch/cornflour and cook over a low heat stirring continuously for 2 minutes.

2 Gradually blend in the milk and cook, stirring, until the sauce thickens, boils and is smooth.

3 Add the fish, ground almonds, mace, parsley, shrimp/prawns and seasoning to taste. Simmer for 10 minutes.

4 Spoon into 4 small dishes or scallop shells. Mix the cheese and bread crumbs together and sprinkle on top. Dot with the remaining butter. Broil/grill until golden brown. Serve immediately with lemon slices and shrimp/prawns to garnish.

CLAMS WITH GRUYÈRE SAUCE

24 clams
2 tbs/25 g butter
1 shallot, finely chopped
2 tsp fresh chopped parsley
⅔ cup/150 ml heavy/double cream
2 tbs/20 g Gruyère cheese, grated
salt
ground black pepper
1 tbs/15 g dried bread crumbs

Serves 4

1 Open the clams, wash off any grit and return them to their half shells.

2 Melt the butter in a small saucepan and cook the shallot until soft. Add the parsley, cook for another minute and then add the cream. Simmer for 1 minute before adding the cheese and seasoning to taste.

3 Place the clams in a heatproof dish and pour the sauce over them. Sprinkle with the bread crumbs. Broil/grill for about 5 minutes and serve at once.

WENSLEYDALE TOPPERS

6 tbs/75 g all-purpose/plain flour
4 tbs/25 g porridge oats
4 tbs/50 g butter
1¼ cups/125 g Cheddar cheese, grated
1 egg yolk
1¼ cups/125 g Wensleydale cheese, crumbled
¼ cucumber, peeled, finely chopped and drained
2–4 tbs/30–60 ml sour cream
salt
ground black pepper
½ cup/50 g peeled shrimps/prawns
pinch cayenne pepper

Makes 30

1 Mix together the flour and oats, then rub in the butter until the mixture resembles fine bread crumbs. Stir in the Cheddar cheese and egg yolk to form a light dough/batter.

2 Roll out on a lightly floured work surface to about ⅛in/0.25cm thick. Cut out 2in/5cm circles using a plain cookie/biscuit cutter, then place them slightly apart on buttered baking trays.

3 Bake at 400°F/200°C/Gas Mark 6 for 10–15 minutes. Cool on a wire rack.

4 Meanwhile , mix the Wensleydale cheese with the cucumber and sour cream. Add seasoning to taste.

5 Top each cookie/biscuit with a little of the cheese and cucumber mixture and garnish with a peeled shrimp, if liked. Sprinkle with a little cayenne pepper.

QUICK CHEDDAR MUSHROOMS

2 tbs/25 g butter
½ cup/50 g fresh whole meal bread crumbs
⅔ cup/150 ml milk
1¼ cups/125 g Cheddar cheese, grated
1 egg, beaten
salt
ground black pepper
4 large open mushrooms, broiled/grilled or fried
tomatoes, lettuce and watercress, to garnish

Serves 2

1 Melt the butter in a saucepan, add the bread crumbs and milk. When very hot add the grated cheese, egg and seasoning. Stir until thick and creamy.

2 Spoon the cheese mixture into the mushroom caps and garnish with the tomatoes, lettuce and watercress.

STUFFED MUSHROOMS

8 large open mushrooms
1 clove garlic, crushed
2 tbs/25 g butter
5 tbs/65 g fresh bread crumbs
1¼ cups/125 g Mycella cheese, crumbled
2 tsp lemon juice
2 tsp fresh chopped parsley
ground black pepper
lemon twists

Serves 4

1 Remove the mushroom stalks and chop. Lightly fry with the garlic in the butter until soft.

2 Remove the saucepan from the heat, add the cheese and stir in the remaining ingredients.

3 Spoon the mixture into the cavity of the mushrooms. Place them in a well-buttered ovenproof dish. Bake at 375°F/190°C/Gas Mark 5 for 20 minutes. Serve garnished with lemon twists.

FRIED CAMEMBERT

4 individual portions wrapped Camembert
¼ tsp cayenne pepper
1 egg, beaten
¾ cup/90 g fresh white bread crumbs
4 thin fingers dry hot toast
deep oil for frying

Serves 4

1 Do not remove the rind from the Camembert.

Quick Cheddar Mushrooms

Sprinkle each piece with cayenne pepper and then dip in the beaten egg. Toss in the bread crumbs to completely cover.

2 Put the Camembert gently in a frying basket and fry in hot oil at 400°F/200°C for 2 minutes or until a light golden brown.

3 Serve immediately with the toast.

ROQUEFORT MOUSSE

2 tbs/25 g unflavoured gelatin/gelatine
1 cup/250 ml cream
3 eggs, separated
3 cups/300 g Roquefort cheese
1 small bunch chives, chopped
¼ cup/65 ml heavy/double cream

Serves 6
1 Tie a double band of wax/greaseproof paper around each of six individual soufflé dishes to come 1in/2.5cm above the rim. Lightly oil the inside of the paper.

2 Sprinkle the gelatin over the cream in a small bowl. Leave to stand for 5 minures. Set the bowl over a pan of hot water and stir until the gelatin has completely dissolved.

3 Whisk the egg yolks until pale, then gradually whisk in the cream and gelatin mixture. Pour the

mixture into a saucepan and stir over a very low heat until thickened.

4 Mash the cheese and add the thickened mixture and chives. Leave to cool, then chill until beginning to set. Whisk the egg whites until stiff. Whip the heavy/double cream until it is just thick.

5 Fold the cream and egg whites through the cheese mixture and divide between the prepared soufflé dishes. Chill until set. Remove the paper before serving.

HERBY CHEESE DIP WITH CRUDITÉS

1 tbs fresh chopped parsley
1 tbs fresh chopped mint
2 cups/175 g Cheddar cheese, grated
¾ cup/75 g cottage cheese
¾ cup/150 ml milk
1 clove garlic, crushed
salt
ground black pepper

Serves 4
1 Put the herbs and cheese into a bowl. Beat until smooth. Add the milk, garlic and seasonings.

2 Chill well and serve surrounded with crudités such as raw carrot sticks, cucumber sticks, celery, cauliflower florets, radishes and corn chips.

CHEDDAR CHEESE AND CELERY DIP

4 tbs/50 g butter
2½ cups/225 g Cheddar cheese, grated
2 tsp made mustard
1 cup/125 g celery, finely chopped
⅔ cup/150 ml light/single cream
salt
ground black pepper
2 tbs/25 g salted peanuts, chopped

Serves 6–8
1 Beat the butter until creamy. Stir in the cheese, mustard and celery.

2 Gradually beat in the cream and season to taste. Serve sprinkled with peanuts, with fresh vegetable sticks.

AVOCADO DIP

1 large ripe avocado
2 tsp lemon juice
1¼ cups/125 g Danish Blue cheese
¼ cup/65 ml light/single cream
cayenne pepper

Serves 4
1 Halve the avocado and scoop out the flesh. Place in a bowl and mash with the lemon juice until smooth.

2 Mash the cheese, add it to the avocado and beat until smooth. Stir in the cream and a little cayenne pepper, to taste.

3 Turn into the serving dish, cover with polythene film and chill for 1 hour before serving. Serve with "dippers" such as raw cauliflower, carrot and cucumber sticks, or crackers/savoury biscuits.

AVOCADO BLUES

1½ cups/150 g Blue Brie cheese
2 tbs/30 ml mayonnaise
3 tbs/45 ml thick unflavoured/natural yogurt
ground black pepper
1–2 tsp lemon juice
2 cups/225 g peeled shrimp/prawns, thawed if frozen
3 ripe avocado pears
lettuce leaves
sliced cucumber

Serves 6
1 Have the cheese at room temperature. Remove the rind and soften the cheese in a bowl.

2 Add the mayonnaise, yogurt, pepper and lemon

juice to taste. Mix well. Reserve a few shrimp/prawns to garnish and stir the remainder into the cheese mixture.

3 Halve the avocados and remove the stones. Brush with a little more lemon juice to prevent browning. Pile the shrimp/prawn mixture over the avocados.

4 Serve the avocados on lettuce leaves garnished with sliced cucumber and the reserved shrimp/prawns.

HOT AVOCADO WITH CHESHIRE CHEESE

⅓ cup/90 ml heavy/double cream
1 cup/75 g Cheshire cheese, grated
¼ tsp paprika pepper
ground black pepper
salt
4 slices wholemeal bread
butter for spreading
2 avocado pears

Serves 4
1 Lightly whip the cream, fold in the grated cheese with the paprika, pepper and a little salt.

2 Toast the wholemeal bread, remove the crusts and butter lightly. Peel, stone and slice the avocado pears and place on the toast.

3 Spoon the cream cheese on top and place under the broiler until glazed. Serve hot.

TOMATO COUPE

14 oz/350 g can tomatoes
1 strip lemon rind
1 bay leaf
1 small clove garlic, crushed
1½ tbs/20 g unflavoured gelatin/ gelatine
¼ cup/65 ml white wine
¼ cup/65 ml boiling water
salt
pinch sugar
ground black pepper
1¼ cups/125 g Cheddar cheese, grated
6 scallions/spring onions, sliced

Serves 6–8
1 Pour the contents of the can of tomatoes into a saucepan. Add the lemon rind, bay leaf and garlic. Crush the tomatoes, cover the saucepan, bring to the boil and simmer for 10 minutes.

2 Sprinkle the gelatin over the wine and boiling water and leave to stand.

3 Rub the tomatoes through a sieve and measure

the pulp. Add enough water to bring to to 2 cups/500 ml. Add sugar, salt and pepper to taste and stir in the soaked gelatin. Stir until completely dissolved.

4 Cool the mixture then pour into coupe glasses or small dishes to about one third full. Leave to set.

5 Mix the cheese with the onions. When the tomato jelly is firm, top each dish with the mixture. Chill slightly before serving with brown bread and butter.

STILTON SOUP I

1½ cups/375 ml milk
1 slice onion
6 peppercorns
½ bay leaf

2 tbs/25 g butter
2 tbs/25 g flour
1 cup/250 ml chicken stock
1¼ cups/125 g Stilton cheese,
crumbled

Serves 4

1 Place the milk in a saucepan with the onion, peppercorns and bay leaf. Bring the milk to boiling point then remove from the heat and allow to infuse for 15 minutes. Strain into a jug.

2 Melt the butter, add the flour and carefully blend in the strained milk. Bring to the boil, simmer for a few minutes, adding enough stock to bring to a light creamy consistency. Remove from the heat.

3 Add the crumbled cheese and season to taste. Serve hot, or iced.

Stilton Soup (left) and Tomato Coupe

STILTON SOUP II

2 tbs/25 g butter
1 onion, finely chopped
5 sticks celery, finely
chopped
2 tbs/25 g all-purpose/plain flour
¼ cup/65 ml dry white wine
2¼ cups/600 ml chicken stock
⅔ cup/150 ml milk
1¼ cups/125 g Stilton cheese, crumbled
salt
ground black pepper
⅓ cup/75 ml heavy/double cream

Serves 4–6

1 Melt the butter in a saucepan. Add the onion and celery and cook until soft but not browned – about 5 minutes.

2 Add the flour and cook for a further minute, then remove the pan from the heat.

3 Stir in the wine and stock and return to the heat. Bring to the boil, stirring continuously until the soup thickens, then simmer over low heat for 30 minutes.

4 Cool slightly and liquidize or press the soup through a sieve. Return to the rinsed-out saucepan.

5 Add the milk and heat gently. Stir in the Stilton until melted, the seasoning and the cream. Do not let the soup boil at this stage, or it will curdle. Serve hot or chilled.

LEEK AND WHITE STILTON SOUP

3 medium leeks, trimmed, washed
and chopped
2 tbs/25 g butter
2 tbs/25 g all-purpose/plain flour
2¼ cups/600 ml milk
1 chicken stock cube
⅔ cup/150 ml boiling water
1¼ cups/125 g White Stilton cheese,
finely grated
2 tbs/30 ml light/single cream
4–6 tbs/25–50 g fresh croûtons
2 tsp fresh chopped chives

Serves 4

1 Cook the leeks in a little boiling water until tender. Drain.

2 Melt the butter in a saucepan, add the leeks and cook, stirring over low heat for 5 minutes. Add the flour and stir over low heat for a few more minutes.

3 Gradually add the milk, stirring continuously over low heat. If the mixture shows any signs of forming lumps, remove the saucepan from the heat and beat thoroughly before adding more liquid.

4 Dissolve the stock cube in the boiling water and add to the soup. Sieve or liquidize until smooth.

5 Return the soup to the saucepan and bring to the boil. Remove from the heat and add the grated cheese slowly, stirring until melted.

6 Serve immediately, topped with a little cream and garnished with croûtons – small cubes of bread fried in butter – and/or chives.

CHEESE AND ONION SOUP

1 large onion, chopped
2 tbs/25 g butter
2 tbs/25 g flour
1 tsp mustard powder
2¼ cups/600 ml milk
⅔ cup/150 ml chicken stock
salt
ground black pepper
1¼ cups/125 g Lancashire cheese,
crumbled
paprika pepper

Serves 4

1 Fry the onion in the butter until soft. Add the flour and mustard and cook slowly for 2 minutes. Blend in the milk and stock and bring to the boil, stirring continuously.

2 Season to taste and leave to simmer gently for 15 minutes.

3 Remove from the heat and add the cheese, stirring until melted. Ladle into warm soup bowls and serve sprinkled with paprika pepper.

CHEESE AND VEGETABLE SOUP

4 carrots, diced
2 onions, finely chopped
2 sticks celery, finely
chopped
1¾ cups/450 ml water
1 tsp salt
2 tbs/25 g flour
1¼ cups/300 ml milk
1¼ cups/125 g Cheddar cheese, finely
grated
2 tbs/25 g butter
salt
ground black pepper

Serves 4

1 Place vegetables, water and salt in a saucepan and simmer for 20–30 minutes.

2 Mix the flour to a smooth paste with the milk,

Add to the saucepan, stirring continuously, and bring the soup to the boil. Simmer for 5 minutes.

3 Remove from the heat and add the cheese and butter. Stir until both have melted.

4 Season to taste. Serve in warmed soup bowls.

CHEESE AND CRAB SOUP

4 tbs/50 g butter
1 small onion, finely chopped
4 tbs/50 g all-purpose/plain flour
5 cups/1 litre chicken stock
2¼ cups/125 g white crab meat
1¼ cups/125 g Lancashire cheese, crumbled
salt
ground black pepper
chopped chives

Serves 4–6
1 Melt the butter in a saucepan. Add the onion, then cook gently until soft but not browned. Add the flour, stirring constantly, and pour in the stock, still stirring.

2 Bring to the boil, then simmer for 5 minutes. Put the crab meat and crumbled cheese in a liquidizer or food processor. Add enough soup to moisten the ingredients and blend them into a smooth purée.

3 Return the soup to the saucepan, then simmer gently for 5 minnutes. Add seasoning to taste and serve garnished with chopped chives.

PESTO

Toss this sauce into freshly cooked spaghetti or noodles just before serving.

1 tbs/15 g pine nuts/kernels
1 large bunch fresh basil, chopped
2 cloves garlic, crushed
4–6 tbs/50–75 g Parmesan cheese, grated
1¼ cups/300 ml olive oil

Serves 4
1 Toast the pine nuts in a dry heavy saucepan, shaking the saucepan all the while.

2 Using a blender, or a pestle and mortar, grind the nuts, basil and garlic to a paste. Gradually incorporate the cheese. Dilute with olive oil.

Main Meals

MOUSSAKA

3 large eggplants/aubergines, sliced
salt
olive oil
2 large onions, thinly sliced
1½ lb/¾ kg ground/minced lamb or beef
1 tsp ground cinnamon
ground black pepper
1 large ripe tomato skinned and chopped
2 tbs/30 ml tomato paste/purée
2 tbs fresh chopped parsley
2 tbs/25 g butter
flour
1½ cups/250 ml hot milk
1 egg yolk, beaten
1¼ cups/125 g Kephalotiri cheese, grated (or use mixture of Gruyère and Parmesan)
freshly grated nutmeg

Serves 4–6
1 Place the eggplant/aubergine slices in a colander, sprinkling each layer with salt. Weight with a plate and leave to drain for 30 minutes.

2 Heat 2 tablespoons of oil in a large deep frying pan. Add the onions and fry, stirring, until they are soft and golden. Add the meat and cinnamon and season to taste. Fry until browned.

3 Add the tomato, tomato paste/purée and parsley and continue to simmer for 20 minutes.

4 Melt the butter in a saucepan. Blend in 2 tablespoons flour and stir over a low heat for 1 minute. Gradually beat in the milk. Bring to the boil, stirring continuously until the sauce is thick and smooth.

5 Allow the sauce to cool slightly. Beat in the egg yolk and cheese and season to taste with a pinch of nutmeg.

6 Rinse the eggplant/aubergine slices and dry them on kitchen paper. Coat in flour and fry in oil until golden brown on both sides. Drain well.

7 Line the base and sides of a deep, round casserole dish with the slices. Layer the meat mixture and the rest of the slices into the dish, ending with a layer of eggplant/aubergine slices. Pour the sauce over the top.

8 Bake at 375°F/190°C/Gas Mark 5 for 40 minutes or until the top is bubbling with a rich golden crust.

ENGLISH CHEESE ROLL

2 onions, finely chopped
½ red pepper, cored,
    deseeded and chopped
2 tbs/25 g butter
1 cup/125 g fresh bread crumbs
3 tbs/45 ml light/single cream
1 tsp dried oregano
    salt
    ground black pepper
¾ **lb/350 g** ground/minced beef
¼ **lb/125 g** bacon, ground/minced
2 tbs/20 ml tomato paste/purée
1 egg, beaten
2 tomatoes, thinly sliced
1½ **cups/150 ml** Cheddar cheese, grated
4 tbs/60 ml spicy tomato ketchup
1 tbs/15 g soft brown sugar
pinch dry mustard
    fried onion rings, to
    garnish

Serves 4–6

1 Sauté the onion and pepper in the butter until soft but not browned. Drain well.

2 Mix the bread crumbs, cream, oregano, seasoning, beef, bacon, 1 tablespoon tomato paste/purée, egg, and half the onion and pepper mixture. Combine thoroughly.

3 Place the mixture on a sheet of wax/greaseproof paper placed on a damp tea towel. Cover with another sheet of wax/greaseproof paper and shape the mixture into an oblong 12 × 8in/30.5 × 20.5cm. Remove the top layer of paper.

4 Mix the remaining onion and pepper with 1 tablespoon tomato paste/purée and spread over two-thirds of the meat mixture to within 1in/2.5cm of the outer edges.

5 Arrange the tomatoes on top and sprinkle with cheese, leaving one third of the meat uncovered. Starting from the filled end, carefully roll up lengthways like a jelly/swiss roll. Wrap in a piece of foil and lift on to a baking tray.

6 Bake at 350°F/180°C/Gas Mark 4 for 35 minutes. Mix tomato ketchup, sugar and mustard together. Open the foil and brush this mixture evenly over the meat roll. Return to the oven, uncovered, for a further 20 minutes until the top is slightly brown. Serve garnished with fried onion rings.

BLUE BURGERS

1 lb/450 g ground/minced beef
½ **cup/50 g** fresh bread crumbs
1 small onion, finely chopped
½ **tsp** made mustard
1 tsp Worcestershire sauce
    ground black pepper
1 egg, beaten
6 tbs/50 g Danish Blue cheese

Serves 4

1 Place all the ingredients, except the cheese, in a bowl. Mix well.

2 Divide the cheese into 4, and mould into 4 discs about ¾in/2cm in diameter.

3 Divide the meat mixture into four. Enclose each cheese disc in a portion of meat. Form into neat burger shapes. Chill for 30 minutes.

4 Broil/grill or fry for about 10 minutes, turning frequently until cooked through.

5 Serve on buns/bread rolls with relish/chutney and salad.

VEAL ESCALOPES WITH CHEESE AND SPINACH

4 thin veal scallops/
    escalopes
1 small onion, finely chopped
6 tbs/80 g butter
½ **cup/120 ml** medium dry sherry
2 tsp flour
¾ **cup/175 ml** stock
½ **tsp** tomato paste/purée
1 bay leaf
    salt
    ground black pepper
½ **lb/250 g** chopped frozen spinach,
    thawed and drained
1–2 tbs/15–30 ml heavy/double cream
3 large ripe tomatoes, peeled
1 clove garlic, crushed
4 thin slices Cheddar cheese

Serves 4

1 Brown the scallops/escalopes in 3 tbs/40 g of the butter adding the onion just before they are ready. Add the sherry and boil rapidly until the quantity of liquid is reduced by half.

2 Remove the scallops/escalopes, stir in the flour, stock and tomato paste/purée. Bring to the boil, add the bay leaf and season. Replace the veal, cover and simmer gently for 10–12 minutes until tender.

3 Melt another 2 tbs/25 g of butter in a pan. Add the spinach, stirring until dry. Add the cream and season well.

4 Slice the tomatoes and sauté them briskly for 30 seconds with the garlic in the remaining butter. Place the spinach down the centre of a serving dish. Arrange the scallops/escalopes, drained of sauce, on the spinach. Cover with the tomato mixture. Lay the cheese on top and broil/grill until brown.

5 Bring the sauce to the boil and strain. Pour it round the spinach on the dish.

VEAL ESCALOPES IN MUSHROOM SAUCE

10	veal scallops/escalopes
5 slices	cooked ham
½ cup/125 g	butter
2 sticks	celery, chopped
1	dessert apple, peeled, cored and chopped
2½ cups/225 g	Lancashire cheese, grated
	salt
	ground black pepper
2	onions, chopped
5 tbs/65 g	whole meal flour
3 cups/750 ml	milk
½ lb/250 g	button mushrooms, sliced
5 tbs/75 ml	heavy/double cream
	watercress, to garnish

Serves 10

1 Place each scallop/escalope between two sheets of polythene film and beat until thin. Cut each slice of ham in half. Place a piece of ham on each scallop/escalope.

2 Melt 1 tablespoon butter in a large frying pan and gently fry the celery and apple for 3–4 minutes. Remove from the pan and cool. Mix in the cheese and seasoning.

3 Place some of the stuffing on to each scallop/escalope and roll up. Secure with wooden cocktail sticks or string.

4 Melt the remaining butter in the frying pan. Add the veal rolls and brown on all sides. Remove from the pan. Add the onion and cook until softened. Stir in the flour and cook for 2–3 minutes.

5 Add the milk gradually to the pan, stirring continuously. Bring to the boil. Add seasoning and the veal rolls. Simmer, covered for 10 minutes.

6 Add the mushrooms to the pan. Simmer for a further 5 minutes. Stir in the cream. Serve garnished with watercress.

Veal Escalopes in Mushroom Sauce

Easter Lamb Special

EASTER LAMB SPECIAL

2 small best ends of lamb,
4–5 cutlets each
1 orange
Stuffing
1 small onion, chopped
1 tbs/15 g butter
½ **cup/50 g** fresh bread crumbs
½ orange, grated rind only
3 tsp fresh chopped parsley
¼ **cup/30 g** walnuts, chopped
1¼ **cups/125 g** Danish Blue cheese,
crumbled
ground black pepper
½ egg, beaten

Serves 4–5

1 Soften the onion in the butter. Add the remaining stuffing ingredients. Peel the orange, cut 4 thin slices and reserve for garnish. Chop remaining flesh and add to stuffing.

2 Trim off any fat between the top 1½in/4cm of cutlet bones. Interweave the cutlet bones of the best ends. Tie the joint together with string at each end to make a Guard of Honour. Fill the cavity of the joint with the stuffing.

3 Cover the ends of the bones with foil to prevent discolouration during roasting.

4 Stand the joint in a roasting tin and cook at 350°F/180°C/Gas Mark 4 for 1¾ hours or until tender.

5 Remove the string and foil from the joint. Place on a serving dish and garnish with the reserved orange slices.

CHEESY LAMB PIZZAS

1 shoulder of lamb, boned
and ground/minced
2 tbs/30 ml tomato paste/purée
½ **tsp** dried oregano
salt
ground black pepper
1½ **lb/¾ kg** bread dough, made from
an instant packet mix
2 onions, sliced
2½ **cups/225 g** Cheddar cheese, sliced
tomato relish/chutney

Serves 12

1 Fry the meat, without any added fat, gradually turning up the heat. Stir in the tomato paste/purée, oregano and seasoning. Simmer gently for 10 minutes.

2 Make 12 dough rolls, as directed on the packet. Shape into rounds and flatten each to the size of a

saucer. Place on a greased baking tray. Cover with oiled polythene film. Leave to rise in a warm place for 30 minutes.

3 Divide the lamb mixture equally between the pizza bases. Top with a few slices of cheese and a spoonful of relish.

4 Bake at 425°F/220°C/Gas Mark 7 for 15–20 minutes. Serve with salad.

CHEESY CHOPS

8 best end lamb cutlets
1 clove garlic, crushed
8 thin slices Cheddar cheese
salt
ground black pepper

Serves 4

1 With a sharp knife, cut through each chop from the outside edge to the bone, to make a pocket. Rub the garlic inside the pockets.

2 Place a slice of cheese inside each chop and season the outside of the chops. Broil/grill the chops until tender. Serve immediately.

CHEESY LAMB CALYPSO

1 lb/500 g fillet lamb
1 large onion, sliced
2 tbs/25 g butter
1½ cups/175 g cooked patna rice
2 bananas, sliced
1¼ cups/125 g Cheddar cheese, grated
½ cup/50 g fresh white bread crumbs

Serves 4

1 Either use an attractive frying pan that may also be put under a broiler/grill, or an ordinary pan and transfer the meat later.

2 Fry the onion gently in the butter until soft. Increase the heat slightly and fry the meat, stirring occasionally for 5 to 10 minutes.

3 Add the rice, banana and seasoning and mix well. Moisten with a little water if needed. Mix together the cheese and bread crumbs and sprinkle over the meat mixture. Grill under a hot broiler until lightly browned. Serve with a tossed green salad.

SUMMER LAMB PARCELS

4 lamb leg steaks
salt
ground black pepper
2 onions, sliced

1¼ cups/125 g Cheddar cheese, sliced
3 tsp fresh chopped parsley

Serves 4

1 Cut 4 pieces of foil large enough to parcel each leg steak. Place a steak in the centre of each piece of foil and season well.

2 Divide the onion between the steaks and top each with slices of cheese. Seal the edges of the foil to form individual parcels.

3 Place on a baking tray and bake at 350°F/180°C/Gas Mark 4 for 1 hour. Remove the meat from the parcels and sprinkle liberally with the parsley. Serve with crusty bread and salad.

THATCHED PORK CHOPS

4 pork loin chops
salt
ground black pepper
2 cooking apples, peeled, cored and chopped
1¼ cups/125 g Cheddar cheese, grated

Serves 4

1 Season the chops and broil/grill for 10–15 minutes on each side until tender.

2 Meanwhile place the apples in a saucepan with 3 tablespoons water. Cover and cook gently until the apples form a thick pulp. Mix in half the cheese.

3 Spread the apple mixture over the cooked chops. Sprinkle the remaining cheese over the top.

4 Return the chops to the broiler/grill and cook until the cheese melts.

Cheesy Lamb Calypso

Stuffed Pork Burgers

STUFFED PORK BURGERS

1 lb/500 g ground/minced pork
3 tbs/40 g dry bread crumbs
1 egg, beaten
3 tbs/25 g Cheddar cheese, grated
2 rashers back bacon
3 tsp fresh chopped parsley
½ clove garlic, crushed

Serves 4

1 Mix together the pork, bread crumbs and egg. Divide the mixture into 4 burgers, making a well in each. Blend the cheese, bacon, parsley and garlic, and spoon into the hollow in each burger.

2 Press the meat to enclose the filling and reshape to burgers. Chill for 30 minutes.

3 Broil/grill for 20 minutes until tender. Serve hot in burger rolls/baps with a green salad.

PORK AND CHEESE ROLL

1 lb/500 g ground/minced pork
1 onion, chopped
1 clove garlic, crushed
4 tsp watercress, chopped
salt
ground black pepper
2 eggs, beaten
½ lb/225 g packet prepared puff pastry
1 tbs/15 ml Worcestershire sauce

1¼ cups/125 g Gouda cheese, grated
2 cups/125 g button mushrooms, sliced

Serves 6

1 Mix the pork, onion, garlic and watercress. Season well, Add one egg and the Worcestershire sauce to the meat.

2 Roll the pastry out to a large oblong and place half the meat down the centre. Layer the cheese and mushrooms on top and cover with the remaining meat.

3 Brush the sides of the pastry with the remaining egg and fold over the meat. Seal the edges well. Turn over and place on a greased baking tray. Brush with egg and garnish with any remaining pastry trimmings.

4 Bake at 400°F/200°C/Gas Mark 6 for 30 minutes. Turn the oven down to 350°F/180°C/Gas Mark 4 and cook for a further 30–40 minutes.

PORK FILLET IN PASTRY

1 lb/450 g pork fillet
2 tbs/25 g butter
1 cup/75 g Stilton, sliced
salt
ground black pepper
½ lb/225 g packet prepared puff pastry
1 egg, beaten
watercress sprigs

Serves 3–4

1 Fry the pork fillet in the butter until sealed and golden. Drain on kitchen paper and cool.

2 Make a slit down one side of the meat and fill with slices of cheese. Season the meat all over.

3 Roll out the pastry into an oblong large enough to enclose the meat. Place the meat in the centre of the pastry and fold the edges over. Seal with a little egg and place on a damp baking sheet with the join underneath.

4 Decorate with pastry trimmings and brush all over with egg. Bake at 425°F/220°C/Gas Mark 7 for 45–50 minutes. Garnish with watercress. Serve immediately.

PORK MOZZARELLA

3¼ lb/1.5 kg pork tenderloin, sliced
1 cup/125 g seasoned flour
⅓ cup/100 ml oil
¾ cup/175 g butter
1 large onion, chopped
1 lb/500 g mushrooms, finely chopped
¾ cup/175 ml dry white wine

salt
ground black pepper
2 tsp fresh chopped parsley
3 cups/300 g Mozzarella cheese, grated
1 cup/150 g hazelnuts, chopped
2 tsp paprika pepper
20 sage leaves
2 cups/500 ml thick, rich stock

Serves 10

1 Flatten the sliced pork, flour and fry gently in the hot oil and 8 tablespoons of the butter.

2 To make a duxelle stuffing, fry the onion in 4 tablespoons butter until soft. Add the mushrooms and cook for 3 minutes. Pour on the wine.

3 Boil the mixture rapidly to reduce it to a paste, season and add the parsley. Spread a little of the duxelle in the centre of each slice of pork.

4 Combine the cheese, nuts and paprika. Cover the pork with this mixture and flash under the broiler to melt.

5 Fry the sage leaves in the remaining butter for 5 to 6 seconds. Put the pork into a serving dish, surround with a little stock and decorate with the sage leaves.

PORK STEAKS DERBY

Potato base
2 onions, sliced
1½ lb/700 g potatoes, sliced
3 tbs/40 g butter
⅔ cup/250 ml hot milk

Stuffing
1 small cooking apple, peeled, cored and diced
2 small sticks celery, chopped
1¼ cups/125 g Sage Derby cheese, grated
4 thick pork steaks
2 tbs/25 g butter

Garnish
1 tbs/15 g butter
1 large crisp dessert apple, cored and sliced
castor sugar

Serves 4

1 Place the onions in a saucepan, cover with cold water, bring to the boil and cook for 2–3 minutes. Drain well.

2 Rub a fireproof dish thickly with half the butter and put in the onions and potatoes, in layers, seasoning with salt and pepper. Finish with a layer of potato. Dot the top with the rest of the butter and pour in the hot milk.

3 Bake the potato base at 375°F/190°C/Gas Mark 5 for 30 minutes while preparing the pork.

4 For the stuffing mix together the apple, celery and half the cheese. Cut a pocket in the side of each pork steak, insert the stuffing and sew up or secure with a wooden cocktail stick.

5 Brown the steaks in the butter, allowing 5 minutes on each side. Arrange the steaks on top of the half-cooked potatoes. Sprinkle with the remaining cheese and return the dish to the oven for a further 30 minutes.

6 For the garnish: melt the butter in a frying pan. Put in the apple, sprinkle with castor sugar and fry until golden brown. Garnish with the apple rings.

CHEESY PORK SLICES

2½–3 lb/1.5 kg loin of pork, boned, rolled and rind removed
2 tbs/30 ml oil
2 carrots, diced
1 onion, roughly chopped
1 bouquet garni
salt
ground black pepper
3 cups/150 g button mushrooms, sliced
1 onion, diced
2 tbs/25 g butter

Sauce
1 cup/250 ml milk
2 tbs/25 g butter
2 tbs/25 g flour
1 cup/75 g Cheddar cheese, grated

Serves 4

1 Heat the oil in a flameproof casserole and brown the pork well. Add the carrots, chopped onion, bouquet garni and enough water to just cover the vegetables. Cover.

2 Cook at 400°F/200°C/Gas Mark 6 for 30 minutes then turn the oven down to 350°F/180°C/Gas Mark 4 and cook for a further 1½ hours.

3 Cook the mushrooms and diced onion together in the butter until soft.

4 Make the sauce: in a clean saucepan melt the butter. Stir in the flour and cook for 1 minute. Gradually add the milk, stirring continuously until a smooth sauce is formed. Cook over a gentle heat for 2 minutes.

5 Cut the cooked pork into 8 thick slices. Arrange on a serving dish, with the mushroom and onion mixture between each slice.

6 Pour the sauce over the top, sprinkle with cheese and return to the oven for 30 minutes at 400°F/200°C/Gas Mark 6. Serve with fresh green beans and sauté potatoes.

DANISH PLAIT

Filling
3 tbs/40 g butter
1 stick celery, finely chopped
2 medium leeks, trimmed and sliced
1½ cups/225 g cooked ham, chopped
1 cup/125 g fresh bread crumbs
1¼ cups/125 g Danish Blue cheese,
crumbled
½ tsp dried sage
salt
ground black pepper
1 large egg, beaten

Pastry
1¼ sticks/150 g butter
3 cups/300 g wholemeal flour
poppy seeds

Serves 6–8
1 Melt the butter and fry the celery for 3 minutes. Add the leeks and cook until slightly soft. Remove the saucepan from the heat. Add the ham, bread crumbs, cheese, sage, seasoning and half the egg. Mix well. Cool completely.

2 For the pastry: rub the butter into the flour. Add just enough cold water to mix to a firm dough.

3 Roll pastry out to a rectangle, 11 × 14in/ 28 × 35cm. Place the filling down the centre, leaving a 2in/5cm border at the short edges. Cut the two long sides into 3in/7.5cm strips ready for plaiting.

4 Brush the pastry with the remaining egg. Fold the short sides over the filling.

5 Starting at the top end, cross alternate strips of pastry from either side over the filling to form a plaited effect, pressing down lightly to seal. Brush with remaining egg and sprinkle with poppy seeds.

6 Transfer to a baking tray and bake at 400°F/200°C/Gas Mark 6 for 35 minutes until dark golden. Serve warm, cut into slices.

Danish Plait

WHEATY BACON PIZZA

8 rashers streaky bacon, derinded
2 cups/125 g mushrooms, sliced
1 onion, sliced
15 oz/425 g can crushed tomatoes,
drained
1 clove garlic, crushed
½ tsp dried oregano
salt
ground black pepper
1 cup/75 g Cheddar cheese, grated

Scone base
4 tbs/50 g butter
1½ cups/175 g wholewheat flour
pinch freshly grated nutmeg
freshly chopped parsley

Serves 4
1 Cut half the bacon into small pieces. Place in a cold saucepan and heat slowly to allow any fat to drain out. Add the onion and mushroom and fry until softened.

2 Stir in the tomatoes, garlic, oregano and seasoning.

3 For the base; rub the margarine into the flour and nutmeg. Add just enough cold water to mix to a soft dough.

4 Place an 8in/20cm flan ring on a baking sheet and press in the dough to fill the base and sides.

5 Place the bacon mixture inside and arrange the remaining bacon rashers in a lattice design on top. Sprinkle with the cheese.

6 Bake at 400°F/200°C/Gas Mark 6 for 30 minutes. Sprinkle with chopped parsley and serve hot.

BACON AND SAUSAGE IN CHOUX PASTRY

6 sausages
6 rashers back bacon
⅔ cup/150 ml water
4 tbs/50 g butter
5 tbs/65 g flour
pinch of salt
2 eggs, beaten
3 tbs/25 g Cheddar cheese, grated
3 tbs/25 g Parmesan cheese, grated

Serves 4
1 Wrap the sausages in the bacon and broil/grill gently for 10 minutes.

2 Place the water and butter in a small saucepan and bring to a rapid boil. When the butter has melted, quickly add all the flour and salt at once and beat vigorously until the mixture forms a ball.

3 Remove the saucepan from the heat and allow to cool for 10 minutes. Gradually beat in the eggs, mixing thoroughly after each addition, until a smooth glossy paste is formed. Add just enough of the egg to give a soft mixture, firm enough to just hold its shape. Stir in the cheeses.

4 Spread the mixture over the bottom of a shallow ovenproof dish. Place the sausages down the centre of the dish and cook for 30 minutes at 400°F/200°C/ Gas Mark 6 until the pastry is risen and golden. Serve immediately.

SAUSAGES IN CHEESY BATTER

1 cup/125 g flour
1 tsp salt
2 eggs
1 tsp made mustard
1 cup/250 ml milk
1¼ cups/125 g Leicester cheese, grated
1 lb/500 g pork sausages

Serves 6

1 Sift the flour and salt into a mixing bowl. Make a well in the centre and drop in the eggs and mustard. Mix to a smooth batter with a wooden spoon.

2 Add the milk a little at a time and whisk the mixture until smooth.

3 Broil, grill or fry the sausages until lightly brown. Grease 8 individual shallow pans or 1 large one.

4 Whisk the batter until bubbles form on the surface and then whisk in half the cheese. Pour in sufficient batter to half fill each pan.

5 Place the sausages in the centre and scatter the remaining cheese over the sausages. Bake at 425°F/ 220°C/Gas Mark 7 for 30 minutes or until well risen and golden brown. A skewer inserted in the batter will come out clean when cooked. Serve immediately.

BLUE CHEESE GAMMON

6 tbs/75 g butter, softened
1 cup/75 g Stilton, crumbled
salt
ground black pepper
4 ham/gammon steaks
oil
6 scallions/spring onions, chopped
2 oranges, grated rind and juice
4 orange slices
watercress, to garnish

Serves 4

1 Mix the softened butter with the cheese and

Blue Cheese Gammon

seasoning. Form into a sausage shape and roll up in wax/greaseproof paper or foil, twisting each end of the paper to seal. Chill for 1 hour in the freezer, until firm.

2 Snip the fat of the ham/gammon steaks at regular intervals – this prevents curling during cooking. Brush the steaks with oil and place on a barbecue or under the broiler/grill.

3 Cook for about 6 minutes. Turn the steaks, brush with oil and sprinkle with the chopped scallions/spring onion, orange rind and juice.

4 Continue cooking until ham/gammon steaks are tender. To serve, top each steak with a slice of orange and a slice of blue cheese butter. Garnish with watercress.

Spinach, Cheese and Ham Torta

SPINACH, CHEESE AND HAM TORTA

3 cups/300 g wholemeal flour
3 cups/300 g all-purpose/plain flour
1¼ cups/300 g butter
½ tsp salt
⅓ cup/100 ml iced water

Filling
5 cups/450 g Mozzarella cheese, sliced
2 cups/275 g spinach, trimmed and
blanched
salt
ground black pepper
freshly grated nutmeg
1 clove garlic, crushed
¾ cup/175 ml béchamel sauce
2½ cups/350 g ham, minced
1 tsp mustard
3 tsp tomato paste/purée
1 tsp Worcestershire sauce
1 egg

Serves 12

1 Combine the flours and rub in the butter to resemble fine bread crumbs. Stir in the salt and just enough water to make a smooth firm dough. Wrap in polythene and chill for 30 minutes.

2 Line a deep 10in/25cm ring or loose-based cake pan using two-thirds of the pastry.

3 Cover the base with one quarter of the cheese. Coarsely chop the spinach, drain well, season and mix in the garlic. Spread evenly over the cheese in the pastry case.

4 Cover the spinach with the remaining cheese. Bind the béchamel, ham, mustard, tomato paste/purée, Worcestershire sauce and egg together and spread evenly over the cheese.

5 Use the remaining pastry to make a lid for the pie and seal the edges well. Decorate the top with pastry trimmings.

6 Bake at 375°F/190°C/Gas Mark 5 for 1¼ hours. Serve warm or cold.

FARMER'S LOAF

2 ham/gammon rashers
6 tbs/75 g butter, softened
5 cups/450 g cottage cheese
2 tsp fresh chopped parsley
½ tsp fresh chopped thyme
½ tsp salt
½ tsp ground black pepper
6 eggs

Serves 4–6

1 Fry the ham/gammon rashers. Remove all the fat and rind. Chop the ham/gammon finely and allow to become cold.

2 Blend the butter and cheese in a blender or with a wooden spoon. Mix in the ham/gammon, herbs and seasoning. In a separate bowl, beat the eggs until they froth and then mix them, little by little, into the butter and cheese until the mixture is like heavy cream

3 Butter a 4 cup/900 ml mould or pudding bowl and pour the mixture into it. Cover with foil and stand it in a baking tin containing about 1½in/3.5cm of hot water.

4 Bake at 350°F/180°C/Gas Mark 4 for 1½ hours. Test with a skewer to make sure it is set. It should turn out perfectly. Serve hot with a hollandaise sauce or cold with salad and mayonnaise.

CHICKEN FILLETS MOZZARELLA

2½ cups/225 g Mozzarella cheese, grated
or diced
1 cup/150 g ham, finely diced
1 tbs/20 g coarse grain mustard
10 boned chicken breasts
1 cup/125 g seasoned flour
2 eggs, beaten
1½ cups/225 g wholemeal bread crumbs
oil for deep frying

Serves 10

1 Combine the cheese, ham and mustard. Remove the fillet from each chicken breast and flatten. Make a deep incision where the fillet has been removed, to form a pocket.

2 Fill the pocket with the cheese mixture, lay the flattened fillet over and coat with the flour, egg and finally toss in the bread crumbs.

3 Deep fry at 325°F/160°C for 8 minutes until the chicken is cooked and golden brown.

4 Drain on kitchen paper and serve on a bed of very thin fries, garnished with watercress.

CHICKEN IN CHOUX PASTRY

Choux paste
½ cup/125 ml water
4 tbs/50 g butter
5 tbs/70 g flour
2 eggs, beaten
½ cup/50 g Cheddar cheese, cubed

Filling
1 onion, sliced
½ tbs/5 g butter
1 large mushroom, sliced
2 tsp flour
½ cup/125 ml stock
1½ cups/150 g cooked chicken, chopped
1 tsp chopped parsley
3 tbs/25 g Cheddar cheese, grated
1 tbs/15 g dry bread crumbs

Serves 4

1 Place the water and butter in a saucepan and heat gently until the butter has melted. Bring to the boil and add the flour all at once. Beat until smooth and the paste leaves the sides of the saucepan.

2 Allow the paste to cool slightly. Gradually beat in the eggs until a smooth glossy paste is formed. Stir in the cubes of cheese.

3 For the filling: cook the onion slowly in the butter to soften. Add the mushroom and cook gently for 2–3 minutes. Stir in the flour and pour in the stock.

4 Stir until the sauce is boiling. Remove from the heat and add the chicken and herbs.

5 Butter a fireproof dish. Spoon the choux paste around the sides of the dish leaving the centre clear. Pour the chicken filling into the centre and sprinkle with the bread crumbs and cheese.

6 Bake at 400°F/200°C/Gas Mark 6 for 30–40 minutes until well risen and brown.

Chicken in Choux Pastry

CHICKEN NEAPOLITAN

2 tbs/25 g butter
4 chicken joints
1 small onion, chopped
1 small clove garlic, crushed
8 oz/227 g can tomatoes
1 bouquet garni
salt
ground black pepper
pinch sugar
6 oz/150 g green tagliatelle
olive oil for tossing

Cheese Sauce
1 tbs/15 g butter
1 tbs/15 g flour
1 cup/250 ml milk
1 cup/75 g Leicester cheese, grated
French mustard

Serves 4

1 Melt the butter in a frying pan. Once the sizzling stops, place the chicken joints in the butter, skin side down. Fry until golden.

2 Remove the chicken to a casserole and keep warm. Place the onion in the frying pan and cook until soft. Add the garlic, tomatoes and bouquet garni. Season and bring to the boil.

3 Pour the tomato sauce over the chicken. Cover the casserole and cook at 325°F/170°C/Gas Mark 3 for 30 minutes.

4 Cook the pasta in boiling salted water until tender. Drain, toss in a little oil and black pepper. Place in a fireproof dish.

5 Cut the chicken joints in half and place on top of the pasta. Spoon the tomato sauce over the chicken.

6 Make the cheese sauce: melt the butter in a saucepan. Add the flour and cook for 1 minute. Gradually beat in the milk until smooth. Cook for 2 minutes until a smooth sauce forms.

7 Remove the pan from the heat, beat in all but 1 tablespoon of the cheese, seasoning and mustard. Spoon over the chicken and pasta. Sprinkle with the remaining cheese. Brown in the oven at 375°F/190°C/Gas Mark 5 for 10–15 minutes.

CHICKEN SAGE DERBY

4 boned chicked breasts
1½ cups/150 g Sage Derby cheese, grated
6 tbs/75 g butter, softened
1 oz/25 g streaky bacon, derinded and cut into strips
pinch dried sage
4 tbs/50 g flour
1 egg, beaten
toasted bread crumbs

1 tbs/15 ml oil
watercress sprigs, to garnish

Serves 4

1 Skin the chicken breasts and place in a wet polythene bag. Beat with a rolling pin until flattened.

2 Mix the cheese, 4 tbs/50 g of the butter, bacon and sage together and divide between the pieces of chicken. Roll up neatly and secure each with a wooden cocktail stick.

3 Toss in flour, brush with egg and coat in the bread crumbs. Chill to firm for 30 minutes.

4 Sauté the chicken in the remaining butter and oil until golden. Transfer to an ovenproof dish. Bake at 365°F/190°C/Gas Mark 5 for 20–30 minutes. Garnish with watercress.

POUSSINS/BROILERS WITH STILTON CREAM SAUCE

4 broilers/poussins
salt
ground black pepper
½ cup/125 g butter
½ lb/225 g mushrooms, sliced
¼ cup/60 ml brandy
1¼ cups/300 ml light/single cream
1¼ cups/125 g Stilton cheese, crumbled
parsley sprigs, to garnish

Serves 4

1 Trim the broilers/poussins, season and dot with half the butter. Roast at 400°F/200°C/Gas Mark 6 for 1 hour.

2 Cook the mushrooms in the remaining butter for 5 minutes. Season with salt and pepper. Reduce the heat, add the brandy and marinate the mushrooms for 15 minutes.

3 Increase the heat, stir in the cream, and stir continuously until the sauce thickens. Crumble the Stilton into the sauce; stir until the cheese has melted.

4 Pour half of the sauce over the cooked broilers/poussins and serve the remaining sauce separately. Garnish with parsley and serve immediately.

STUFFED WHITE FISH

1½ cups/150 g fresh bread crumbs
1½ cups/150 g Cheshire cheese, grated
2 onions, finely chopped
1 tsp dried mixed herbs
salt
ground black pepper

4 cups/900 ml milk
2¾ lb/1.3 kg white fish fillets, skinned
6 tbs/75 g butter
½ lb/225 g mushrooms, sliced
1 cup/125 g flour
5 tbs/75 ml tomato paste/purée
fresh chopped parsley

Serves 10

1 Mix together the bread crumbs, cheese, onion, herbs and seasoning with 7 tablespoons of the milk.

2 Place half the fish on the base of a buttered shallow ovenproof dish. Spread the stuffing over the fish and top with the remaining fillets.

3 Melt the butter in a saucepan and fry the mushrooms until soft. Add the flour, remaining milk, tomato paste/purée and seasoning. Heat, stirring continuously, until the sauce thickens and boils. Pour over the fish.

4 Bake at 375°F/190°C/Gas Mark 5 for 20 minutes. Serve garnished with parsley.

SOLE WITH MUSHROOM GARNISH AND CHEESE SAUCE

4 double fillets flounder/plaice or sole, skinned
1½ tbs/20 g butter
1 shallot, finely chopped
½ lb/225 g open mushrooms, finely chopped
small pinch dried thyme
1½ tbs/20 g flour
⅔ cup/150 ml milk
2 tbs/30 ml heavy/double cream
⅓ cup/90 ml light/single cream
1 cup/75 g Derby cheese, grated

Serves 4

1 Wash and dry the fish fillets. Melt the butter and add the shallot. Cook for 1 minute then add the mushrooms, salt, pepper and a little thyme.

2 Allow the mushrooms to cook until the mixture is nearly dry in the saucepan, sprinkle in the flour, mix together and then blend in the milk.

3 Bring to the boil, stirring, and simmer for 2–3 minutes. Adjust the seasoning and spoon the heavy/double cream over the top and leave to cool.

4 Butter a flameproof dish. Place the fillets skinned-side up and spoon the mushroom mixture over them. Fold each in half lengthways and lift carefully into the buttered dish.

5 Mix the light/single cream with the cheese and salt and pepper. Spoon over the fish fillets. Bake at 350°F/180°C/Gas Mark 4 for about 15 minutes. Serve immediately.

MONKFISH, GREEN PEPPERCORNS AND MOZZARELLA

3¼ lb/1.5 kg tail of monkfish, boned and membrane removed
1 cup/125 g seasoned flour
3 tbs/45 ml oil
4 tbs/50 g butter
2 tbs/40 g green peppercorns
4 cups/400 g Mozzarella cheese, thinly sliced

Sauce
1 clove garlic, crushed
2 tbs/30 ml olive oil
¼ cup/60 ml dry vermouth
about 1 lb/500 g tomato flesh, puréed
salt
ground black pepper

Serves 10

1 Cut the monkfish into slices, allowing 2–3 slices per portion. Coat in the seasoned flour. In a frying pan, heat the oil and butter and fry the fish until tender, lightly colouring it.

2 Place the cooked fish on individual plates, sprinkle each piece with a few peppercorns, cover with slices of Mozzarella and place under the broiler/grill until melted.

3 To make the sauce: fry the garlic in the oil. Add the vermouth and rapidly boil until the liquid is reduced by half. Add the tomato flesh, heat, season and pour round the fish.

Stuffed White Fish

*Spiced Fish (left) and
Haddock with Banana
and Almonds*

SPICED FISH

1 lb/450 g cod fillet, skinned and cut
into strips
2 tsp turmeric
3 tbs/45 ml oil
2 onion, chopped
2in/5cm piece cinnamon stick
½ tsp chili powder
2 sticks celery
2 carrots, chopped
½ cup/150 ml unflavoured/natural
yogurt
⅓ cup/50 g mixed nuts, chopped
salt
ground black pepper
1¼ cups/125 g Cheddar cheese, grated
1 lb/450 g potatoes, cooked and
mashed

Serves 4

1 Coat the fish in turmeric and fry quickly in oil for
5 minutes, turning once. Remove from frying pan.

2 Fry the onions and cinnamon stick in the oil until
golden brown. Add the chili powder, celery, carrot
and fry for 10 minutes. Remove from the heat.

3 Stir in the yogurt, a tablespoon at a time. Add
¼ cup/60 ml water, the nuts and seasoning to taste.
Add the fish and simmer for 5–10 minutes.

4 Transfer to an ovenproof casserole and sprinkle
with half the cheese. Add the remaining cheese to the
mashed potatoes and pipe around the edge of the
dish. Broil/grill until golden brown.

HADDOCK WITH
BANANA AND
ALMONDS

2 bananas, cut in half
lengthways
5 tbs/65 g butter
1 lb/450 g haddock fillet
salt
ground black pepper
¼ lb/125 g streaky bacon, derinded
2 onions, sliced
1½ tbs/40 g flour
1¼ cups/300 ml milk
1½ cups/150 g Cheddar cheese, grated
2 tbs/30 ml sherry
½ cup/25 g flaked almonds

Serves 4

1 Fry the bananas quickly in 2 tablespoons butter
until golden brown.

2 Poach the fish in salted water for 10 minutes or
until tender. Reserve ⅔ cup/150 ml of the liquor for

stock. Flake the fish, discarding any skin and bones.

3   Layer the fish and bananas alternately in a buttered 5 cup/1 litre ovenproof dish, seasoning to taste.

4   Fry the bacon rashers in their own fat, remove from the frying pan and fry the onions until soft. Arrange the bacon and onions over the fish and bananas.

5   Place the remaining butter, flour, milk and fish liquor into a saucepan. Heat, stirring continuously, until the sauce thickens, boils and is smooth. Stir in 1¼ cups/125 g of the cheese and the sherry, off the heat, and pour the sauce over the fish. Sprinkle with remaining cheese and almonds.

6   Bake at 400°F/200°C/Gas Mark 6 for 15–20 minutes until the topping is golden brown.

SMOKED HADDOCK IN SCALLOP SHELLS

1¼ lb/600 g mashed potato
1½ lb/750 g smoked haddock, cooked and flaked
½ cup/125 ml béchamel sauce
½ cup/125 ml heavy/double cream
10 slices Mozzarella cheese

Verdi (green) Soufflé
½ cup/125 g butter
1 cup/125 g flour
2 cups/500 ml milk
6 eggs, separated
1 cup/150 g spinach, cooked and chopped
salt
ground black pepper
freshly grated nutmeg
1¼ cups/125 g Mozzarella cheese, grated

Serves 10
1   Pipe the potato around the sides of 10 scallop shells.

2   Combine the flaked haddock, sauce and cream and divide between the shells, placing a slice of Mozzarella on top of each.

3   Make the soufflé: melt the butter in a saucepan. Stir in the flour and cook for 1 minute. Remove from the heat and gradually beat in the milk to form a smooth sauce. Bring to the boil and simmer for 2 minutes. Remove from the heat.

4   Beat in the egg yolks, spinach, seasoning and grated Mozzarella. Whisk the egg whites stiffly and fold into the sauce mixture.

5   Coat the cheese slices with the soufflé mixture. Bake at 400°F/200°C/Gas Mark 6 for 10 minutes until the tops are brown. Serve immediately.

SALMON FLAN

Pastry
1½ cups/175 g all-purpose/plain flour
6 tbs/75 g butter
2 tbs/25 g vegetable shortening
1 egg yolk
2–3 tbs/30–45 ml iced water

Filling
3 large ripe tomatoes
1 onion, thinly sliced
2 tbs/25 g butter
⅔ cup/150 ml light/single cream
2 eggs
7½ oz/190 g can salmon, drained

Topping
6 tbs/50 g Lancashire cheese, grated
¼ cup/25 g fresh bread crumbs
salt
ground black pepper
paprika pepper

Serves 6
1   For the pastry; sift the flour into a mixing bowl. Rub in the fats to resemble fine bread crumbs. Mix the egg yolk and the water together and stir into the flour to make a firm dough. Chill for 30 minutes.

2   Roll the pastry out and use to line a flan ring. Bake blind at 400°F/200°C/Gas Mark 6 for 10 minutes.

3   For the filling; scald and skin the tomatoes, cut in half, remove the seeds, slice and set aside. Cook the onion slowly in the butter then stir in the cream.

4   Remove the saucepan from the heat. Add seasonings and the beaten eggs.

5   Arrange the tomatoes and fish on the bottom of the partially cooked pastry case. Season well, and pour in the onion and egg mixture.

6   Mix the topping ingredients and sprinkle over the flan. Bake at 375°F/190°C/Gas Mark 5 for 20–25 minutes until set and golden brown.

Smoked Haddock in Scallop Shells

BAKED SCALLOPS

6 **large** scallops (off the shell)
1 cup/300 ml water
1 slice onion
6 peppercorns
pinch salt
1 tsp lemon juice
⅔ cup/150 ml heavy/double cream
6 tbs/50 g Cheshire cheese, grated
2 tbs/25 g fresh bread crumbs
6–8 rashers streaky bacon

Serves 3–4

1 Wash the scallops and place in a saucepan with the water, onion, peppercorns, salt and lemon juice. Bring slowly and gently to the boil, turn off the heat. Cover the pan and leave for 5–7 minutes.

2 Lift the scallops from the pan, cut the white part into 2–3 slices and leave the coral whole.

3 Place in a shallow fireproof dish, season the cream with salt and pepper and pour over the scallops. Sprinkle the cheese and crumbs over and bake at 350°F/180°C/Gas Mark 4 for 10–15 minutes.

4 Broil/grill or fry the bacon rashers until crisp. Cut in half and scatter over the top of the scallops.

CHEESE SOUFFLÉ WITH FILLETS OF PLAICE

4 fillets flounder/plaice, skinned
salt
ground black pepper
4 eggs, separated
1 cup/75 g Cheddar cheese, grated
parsley sprigs

Serves 4

1 Roll up the fish, season with salt and pepper and place in a well buttered 5 cup/1 litre soufflé dish and cover.

2 Bake at 350°F/180°C/Gas Mark 4 for 5 minutes. Drain off and discard any liquid.

3 Place the egg yolks in a bowl and beat in the cheese. Whisk the egg whites until stiff and gently fold into the egg yolk mixture. Pour over the fish.

4 Return to the oven and bake at 425°F/220°C/Gas Mark 7 for 12 to 15 minutes until well risen. Serve immediately, garnished with parsley sprigs.

BAKED LASAGNE

2 tbs/25 g butter
3 oz/75 g bacon, chopped
1 onion, chopped
1 carrot, chopped
1 stick celery, chopped
1 clove garlic, crushed
½ lb/225 g ground/minced beef
¼ lb/125 g chicken livers, chopped
2 tbs/30 ml tomato paste/purée
⅓ cup/120 ml white wine
15 oz/425 g can tomatoes
salt
ground black pepper
pinch freshly grated nutmeg
6 oz/175 g lasagne sheets
2½ cups/225 g Mozzarella cheese, sliced
5 tbs/75 ml light/single cream

Serves 6

1 Melt the butter in a pan and fry the bacon, onion, carrot and celery for about 10 minutes until tender.

2 Add the garlic, beef and chicken livers, fry until brown. Stir in the tomato paste, wine, tomatoes and seasonings. Stir until the mixture boils then cover and simmer gently for 40 minutes.

3 Cook the lasagne, a few sheets at a time in boiling, salted water. Drain and put a layer into a well-buttered casserole dish. Cover with a layer of Mozzarella cheese, then a layer of meat sauce to which the cream has been added.

4 Continue in layers finishing with a thick layer of Mozzarella cheese. Dot with a little more butter and bake at 350°F/180°C/Gas Mark 4 for 30 minutes. Serve with a green salad.

SPAGHETTI CAMPANIA

4 tbs/50 g butter
1 onion, sliced
1 cup/50 g button mushrooms, sliced
1¼ cups/175 g cooked ham, diced
2 tomatoes, skinned and chopped
1–2 cloves garlic, crushed
1 tsp dried oregano
salt
ground black pepper
2 tbs/25 g wholemeal flour
1¾ cups/450 ml milk
6 tbs/50 g Cheddar cheese, grated
6 oz/175 g wholemeal spaghetti, cooked
¼ cup/25 g wholemeal bread crumbs

Serves 4

1 Melt half the butter in a frying pan, fry the onion and mushrooms. Stir in the ham, tomatoes, garlic, oregano and seasoning.

2 Place flour, remaining butter and milk in a saucepan. Heat, stirring continuously until the sauce thickens, boils and is smooth. Cook for 2–3 minutes. Remove the saucepan from the heat, add the cheese and stir in the ham mixture.

3 Place the spaghetti on a warmed serving dish, pour over the sauce and sprinkle with bread crumbs. Broil/grill for 5 minutes until golden. Serve hot with a green salad.

CHEESY PASTA

½ lb/225 g tagliatelle
2 tbs/25 g butter
1 onion, chopped
1 clove garlic, crushed
2 oz/50 g cooked ham, cut into strips
1 cup/50 g mushrooms, sliced
3 eggs

⅔ cup/150 ml unflavoured yogurt
salt
ground black pepper
1 cup/75 g Leicester cheese, finely grated

Serves 2

1 Boil the pasta in salted water for 5 minutes, drain.

2 Heat the butter and fry the onion and garlic until soft. Add the ham and mushrooms and cook for a further 3 minutes. Stir in the drained pasta and heat through.

3 Beat the eggs with the yogurt and seasoning. Add to the pasta and cook gently until the egg just starts to set. Sprinkle with cheese and serve at once.

Snacks and Light Meals

CHEESE STRAWS

1 cup/125 g wholemeal flour
salt
cayenne pepper
4 tbs/50 g butter
6 tbs/50 g Cheddar cheese, grated
1 egg yolk

Serves 4–6

1 Season the flour with salt and cayenne pepper. Rub in the butter. Mix in the cheese and egg yolk, Add just enough cold water to mix to a stiff dough.

2 Roll out thinly and cut into rectangles 7in/18cm × 4in/10cm. Place on greased baking trays.

3 Cut the rectangles into straws ¼in/5mm wide. Bake at 400°F/200°C/Gas Mark 6 for 10–15 minutes. Allow to cool on a wire rack.

COTTAGE SCRAMBLE

¼ lb/125 g streaky bacon, derinded and chopped
salt
ground black pepper
6 eggs, lightly beaten
2½ cups/225 g cottage cheese
4 slices wholemeal bread
watercress sprigs, to garnish

Serves 4

1 Fry the bacon in a small saucepan for 3 minutes in its own fat. Season the eggs and pour over the bacon.

2 Cook gently, stirring occasionally, until the egg is scrambled. Stir in the cottage cheese and continue to cook over low heat until the cheese is heated through.

3 Toast the bread. Divide the egg mixture between the toast slices. Garnish with watercress. Serve immediately.

WEST COUNTRY PIES

½ lb/225 g shortcrust pastry
6 oz/175 g bacon rashers, derinded, chopped
2½ cups/225 g Cheddar cheese, finely sliced
1 cooking apple, peeled and thinly sliced
pinch cayenne pepper
salt
beaten egg to glaze

Serves 8

1 Roll out two thirds of the pastry to ¼in/7.5cm circles and line the bases of eight small cake pans. Prick the bases with a fork.

2 Place a layer of bacon pieces on the base of each of the pies, top with a layer of cheese then a layer of apple. Sprinkle with a little cayenne pepper and salt to taste.

3 Roll out the remaining pastry and cut 8 lids to fit. Brush the pies with a little water and press the lids on the pies. Decorate with pastry trimmings.

4 Brush the pies with beaten egg and bake at 425°F/220°C/Gas Mark 7 for 30–35 minutes, until golden brown.

GLOUCESTERSHIRE CHOWDER

2 medium potatoes, diced
2½ cups/600 ml water
salt
ground black pepper
1 bay leaf
1 tsp dried sage
1 tsp ground cumin
1 large onion, chopped
2 tbs/25 g butter
¼ lb/100 g sweetcorn, frozen or canned
2 oz/50 g frozen peas
⅔ cup/150 ml light/single cream
1¼ cups/125 g Double Gloucester cheese, grated
½ tsp freshly grated nutmeg

Serves 4

1 Place the potatoes, water and seasoning in a saucepan with the bay leaf, sage and cumin. Bring to the boil and simmer for about 15 minutes. Remove the bay leaf.

2 Fry the onion in the butter until soft but not browned. Add the boiled potatoes and their cooking liquid. Add the corn and peas, then simmer for 5 minutes. Add a little more water if the soup is too thick.

3 Stir in the cream, cheese and nutmeg. Stir over a very gentle heat until the cheese has melted. Serve immediately.

HAM ROLLS WITH DOUBLE GLOUCESTER

8–10 slices cooked ham/gammon

Filling
4 sticks celery, finely chopped
1¾ cups/175 g Double Gloucester, coarsely grated
2 tbs/25 g pine nuts/kernels
2 tsp unflavoured gelatin/ gelatine
3 tbs/45 ml water
2 tbs/30 ml mayonnaise
¼ cup/65 ml sour cream

Dressing
⅓ cup/90 ml salad oil
1–2 tbs/15–30 ml wine vinegar
salt
ground black pepper
mustard powder
3–4 tomatoes
3 tsp fresh chopped parsley
1 tsp fresh chopped mint and chives

Serves 4–6

1 Mix the celery with the cheese and pine nuts. Soak the gelatin in the water for 2–3 minutes. Stand the bowl in a pan of hot water and stir until dissolved.

2 Add the mayonnaise and sour cream to the gelatin. Add seasoning. When just beginning to set, stir in the cheese mixture.

3 Divide the filling between the slices of ham, roll up like cigars and place in a shallow serving dish. Cover with polythene film and chill.

4 Make the dressing: whisk the oil, vinegar and seasonings together. Skin and deseed the tomatoes. Chop the flesh and add to the dressing with the herbs. Spoon over the rolls just before serving.

CHEESE MILLE FEUILLES

½ lb/225 g puff pastry
2½ cups/225 g Stilton cheese
6 tbs/75 g butter
2 tbs/30 ml heavy/double cream, lightly whipped
1–2 tbs/15–30 ml milk
1¼ cups/125 g Lancashire cheese, grated
salt
ground black pepper
cayenne pepper
mustard powder
3 tsp relish/chutney, chopped

Serves 6

1 Roll out the pastry thinly to a large even sheet, rectangular in shape, to fit your largest baking tray. Prick the surface with a fork.

2 Bake at 425°F/220°C/Gas Mark 7 for 10–15 minutes until deep golden brown. Allow to cool slightly, then cut and trim into 3 even strips. Set aside and reserve trimmings.

3 Remove the rind from the Stilton and crumble the cheese. Cream the butter and gradually work in the cheese. Season well. If necessary add a little of the cream to make the mixture easier to spread. Set aside.

4 Beat the milk into the Lancashire cheese, season and add the relish.

5 Spread half the Stilton cheese mixture evenly over one of the strips of pastry. Place the second strip on top, spread with the Lancashire cheese. Cover with the last strip of pastry.

6 Press down gently with a baking sheet to form the layers before spreading the remaining Stilton cheese mixture over. Mark with a knife or decorate with sliced gherkins, olives etc.

7 Crumble the reserved trimmings finely and place in a narrow band on the top along the long edges. Press in lightly. Cut into wide slices and serve.

Ham Rolls with Double Gloucester (left) and Cheese Mille Feuilles

POTATO AND CHEESE SAUSAGE SOUFFLÉS

$\frac{3}{4}$ **lb/350 g** mashed potato
1$\frac{3}{4}$ **cups/175g** cheese, grated
4 cooked sausages, skinned and chopped
salt
ground black pepper
$\frac{1}{4}$ **cup/15 g** fresh chopped parsley
2 tbs/25 g butter
4 eggs, separated
1 small onion, cut in rings

Serves 4

1 Beat the mashed potato with two thirds of the cheese, the sausages, seasoning, parsley, butter and egg yolks.

2 Whisk the egg whites until stiff and fold into the mixture.

3 Spoon the mixture into 4 greased deep individual ovenproof dishes. Top each one with a few onion rings and sprinkle with the remaining cheese.

4 Bake at 375°F/190°C/Gas Mark 5 for 35–40 minutes, until risen and golden. Serve immediately.

KIPPER AND MUSHROOM SAVOURY

6 oz/175 g kipper fillets
1 cup/50 g button mushrooms, thickly sliced
salt
ground black pepper
2 tbs/25 g butter
1 tbs/15 g flour
$\frac{2}{3}$ **cup/150 ml** milk
5 tbs/45 g Cheddar cheese, grated
hot buttered toast, to serve

Serves 4

1 Poach the kippers and divide into neat fillets, removing the skin and bones.

2 Fry the mushrooms in half the butter, with seasoning, for 1 minute.

3 Melt the remaining butter in a saucepan, add the flour and gradually blend in the milk. Stir until boiling, add the cheese and seasoning.

4 Arrange the mushrooms and then the kipper fillets on fingers of hot toast. Spoon over the sauce and place quickly under a hot broiler/grill. Serve hot.

Tomatoes Filled with Mozzarella and Crab

TOMATOES FILLED WITH MOZZARELLA AND CRAB

20 tomatoes
$\frac{1}{3}$ cucumber, peeled and finely diced
2$\frac{1}{2}$ cups/225 g Mozzarella cheese, finely diced
2 cups/225 g white crab meat
2 cups/225 g dark crab meat
$\frac{1}{3}$ **cup/90 ml** vinaigrette dressing
6 tsp fresh chopped chives
$\frac{2}{3}$ **cup/180 ml** sour cream
10 lettuce leaves
10 thin slices Mozzarella cheese

Serves 10

1 Cut the top quarter off the tomatoes and scoop out the flesh and seeds. Mix the cucumber, diced Mozzarella and crab meat. Stir in the vinaigrette and fill the tomatoes with the mixture.

2 Stir the chives into the sour cream and spoon some on top of each tomato. Replace the tomato lids at an angle.

3 Place a flattened lettuce leaf on each plate. Put 2 tomatoes on each and lay a small slice of mozzarella between them. Serve with brown bread and butter.

BAKED EGGS ARNOLD BENNETT

$\frac{1}{2}$ **lb/225 g** smoked haddock fillet
2 cups/125 g mushrooms, thickly sliced
6 scallions/spring onions, trimmed, thinly sliced
1$\frac{1}{2}$ tbs/20 g butter
salt
ground black pepper
5 eggs
$\frac{1}{4}$ **cup/65 ml** heavy/double cream
3 tbs/25 g Cheddar cheese, finely grated

Serves 4

1 Cover the fish with cold water. Bring slowly to the boil, remove from the heat and allow to stand for 10 minutes.

2 Fry the mushrooms and scallions/spring onions quickly in the butter. Season.

3 Flake the fish, removing skin and bones and add to the mushroom and onion. Separate 1 egg and mix the yolk with half the cream. Stir this into the fish mixture.

4 Spoon the mixture into a buttered ovenproof dish. Make 4 hollows in the mixture with a spoon. Lightly whip the remaining cream, add the cheese and season. Whisk the egg white stiffly and fold into the cheese mixture.

5 Break an egg carefully into each hollow, spoon over the cream and sprinkle with a little more grated cheese.

6 Bake at 400°F/200°C/Gas Mark 6 for 6–10 minutes until the white is just set. Serve immediately.

DANISH MARINERS' PARCELS

13 oz/370 g puff pastry
1¾ cups/175 g Mycella cheese, crumbled
3½ oz/100 g can salmon, drained
¾ cup/125 g frozen mixed vegetables, thawed
½ cup/50 g fresh bread crumbs
ground black pepper
1 egg, beaten

Serves 6

1 Roll the pastry to a 15 × 10in/38 × 26cm rectangle. Trim the edges and cut into six 5in/13cm squares.

2 Mix the cheese, salmon, vegetables, bread crumbs, pepper and half the egg. Divide the mixture between the pastry squares.

3 Brush the edges of the pastry with egg. Fold the pastry over, corner to corner to make triangular parcels. Decorate with pastry trimmings. Glaze with the remaining egg.

4 Place on baking trays and bake at 400°F/200°C/Gas Mark 6 for 25–30 minutes until golden brown. Serve hot or cold.

SOUFFLÉD CHEESE AND PASTA PUDDING

1 medium cauliflower, trimmed
salt
2 tsp made mustard
3 eggs, separated
ground black pepper
¼ lb/125 g short cut macaroni
4 tbs/50 g butter
4 tbs/50 g flour
1¼ cups/300 ml milk
1¼ cups/125 g Cheddar cheese, grated

Serves 4

1 Divide the cauliflower into florets and cook in boiling salted water until tender. Drain and mash. Beat in the mustard and egg yolks. Season.

2 Cook the macaroni in plenty of boiling salted water until tender. Drain thoroughly.

3 Melt the butter in a saucepan and stir in the flour. Cook for 1 minute. Gradually add the milk, stirring

continuously until a smooth sauce forms. Stir in macaroni, half the cheese and the mashed cauliflower.

4 Whisk the egg whites stiffly and fold into the sauce mixture. Spoon into a greased ovenproof dish. Sprinkle with the remaining cheese.

5 Bake at 375°F/190°C/Gas Mark 5 for 35–40 minutes until risen and golden. Serve immediately with a green salad.

BACON AND LEEK QUICHES

1 lb/450 g shortcrust pastry
2 leeks, finely sliced
2 tbs/25 g butter
½ lb/225 g boiled bacon from a joint, finely diced
ground black pepper
¾ cup/175 ml milk
3 eggs
6 tbs/50 g Cheddar cheese, grated

Serves 6

1 Line 8 small deep cake pans with the shortcrust pastry.

2 Fry the leek in the butter until soft and divide between the pastry cases. Sprinkle over the chopped bacon and season.

3 Beat together the milk, eggs and cheese and pour into the pastry cases. Bake at 375°F/190°C/Gas Mark 5 for 40 minutes until golden brown. Serve hot or cold.

Danish Mariners' Parcels

FARMHOUSE QUICHE

½ lb/225 g shortcrust pastry
1 onion, chopped
¼ lb/125 g streaky bacon, derinded and chopped
1 cup/50 g mushrooms, sliced
2 tbs/25 g butter
1 tbs/15 g sage and onion stuffing mix
7½ oz/213 g can tomatoes, drained
1¾ cups/175 g Cheddar cheese, grated
1 dessert apple, peeled and chopped
3 eggs, beaten
⅓ cup/90 ml milk
salt
ground black pepper
1 tsp made mustard
sprig of watercress

Serves 4–6

1 Roll out the pastry and use to line a 9in/23cm tart pan/flan dish.

2 Fry the onion, bacon and mushrooms in the butter until soft. Stir in the stuffing mix and tomatoes. Allow to cool.

3 Sprinkle half of the cheese over the base of the tart, then spread the apple over followed by the onion mixture and the remaining cheese.

4 Beat together the eggs, milk, seasoning and mustard and pour over the tart.

5 Bake at 400°F/200°C/Gas Mark 6 for 50 minutes. Garnish with watercress and serve hot or cold.

ONION TART/FLAN

6 tbs/75 g butter
1½ lb/700 g large mild onions, thinly sliced
6 tsp finely chopped parsley
2 tsp dried basil
½ lb/450 g shortcrust pastry
1¼ cups/300 ml light/single cream
3 large eggs
6 tbs/50 g Gruyère cheese, grated
salt
ground black pepper

Topping
3 tbs/25 g Gruyère cheese, grated
4 tbs/50 g fresh white bread crumbs

Serves 6–8

1 Melt the butter in a large saucepan. Add the onions and cook gently, tightly covered, for 15 minutes. Stir frequently.

2 When the onion is soft, uncover the saucepan and continue to fry until they become very soft without

colouring or losing their shape.

3 Remove the pan from the heat and stir in the parsley and basil.

4 Roll out the pastry and use to line a 10in/25cm flan pan with a removable base. Prick the pastry case with a fork, line with foil and fill with beans.

5 Bake blind at 425°F/220°C/Gas Mark 7 for 15 minutes. Remove the foil and beans and return to the oven for a further 5 minutes.

6 Beat the cream lightly with the eggs and cheese and mix into the onion mixture. Season. Pour the filling into the pastry case set on a baking tray.

7 For the topping: mix the cheese and crumbs and sprinkle over the tart. Bake at 375°F/190°C/Gas Mark 5 for 35 minutes until the filling is puffed and set.

PRAWN AND SMOKED SALMON TART/FLAN

¼ lb/125 g cheese flavoured crackers/biscuits
5 tbs/65 g butter, melted
6 tbs/50 g Cheddar cheese, grated
salt
ground black pepper
½ tsp made mustard

Filling
3 tbs/40 g butter
6 eggs
3 tbs/45 ml heavy/double cream
1½ cups/175 g peeled shrimp/prawns
1¼ cups/125 g Cheshire cheese, crumbled
¼ lb/75 g thinly shredded smoked salmon

Serves 6

1 Make the case: crush the crackers/biscuits finely. Stir in the melted butter, cheese and seasonings.

2 Press the mixture over the base and sides of a 9in/23cm tart pan, using the back of a spoon. Bake at 350°F/180°C/Gas Mark 4 for 10 minutes. Allow to cool.

3 Make the filling: melt the butter in a saucepan. Beat the eggs with more seasoning and the cream and pour into the saucepan. Stir slowly over a gentle heat until the mixture becomes creamy and thick. Do not overcook.

4 Remove from the heat, stir in the shrimp/prawns and Cheshire cheese. Pour into the crumb crust case and allow to cool.

5 Scatter the surface of the tart with the shredded smoked salmon.

CHEESE SAUSAGE TART/FLAN

6 oz/175 g shortcrust pastry
½ lb/225 g sausage meat
2 eggs, beaten
1 small onion, chopped
½ tsp dried mixed herbs
salt
ground black pepper
1¼ cups/125 g Double Gloucester
cheese, grated
2 tomatoes, sliced

Serves 4–6

1 Roll out the pastry on a lightly floured surface and use to line an 8in/20cm tart pan/flan dish, reserving the trimmings for decoration.

2 Break up the sausage meat with a fork and work in the eggs, onion, herbs and seasoning. Pour into the prepared crust.

3 Sprinkle the cheese over the top of the tart. Roll the pastry trimmings out and cut into strips. Arrange them in a lattice design over the tart. Place the slices of tomato between the pastry strips.

4 Bake at 425°F/220°C/Gas Mark 7 for 30–35 minutes. Serve hot or cold.

DANISH LATTICE FLAN

Pastry
½ cup/125 g butter
2 cups/225 g wholemeal flour
1 small onion, grated
3–4 tbs/45–60 ml iced water
Filling
½ lb/225 g cauliflower florets
2 tbs/25 g butter
2 tbs/25 g flour
1¼ cups/300 ml milk
1¼ cups/125 g Danish Blue cheese,
crumbled
ground black pepper
¼ tsp mustard powder
¼ lb/125 g cooked ham, chopped
3 tsp fresh chopped parsley
beaten egg or milk, to
glaze

Serves 6–8

1 Make the pastry: rub the butter into the flour. Stir in the onion and add just enough water to give a firm mixture.

2 Knead on a lightly floured surface. Roll out two thirds of the pastry and use to line an 8in/20cm tart pan/tin. Chill for 20 minutes.

3 Cook the cauliflower until just tender. Leave to drain thoroughly.

Danish Lattice Flan

4 Melt the butter in a saucepan and add the flour. Cook for 1 minute, remove from the heat and gradually stir in the milk. Return to the heat and bring to the boil, stirring.

5 Remove from the heat and stir in the cheese, pepper and mustard. Gently stir in the ham and parsley.

6 Line the pastry case with foil and bake blind at 400°F/200°C/Gas Mark 6 for 10 minutes. Remove the foil.

7 Roll out the remaining pastry and cut into ½in/1cm strips. Pour the cheese mixture into the tart case and arrange the strips of pastry over the top. Glaze with egg or milk.

8 Bake for 15 more minutes, then turn the oven down to 350°F/180°C/Gas Mark 4 for a final 20 minutes.

CHEESE FONDUE

1 clove garlic, bruised
1 bottle dry white wine
7½ cups/700 g Gruyère cheese, grated
7½ cups/700 g Emmental cheese, grated
ground black pepper
freshly grated nutmeg
⅓ cup/90 ml kirsch
2 large French bread sticks, cut
into cubes

Serves 6

1 Begin the fondue on the stove and then transfer it to the fondue stand. Rub the fondue pan with garlic.

2 Pour the wine into the pan, add the cheese and cook over moderate heat until the cheese has melted. Sprinkle in a little pepper or nutmeg and stir in the kirsch. Transfer to the fondue stand on the table.

3 The diners dip cubes of bread into the cheese mixture, on long thin forks.

*Celeriac Croquettes (left)
and Stuffed Mushrooms
Wensleydale*

CHEESE SOUFFLÉ

3 tbs/40 g butter
3 tbs/40 g flour
1¼ cups/300 ml milk
salt
ground black pepper
pinch cayenne pepper
1 tsp made mustard
4 egg yolks
4 tbs/40 g Gruyère cheese, grated
3 tbs/25 g Parmesan cheese, grated
5 egg whites

Serves 4

1 Melt the butter in a saucepan. Stir in the flour and cook for 1 minute. Remove from the heat and gradually stir in the milk until a smooth sauce is formed.

2 Return the saucepan to the heat and bring to the boil, stirring. Remove from the heat and stir in the seasonings.

3 Cool the sauce slightly. Beat in the egg yolks and the cheese. Whisk the egg whites until stiff. Mix 1 tablespoon of the egg whites into the sauce, then fold in the rest.

4 Pour the mixture into a well-buttered 2 pint/1 litre soufflé dish and bake at 375°F/190°C/Gas Mark 5 for 25–30 minutes until golden and well risen. Serve immediately.

CELERIAC CROQUETTES

1 celeriac root, thickly peeled
beaten egg
½ cup/50 g fresh bread crumbs
3 tbs/25 g Derby cheese, finely grated
oil and butter for frying

Serves 4

1 Cut the celeriac into thick wedge-shaped pieces. Cook in salted water until just tender. Drain and dry.

2 Brush the cooked celeriac with beaten egg and roll in a mixture of bread crumbs and cheese.

3 Shallow fry until golden brown. Serve hot.

STUFFED MUSHROOMS WENSLEYDALE

¾ lb/350 g mushrooms, peeled
3 tbs/25 g fresh bread crumbs
1 tbs/15 g butter, melted
1 egg yolk
2 tbs/30 ml cream
2 tsp finely chopped parsley
2 tsp finely chopped chives
1 clove garlic, crushed

salt
ground black pepper
pinch freshly grated nutmeg
1 cup/75 g Wensleydale cheese,
grated
2 tbs/20 g toasted bread crumbs
3 tbs/40 g butter

Serves 4

1 Remove the stalks from the mushrooms and chop with the peelings and one third of the mushrooms. Stir in the crumbs, melted butter, egg yolk and cream. Blend in the herbs, garlic and seasoning.

2 Fill the remaining mushroom cups with this mixture. Arrange them in a buttered flameproof casserole dish. Sprinkle with the cheese, crumbs and dot with the butter.

3 Bake at 375°F/190°C/Gas Mark 5 for 12–15 minutes. Serve as an accompaniment to chicken or lamb dishes.

CAULIFLOWER CHEESE FRITTERS

1 cauliflower, separated
into florets
1 cup/125 g all-purpose/plain flour
1 egg, separated
⅔ cup/300 ml milk
salt
ground black pepper
2 tbs/15 g Parmesan cheese, grated
oil for deep frying

Serves 4–6

1 Cook the cauliflower in boiling salted water for 5 minutes. Drain well and dry on kitchen paper. Set aside.

2 Place the flour, egg yolk, milk, seasonings and cheese in a blender or food processor and work until smooth. Whisk the egg white until stiff and carefully fold into the batter.

3 Dip each floret into the batter and drop it into hot oil at 375°F/190°C. Cook for 4–5 minutes or until golden brown.

4 Remove the fritters from the oil with a slotted spoon, drain on kitchen paper and serve hot.

LIMA/BROAD BEANS AU GRATIN

4 tbs/50 g butter
¾ lb/350 g mushrooms, thickly sliced
1½ tbs/40 g flour
1¼ cups/300 ml stock
1¼ cups/300 ml light/single cream

4 tbs/25 g Parmesan cheese, grated
salt
ground black pepper
1½ lb/350 g shelled lima/broad beans
dry bread crumbs
extra butter

Serves 4–6

1 Melt 1 tablespoon of the butter in a frying pan. Add the mushrooms and fry until just golden. Remove from the pan and reserve.

2 Melt the remaining butter in a large saucepan. Stir in the flour and cook for 1 minute. Remove the pan from the heat and gradually add the stock and cream, stirring continuously.

3 Return the pan to the heat and bring to the boil, stirring. Stir in 2 tablespoons of the cheese and salt and pepper to taste. Add the beans and mushrooms, with their pan liquor and stir in thoroughly.

4 Pour into a heatproof dish. Sprinkle the top with the remaining cheese and enough bread crumbs to cover thinly. Dot with a little extra butter and broil/grill until browned.

POTATO GNOCCHI

1½ lb/700 g floury potatoes
salt
2 tbs/25 g butter
1 egg, lightly beaten
½ tsp baking powder
1½ cups/175 g all-purpose/plain flour
6 tbs/75 g butter, melted
6 tbs/50 g Parmesan cheese, grated
1 tbs/15 g fine dry bread crumbs

Serves 3–4

1 Boil the potatoes in salted water until just tender. Drain and mash them with the butter. Beat in the egg, baking powder and salt.

2 Gradually add the flour to the potato a handful at a time, working it in smoothly with your fingers. As the mixture stiffens, turn it out on to a floured surface.

3 Continue kneading in the flour to make a firm dough. Divide into 4 portions and allow them to rest for 10 minutes.

4 Shape a portion of the dough into a cylinder ½in/1cm in diameter. Cut it into 1in/2½cm lengths.

5 Drop them into a large pan of boiling salted water. They will sink to the bottom and then float to the surface. Once they have done so, simmer them for 3 minutes.

6 Remove the gnocchi with a slotted spoon, rinse them in boiling water and allow to drain. Pour a tablespoon of melted butter and a quarter of the cheese into a heated baking dish. Put the gnocchi in

it and sprinkle with another tablespoon of butter and cheese.

7   Place the baking dish under the broiler/grill to brown the gnocchi while the next batch is cooking. Repeat the process until all the gnocchi are cooked. Top the final layer with a mixture of bread crumbs and cheese. Brown under the broiler/grill. Serve hot.

POTATOES HAGGERTY IN THE PAN

1½ tbs/25 ml oil
1½ lb/¾ kg potatoes, very thinly sliced
1 large onion, finely sliced
1¼ cups/125 g dried hard cheese, grated
ground black pepper
salt

Serves 2

1   Heat the oil in a large frying pan. When it is hot remove the pan from the heat and put the potatoes, onions and cheese in layers, seasoning as you go. End with a layer of potatoes.

2   Return the pan to the heat, cover and cook over low heat. When the vegetables are cooked increase the heat to brown the base. Put under a broiler/grill to brown the top. Serve from the pan.

POTATOES À LA DAUPHINOISE

4 tbs/50 g butter
1 clove garlic, crushed
2 lb/900 g potatoes, thinly sliced and washed
1¼ cups/125 g Gruyère cheese, grated
salt
ground black pepper
freshly grated nutmeg
⅔ cup/300 ml scalded milk or cream
1 egg, beaten

Serves 4

1   Mash half the butter with the garlic clove and use it to grease a shallow baking dish.

2   Place a layer of potatoes in the bottom of the dish and sprinkle with a little of the cheese, salt, pepper and nutmeg. Repeat the layers until you have used all the potatoes and nearly all the cheese.

3   Beat the milk or cream and egg together and strain the mixture over the potatoes. Sprinkle over the remaining cheese.

4   Cut the remaining butter into small pieces and dot it over the top. Bake at 350°F/180°C/Gas Mark 4 for about 1¼ hours or until the potatoes are tender and the top is golden.

DANISH BLUE AND PINEAPPLE DIP

1½ cups/150 g Danish Blue cheese, at room temperature
2 tbs/30 ml mayonnaise
⅔ cup/150 ml sour cream
8 oz/227 g can pineapple, well drained
1 tsp chopped chives
ground black pepper
chopped parsley, to garnish

Serves 4–6

1   Mash the cheese and blend in the mayonnaise and cream.

2   Finely chop the pineapple. Add to the cheese with the chives and mix well. Season to taste.

3   Spoon into a serving dish and chill for at least an hour. Garnish and serve with dippers such as crackers, raw cauliflower sprigs, carrot sticks, celery and cucumber.

BLUE STILTON, WALNUT AND GRAPE CHARLOTTE

4–6 slices white bread, crusts removed
½ cup/125 g butter
2 eggs, separated
salt
ground black pepper
¼ tsp mustard powder
⅔ cup/150 ml milk
1 tbs/15 g unflavoured gelatin/gelatine
1¾ cups/175 g Stilton cheese, crumbled
¼ lb/125 g white grapes, skinned, deseeded and quartered
⅓ cup/50 g walnuts, chopped
⅔ cup/150 ml heavy/double cream
walnut halves, black and green olives and parsley, to garnish

Serves 8

1   Cut each slice of bread into 4 fingers. Melt the butter in a frying pan and fry the bread fingers until evenly golden brown, turning once during cooking. Drain on kitchen paper.

2   Use the bread fingers to line the sides of a 6in/15cm deep cake pan. Reserve one slice for the top.

3   Beat the egg yolks with the seasoning and mustard until pale and creamy. Scald the milk, remove from the heat and pour over the yolks while whisking.

4 Set the egg yolks in a bowl over a pan of simmering water and cook, stirring continuously, until the mixture thickens enough to coat the back of a wooden spoon.

5 Place 2 tablespoons cold water in a small bowl and sprinkle the gelatin over. Stand the bowl in a saucepan of hot water and heat gently until dissolved.

6 Stir the gelatin into the cooked custard with the cheese, grapes and walnuts. Leave to cool and set.

7 Whip the cream and fold into the set custard. Whisk the egg whites until stiff and fold in. Pour the mixture into the prepared cake pan and finish with the reserved slice. Chill until set.

8 Dip in hot water and turn out. Decorate with nuts, olives and parsley. Serve with Melba toast.

STILTON CHEESE SLICE

½ lb/225 g puff pastry
1 cup/75 g Stilton cheese, rind removed and crumbled
1 egg, beaten
2 tbs/25 g butter, softened
salt
ground black pepper
cayenne pepper
beaten egg with salt to glaze

Serves 6

1 Roll the pastry out to a thin oblong and divide into two equal pieces. Mash the cheese until creamy, add the beaten egg, butter and seasoning to taste.

2 Spread this mixture on one half of the pastry, wet the edges and place the other half on top.

3 Press the edges, brush with beaten egg, score across in long narrow fingers. Bake at 425°F/220°C/Gas Mark 7 for 20 minutes and cut into fingers as marked. Serve warm.

CHEESE AND GARLIC LOAF

2 cups/225 g all-purpose/plain flour
1¾ cups/200 g wholemeal flour
2 tsp baking powder
4 tbs/50 g butter
1¾ cups/175 g Cheddar cheese, grated
1 clove garlic, crushed
1 egg, lightly beaten
1¼ cups/300 ml milk

Serves 4–6

1 Mix the flours together with the baking powder. Rub in the butter. Add the cheese and garlic and stir

in just enough egg and milk to form a soft dough.

2 Knead lightly and place in a well buttered large loaf pan. Bake at 400°F/200°C/Gas Mark 6 for 50 minutes until well risen and golden brown.

3 Cool on a wire rack. Serve in slices, buttered.

Danish Cheese Loaf

DANISH CHEESE LOAF

1 cup/125 g wholemeal flour
1 cup/125 g self-raising flour
½ tsp baking powder
1 tsp mustard powder
½ tsp salt
6 tbs/50 g butter
1¼ cups/125 g Danish Blue cheese, crumbled
2 sticks celery, chopped
⅓ cup/50 g walnuts, chopped
1 large egg
⅓ cup/125 ml milk
sesame seeds, optional

Serves 8

1 Sift the flours, baking powder, mustard and salt into a bowl. Rub in the butter until the mixture resembles fine bread crumbs. Add the cheese and stir through the mixture.

2 Mix in the celery and nuts. Beat the egg and milk together and add to the dry ingredients. Mix well to give a fairly stiff batter.

3 Spoon the mixture into a greased and lined 1 lb/450 g loaf pan/tin. Level the top and sprinkle with sesame seeds, if used.

4 Bake at 375°F/190°C/Gas Mark 5 for 1 hour or until well browned and a skewer inserted comes out cleanly.

5 Allow to cool in the pan/tin for 5 minutes. Turn out on to a wire rack. Serve warm or cold, sliced and buttered.

CHEDDAR SUNSET LOAF

2 eggs, beaten
1¼ cups/125 g Double Gloucester cheese, grated
¼ cup/25 g fresh bread crumbs
½ tsp dried oregano
½ tsp soy sauce
1 small onion, chopped
salt
ground black pepper
1½ cups/175g self-raising flour
2 large tomatoes, skinned and sliced
1 cup/75 g Cheddar cheese, sliced

Serves 4–5

1 Mix the eggs, cheese, bread crumbs, oregano, soy sauce, onion and seasonings. Work in the flour a little at a time to make a soft dough.

2 Knead well and divide into 2 pieces. Place one piece in the base of a small buttered loaf pan. Place the tomato over the dough.

3 Arrange the cheese slices on the tomato and top with the remaining dough.

4 Bake at 350°F/180°C/Gas Mark 4 for 40–45 minutes or until firm and golden. Cool on a wire rack. Serve sliced and buttered.

HOT CHEESE AND GARLIC BREAD

2 cloves garlic, crushed
½ cup/125 g butter, softened
1¼ cups/125 g Mozzarella cheese, grated
ground black pepper
3 tsp fresh chopped parsley
1 small crusty bread loaf

Serves 4

1 Mix the garlic, butter, cheese, pepper and parsley. Make cuts down the loaf at ½in/1cm intervals, almost to the base.

2 Spread the butter mixture over each side of the bread slices.

3 Bake at 400°F/200°C/Gas Mark 6 for 15 minutes. Serve immediately.

DANISH BLUE RING

2 cups/225 g self-raising flour
1 tsp baking powder
4 tbs/50 g butter
6 tbs/50 g Danish Blue cheese, crumbled
⅔ cup/150 ml milk

Serves 4–8

1 Sift the flour and baking powder into a bowl. Rub in the butter and stir in the cheese.

2 Mix in enough milk, using a fork, to make a soft but not sticky batter. Knead lightly on a floured surface.

3 Divide the mixture into 8 pieces and form each into a ball. Place one ball in the centre of a well-buttered 8in/20cm round cake pan. Arrange the remaining balls of dough round the outside so they just touch.

4 Brush with milk to glaze. Bake at 400°F/200°C/Gas Mark 6 for 25 minutes until well risen and brown.

5 Serve warm buttered and filled with jelly/jam, or cucumber and blue cheese.

LANCASHIRE CHEESE BISCUITS/SCONES

2 cups/225 g self-raising flour
1 tsp salt
¼ tsp mustard powder
4 tbs/50 g butter
1¼ cups/125 g Lancashire cheese, finely grated
milk, to mix

Serves 4–8

1 Mix the flour with the salt and mustard. Rub in the butter until it resembles bread crumbs. Mix in the cheese, then stir in enough milk to form a soft dough.

2 Roll out the dough to ½in/1cm thick and cut into triangles. Put the biscuits/scones on a greased baking tray and bake at 425°F/220°C/Gas Mark 7 for 10–15 minutes.

CHEESE AND BACON BISCUIT/SCONE

2 cups/225 g all-purpose/plain flour
½ tsp salt
2 tsp baking powder
2 tbs/25 ml corn oil
⅔ cup/150 ml milk
1¼ cups/125 g Cheddar cheese, grated
4 rashers streaky bacon, derinded and chopped

Serves 4–6

1 Sift the flour, salt and baking powder into a bowl. Mix together the oil and milk. Add half the cheese and the bacon to the flour and mix with the liquid to form a soft, elastic batter/dough.

2 Knead lightly on a floured surface and roll out to a circle ½in/1cm thick.

3 Mark the top into wedges with a sharp knife and sprinkle with the remaining cheese.

4 Bake at 425°F/220°C/Gas Mark 7 for 10–15 minutes. Serve warm, split and buttered.

CREAMY FILLED SCONES/BISCUITS

2 cups/225 g self-raising flour
½ **tsp** salt
½ **tsp** mustard powder
1¼ **cups/125 g** Double Gloucester cheese, grated
⅔ **cup/150 ml** milk
walnut halves

Filling
1¼ **cups/125 g** Lancashire cheese, grated
salt
ground black pepper
6 tbs/50 g butter, softened
¼ **cup/60 ml** heavy/double cream

Makes 9–12 scones/biscuits

1 Sift the flour, salt and mustard into a bowl. Rub in the butter and stir in three quarters of the cheese. Mix together with the milk to make a soft mixture.

2 Turn out on to a floured surface, knead lightly and roll out to ½in/1cm thick. Cut out rounds with a cookie/biscuit cutter and place on a baking tray.

3 Sprinkle the scones/biscuits with the remaining cheese and top each with a walnut half.

4 Bake at 450°F/230°C/Gas Mark 8 for 10–12 minutes. Remove and cool on a wire rack.

5 Make the filling: beat together the cheese, seasoning, butter and cream. Split the scones/biscuits and sandwich with the filling.

STRONG ALE AND CHEESE

1¾ **cups/175 g** Double Gloucester cheese, cut in slices
2 tbs/25 g wholegrain mustard
⅔ **cup/300 ml** strong beer or ale
4 large slices fresh toasted white bread, crusts removed

Serves 4

1 Put the cheese into a small shallow fireproof dish so that the slices are about ½in/1cm deep. Spread the mustard over the top.

2 Pour in the ale, which should just cover the cheese. Bake at 450°F/230°C/Gas Mark 8 for 15 minutes.

3 To serve, pour and spoon the cheese mixture over the slices of toast. Serve with a bowl of fresh watercress.

Hot Cheese and Garlic Bread

CHEESE AND BACON TOASTIES

4 slices white bread
8 rashers streaky bacon
1 cup/75 g Leicester cheese, grated
¾ cup/75 g fresh bread crumbs
pinch mustard powder
pinch paprika pepper
shredded lettuce, to garnish

Serves 4

1 Toast the bread on one side. Broil/grill the bacon. Arrange 2 rashers of bacon on the untoasted side of each piece of bread.

2 Mix the cheese, bread crumbs, mustard and paprika. Pile on top of the bacon, and put under a hot broiler/grill for a few minutes, until golden brown.

3 Cut off the crusts and cut each toasty in half to make 2 triangles. Garnish with lettuce.

CRISPY CHEESE CASES

8 large slices white bread, crusts removed
4 slices Mozzarella cheese
4 slices ham
ground black pepper
butter for frying

Serves 4

1 Put a slice of cheese on four slices of the bread. Cover each with ham and a little black pepper.

2 Press the remaining bread slices on top and cut each sandwich in half.

3 Fry the sandwiches in the butter until brown on one side. Turn and brown the other side. Serve hot with salad.

CHARNWOOD SMOKED PÂTÉ WITH ALMONDS

1¼ cups/125 g full fat cream cheese
1¼ cups/125 g low fat curd cheese
⅔ cup/150 ml heavy/double cream
1 tbs/15 g butter
¼ tsp chili powder
¼ tsp dried chervil
1 tsp mustard powder
⅔ cup/125 g whole blanched almonds
1¼ cups/125 g Charnwood smoked Cheddar cheese, grated
parsley sprigs, to garnish

Serves 6

1 Cream the soft cheeses together. Lightly whip the cream and fold into the cheese mixture; set aside.

2 Melt the butter in a frying pan on very low heat and add the chili powder, chervil and mustard powder. Cook for ½ minute.

3 Reserve a few of the almonds for garnish and finely chop the remainder. Add these to the frying pan with the Charnwood cheese and stir until just melted.

4 Remove from the heat and mix thoroughly. Allow to cool slightly, then add to the creamed cheeses and stir through lightly.

5 Divide the mixture between 6 small dishes and chill until set. Toast the reserved almonds. Garnish with the nuts and parsley. Serve with toast.

BACON AND PINEAPPLE TOASTIES

4 large slices white bread
butter, for spreading
4 canned pineapple rings, drained
4 thick slices Cheddar cheese
8 rashers streaky bacon

Serves 4

1 Toast the bread fully on one side and lightly on the other side. Butter the lightly toasted side.

2 Put a pineapple ring on each buttered side and top with a slice of cheese.

3 Broil/grill until the cheese has melted and is golden brown. Broil/grill the bacon rashers until crisp and place on top of the cheese.

HAM AND CHEESE FRIES

4 slices ham
4 slices Gruyère cheese
8 slices bread
2 eggs
½ cup/125 g butter
tomato, to garnish

Serves 4

1 Cut the ham slices in half. Make 4 sandwiches with a slice of ham, a slice of cheese and another slice of ham, between 2 slices of bread.

2 Beat the eggs in a flat dish. Lay each of the sandwiches in the egg, turning over so both sides of the bread soak up the egg.

3 Fry the sandwiches in the butter until golden brown. Serve cut in half, garnished with tomato.

OPEN SANDWICH

1 crispbread
butter
Double Gloucester cheese
slices
shredded lettuce
sliced cucumber
salami slices, made into
cones
Caerphilly cheese, finely
grated, blended with a
little milk
stuffed olives to garnish

Serves 1

1 Spread the crispbread with butter. Arrange on top a layer of Double Gloucester, lettuce and cucumber. Add cones of salami filled with the blended Caerphilly cheese.

2 Garnish with sliced stuffed olives.

SALAD ROLLS

8 large crisp rolls
4 tbs/50 g butter, melted

Cheshire Filling
2–3 tomatoes
2 tbs/25 g sweet relish/pickle
6 tbs/50 g Cheshire cheese, crumbled
4 lettuce leaves

Wensleydale Filling
½ **bunch** watercress, chopped
1 cup/75 g Wensleydale cheese,
crumbled
2 tbs/30 ml thick mayonaise

Serves 4–8

1 Cut the tops off the rolls. Scoop out the soft crumb and brush inside and out with the butter. Bake at 350°F/180°C/Gas Mark 4 for 5–6 minutes. Cool.

2 Cheshire filling: skin and slice the tomatoes. Mix the relish with the cheese. Place the lettuce leaves inside 4 of the rolls. Divide the filling between these rolls. Replace the lids.

3 Wensleydale filling: mix the watercress with the cheese and mayonnaise. Season and use to fill the remaining 4 rolls. Replace the lids.

CHEESE AND RAISIN ROLLS

6 tbs/50 g Blue Cheshire cheese,
crumbled
1 tbs/15 g seedless raisins
½ **stick** celery, diced
3 tsp mayonnaise
2 brown rolls

Serves 2

1 Mix all the ingredients together. Use to fill the brown rolls.

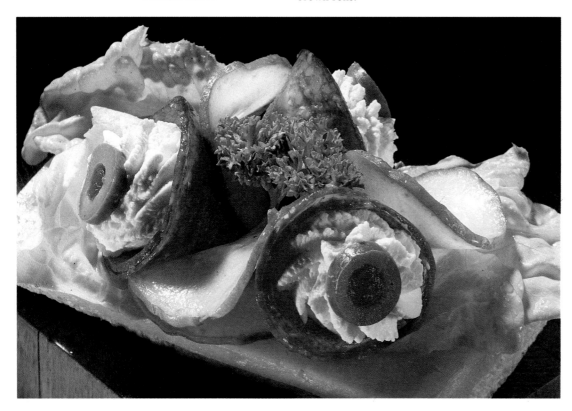

Open Sandwich

WELSH RAREBIT

2½ cups/225 g Cheddar cheese, grated
2 tbs/25 g butter
1 tsp made mustard
3 tbs/45 ml British beer or ale
salt
ground black pepper
cayenne papper
4 slices warm toast

Serves 4

1 Mix the cheese, butter, mustard, beer and seasoning in a small saucepan over a low heat. Stir until completely blended.

2 Pour over the toast and broil/grill until brown.

WHOLEMEAL CHEESE WAFERS

1 cup/125 g wholemeal flour
¼ tsp salt
pinch paprika pepper
2 tbs/25 g butter
2½ cups/225 g Cheddar cheese, finely grated

Serves 4–6

1 Mix the flour and seasonings and rub in the butter. Stir in the cheese and just enough cold water to bind to a firm dough.

2 Knead the dough firmly and roll out to ⅛in/3mm thick. Prick with a fork and cut out into fancy shapes.

3 Place on a greased baking sheet and bake at 450°F/230°C/Gas Mark 8 for 6–8 minutes, until golden brown.

SHERRIED CHESHIRE SPREAD

2½ cups/225 g White Cheshire cheese, crumbled
2 tbs/25 g butter
½ tsp sugar
pinch cayenne pepper
¼ cup/65 ml sherry

Serves 4–6

1 Beat together the cheese and butter. Add the sugar, cayenne pepper and half the sherry. Gradually add the remaining sherry, mixing well until creamy.

2 Serve spread on plain crackers as an appetizer or savoury, or serve with Wholemeal Cheese Wafers.

SANDWICH FILLINGS

Cheese makes a superb sandwich filling especially when combined with other ingredients for added interest. Ready in a moment, easily packed and eaten anywhere, here are a few sandwich filling ideas to liven up any lunch pack. Simply combine the ingredients together and spread generous amounts on to well buttered bread. Ready prepared fillings can be kept in the refrigerator for several days and used as required.

LIVER SAUSAGE AND CHEESE
1¼ cups/125 g Leicester cheese, grated
2 oz/50 g liver sausage, mashed
4 tsp finely chopped cucumber

COUNTRY CHEESE AND HAM
1¼ cups/125 g Wensleydale cheese, grated
½ cup/50 g ham, chopped
2 tbs/25 g butter, softened
3 tsp milk
3 tsp fresh chopped chives

CRUNCHY CHEESE
1¼ cups/125 g Lancashire cheese, grated
1 apple, chopped
1 stick celery, chopped
2 tbs/30 ml unflavoured/natural yogurt

HAWAIIAN DELIGHT
1¼ cups/125 g Caerphilly cheese, grated
¼ cup/60 ml light/single cream
2 oz/50 g pineapple, chopped

CHEDDAR AND ONION
1¼ cups/125 g Cheddar cheese, grated
2 tbs/25 g butter, softened
2 tbs/30 ml mayonnaise
3 scallions/spring onions, finely chopped

CHEESE AND EGG
1¼ cups/125 g Double Gloucester cheese, grated
1 egg, hardboiled, mashed
2 tbs/30 ml salad cream

CHEESE 'N' BEEF
1¼ cups/125 g Leicester cheese, grated
3 oz/75 g corned beef, mashed
2 tbs/30 ml tomato ketchup

CHEESE AND CHICKEN
1¼ cups/125 g Sage Derby cheese, grated
¾ cup/75 g cooked chicken, chopped
2 tbs/30 ml mayonnaise

FRUITY CHEESE
1¼ cups/125 g Cheshire cheese, grated
1 banana, mashed
2 tsp lemon juice
2 tbs/25 g white raisins/sultanas
3 tsp light/single cream

LANCASHIRE, DATE AND WALNUT
1¼ cups/125 g Lancashire cheese, crumbled
4 dates, chopped
1 tbs/15 g walnuts, chopped
3 tbs/45 ml unflavoured/natural yogurt

RED WINDSOR AND WATERCRESS
1¼ cups/125 g Red Windsor cheese, grated
6 tsp fresh chopped watercress
3 tbs/45 ml cream
salt
ground black pepper

CHEESY PEANUT
1¼ cups/125 g Cheddar cheese, grated
2 oz/50 g peanut butter

CHEESE AND BEANS
1 small can butter beans, drained
1¼ cups/125 g Cheddar cheese, grated
1 tbs/15 g butter
2 tbs/30 ml milk
salt
ground black pepper
½ tsp made mustard

CHEESE AND TUNA
1¼ cups/125 g Double Gloucester cheese, grated
3½ oz/90 g can tuna fish, drained and flaked
2 tbs/30 ml mayonnaise
salt
ground black pepper

Cheddar Sandwich Spread (top); Lancashire, Date and Walnut Spread (bottom left); Red Windsor and Watercress Spread (bottom right)

Vegetarian Meals

CHEESE AND LENTIL LOAF

1 tbs/15 ml oil
1 large onion, sliced
1⅓ cups/225 g lentils
2 tbs/15 g dried mixed vegetables
7 oz/200 g can tomatoes
1 tbs/15 ml tomato paste/purée
⅔ cup/150 ml water
1 cup/50 g mushrooms, chopped
2 eggs, beaten
1¼ cups/125 g Leicester cheese, grated
1 cup/125 g fresh brown bread crumbs
2 tsp dried thyme
salt
ground black pepper
slices of green pepper, to garnish

Serves 8

1 Heat the oil in a saucepan and fry the onion until soft. Add the lentils, dried vegetables, tomatoes and their juice, tomato paste/purée and water.

2 Bring to the boil, cover and simmer for 30 minutes or until the lentils are soft. Allow to cool slightly.

3 Stir in the mushrooms, eggs, cheese, crumbs, thyme and seasoning to taste. Mix well and spoon into a buttered large loaf tin.

4 Bake at 350°F/180°C/Gas Mark 4 for 1 hour. Turn out on to a serving dish and serve garnished with slices of green pepper.

CHEESY LOAF

1½ cups/175 g cooked long-grain rice
1 cup/75 g Mozzarella cheese, grated
1 cup/75 g Lancashire cheese, grated
1 egg, beaten
1 cup/225 ml milk
1 tsp dried mixed herbs
1 red or green pepper, cored, deseeded and chopped

Serves 4

1 Mix the rice with the cheeses, egg, milk and herbs.

2 Spoon into a small, greased loaf pan/tin and bake at 375°F/190°C/Gas Mark 5 for 15–20 minutes, or until firm to the touch.

3 Turn out and garnish with pepper.

Cheesy Loaf

VEGETARIAN CORNISH PASTY

½ lb/225 g potatoes, cubed
½ lb/225 g turnips, cubed
½ lb/225 g carrots, cubed
½ lb/225 g parsnips, cubed
1 clove garlic, crushed
2 onions, sliced
oil for frying
salt
ground black pepper
1¼ cups/125 g Cheddar cheese, grated
large pinch thyme
¼ cup/125 g butter
2 cups/225 g wholemeal flour

Serves 4

1 Boil all the cubed vegetables until soft. Drain. Fry the garlic and onion in a little oil until softened.

2 Mix the boiled and fried vegetables. Add a pinch of salt, pepper, half the cheese and the thyme and mash roughly. Do not reduce to a purèe. Cool.

3 Rub the butter into the flour with the remaining cheese. Mix to a dough with just enough water and divide the mixture into 4. Shape each piece of dough into a ball and roll out to a 6in/15cm circle.

4 Divide the filling between the pastry circles. Dampen the edges of the pastry and bring up the sides to form a long shape. Join and seal the edges over the filling, pinching the pastry together.

5 Place on a greased baking tray and bake at 400°F/200°C/Gas Mark 6 for 30 minutes. Serve hot.

CHEESY OATBURGERS

1¾ cups/175 g Leicester cheese, grated
1 small green pepper, cored, deseeded and chopped
1 large tomato, skinned and finely chopped
1 small onion, finely chopped
1⅓ cups/125 g porridge oats
2 eggs
salt
ground black pepper
oil for shallow frying

Serves 2–4

1 Reserve 6 tablespoons of cheese for the topping. Mix the remaining cheese with the pepper, tomato, onion and oats. Add the eggs and mix until well blended. Season generously.

2 Divide the mixture into 4 portions and shape into burgers. If the mixture is too sticky, add a few more oats.

3 Heat about 2 tablespoons oil in a frying pan and gently fry the burgers until golden brown. Turn them carefully and cook until golden on the second side.

4 Sprinkle the reserved cheese over the burgers and place under a hot broiler/grill until the tops are golden brown.

5 Serve with relish and salad.

ROYAL STILTON TAGLIATELLE

½ lb/225 g green tagliatelle
½ cup/125 g butter
1 clove garlic, crushed
⅔ cup/150 ml heavy/double cream
1¼ cups/125 g Stilton cheese, crumbled
3 tsp brandy
⅓ cup/50 g pistachio nuts, chopped

Serves 4

1 Cook the pasta in plenty of boiling salted water until just tender. Drain.

2 Gently heat the butter and add the garlic. Cook for 1 minute. Add the cream and Stilton. Heat gently until the cheese has melted. Stir in the brandy.

3 Gently toss with the cooked pasta and sprinkle with the pistachios. Serve immediately.

BAKED LAYERED CASSEROLE

¼ lb/125 g red kidney beans, soaked overnight in water
½ lb/225 g mushrooms
1 onion, chopped
2 tbs/25 g butter
3 cups/350 g cooked long-grain rice
1¼ cups/125 g Leicester cheese, grated
1¼ cups/300 ml thick white sauce

Serves 4

1 Drain the kidney beans. Place in a saucepan covered with fresh water and bring to the boil for 10 minutes. Reduce to a simmer for 35 minutes. Add salt to taste. Drain.

2 Chop the mushroom stalks and fry with the onion in the butter until soft. Mix with the cooked rice. Stir most of the cheese into the sauce.

3 Arrange a layer of mushrooms in the base of the dish, cover with half the cheese sauce; add a layer of beans and then the mushroom mixture. Top with the remaining cheese sauce. Sprinkle the rest of the cheese on top.

4 Bake at 350°F/180°C/Gas Mark 4 for 25 minutes. Serve hot.

CHEDDAR CHEESE AND WALNUT TART/FLAN

6 oz/175 g shortcrust or wholemeal
pastry
$\frac{2}{3}$ **cup/150 ml** boiling milk
$\frac{1}{2}$ **cup/50 g** fresh white bread crumbs
2 eggs, beaten
1$\frac{1}{4}$ **cups/125 g** Cheddar cheese, grated
$\frac{1}{3}$ **cup/50 g** walnuts, chopped
1 tsp Worcestershire sauce
raw onion rings

Serves 4–6

1 Roll out the pastry and use to line an
8in/20cm tart pan/flan tin. Prick the base. Line with
foil and bake at 400°F/200°C/Gas Mark 6 for 10–15
minutes. Remove the foil.

2 Pour the milk on the bread crumbs and allow to
stand for 5 minutes. Beat well and add the eggs,
cheese, nuts and Worcestershire sauce. Pour into the
tart case.

3 Return to the oven at 375°F/190°C/Gas
Mark 5 for 30 minutes. Garnish with onion rings.

WATERCRESS AND ONION TART/FLAN

6 oz/175 g shortcrust or wholemeal
pastry
1 onion, chopped
1 bunch watercress, chopped
1$\frac{1}{4}$ **cups/125 g** Red Windsor cheese,
grated
2 eggs, beaten
$\frac{2}{3}$ **cup/150 ml** milk
salt
ground black pepper
watercress, onion rings
and tomatoes, to
garnish

Serves 4

1 Roll out the pastry and use to line an
8in/20cm tart pan/flan tin. Prick the base. Line with
foil and bake at 400°F/200°C/Gas Mark 6 for 10–15
minutes. Remove the foil.

2 Combine the chopped onion, watercress and three
quarters of the cheese. Scatter in the tart case.

3 Beat the eggs and milk together, season and pour into the tart case. Sprinkle the reserved cheese on top.

4 Bake at 400°F/200°C/Gas Mark 6 for 30 minutes. Garnish with watercress, onion and tomato. Serve hot or cold.

BROCCOLI AND CASHEW TART/FLAN

6 oz/175 g shortcrust or wholemeal pastry
3 tbs/40 g all-purpose/plain flour
3 tbs/40 g butter
1¾ cups/450 ml milk
salt
cayenne pepper
1¼ cups/125 g Lancashire cheese, crumbled
1 egg, separated
½ lb/225 g cooked chopped broccoli
⅓ cup/50 g cashew nuts, chopped

Serves 4–6
1 Roll out the pastry and use to line an 8in/20cm tart pan/flan tin. Prick the base. Line with foil and bake at 400°F/200°C/Gas Mark 6 for 10–15 minutes. Remove the foil.

2 Place the flour, butter and milk in a saucepan; heat, stirring continuously, until the sauce thickens, boils and is smooth. Cook for 1 minute. Season.

3 Remove the saucepan from the heat, add the cheese and stir until melted. Stir in the egg yolk.

4 Whisk the egg white stiffly and fold into the sauce. Place the broccoli and nuts in the tart case and pour the sauce on top, smoothing evenly.

5 Return to the oven for 30 minutes and serve immediately.

DERBYSHIRE QUICHE

6 oz/175 g shortcrust or wholemeal pastry
1 lb/450 g onions, chopped
1 tbs/15 ml oil
2 tbs/25 g butter
2 eggs, beaten
2 tbs/30 ml light/single cream
1 tsp mustard
salt
ground black pepper
1¼ cups/125 g Sage Derby cheese, cubed

Serves 4–6
1 Roll out the pastry and use to line an 8in/20cm tart pan/flan tin. Prick the base. Line with foil and bake at 400°F/200°C/Gas Mark 6 for 10–15

minutes. Remove the foil.

2 Fry the onions in the oil and butter until soft. Beat the eggs, cream, mustard and seasonings.

3 Mix the onions with the eggs and pour into the tart case. Sprinkle the cheese over the tart and return to the oven for 30 minutes, until set. Serve hot.

CREAMY SAGE AND ONION TART/FLAN

½ cup/100 g butter
2 onions, sliced
1 clove garlic, crushed
1¼ cups/160 g wholemeal flour
2–3 tbs/30–45 ml water
1¼ cups/125 g curd cheese, softened
⅔ cup/150 ml milk
2 eggs, beaten
3 tsp fresh chopped sage

Serves 4
1 Melt 2 tablespoons of the butter and fry the onions and garlic until soft.

2 Place the flour in a bowl and rub in the remaining butter. Add the water and mix to a firm dough. Knead lightly.

3 Roll out and use to line a 6in/15cm tart pan/flan tin.

4 Blend the cheese, milk and egg. Beat in the sage. Drain the onions and place in the pastry case. Pour over the cheese mixture.

5 Bake at 400°F/200°C/Gas Mark 6 for 40 minutes until set and golden.

CHEESE AND TOMATO PIZZA

Base
½ cake/15 g compressed/fresh yeast
¼ cup/60 ml warm water
1 cup/125 g all-purpose/plain flour
1 cup/125 g wholemeal flour
1 tsp salt
2 tbs/25 g butter
¼ cup/60 ml warm milk
Topping
2 tbs/25 g butter
1 onion, chopped
1 clove garlic, crushed
1 lb/450 g tomatoes, skinned, deseeded and chopped
2 tsp fresh chopped basil
salt
ground black pepper
2½ cups/225 g Mozzarella cheese, sliced
black olives, to garnish

Serves 4

1 Cream the yeast with half the warm water. Sift the flours and salt into a bowl. Rub in the butter. Make a well in the centre and pour in the yeast, milk and remaining warm water.

2 Mix to a firm dough, then knead well on a floured surface for 5 minutes. Place in a clean bowl, cover with a damp cloth and leave to rise in a warm place until doubled in size.

3 Knead the dough lightly and divide in half. Roll each piece into an 8in/20cm circle and place on greased baking trays.

4 Melt the butter in a saucepan and fry the onion until soft. Add the garlic, tomatoes, basil and seasoning.

5 Cover each dough circle with tomato topping and top with Mozzarella cheese slices. Leave to prove in a warm place for 30 minutes.

6 Bake at 400°F/200°C/Gas Mark 6 for 20–30 minutes. Top with black olives.

GNOCCHI WITH DOUBLE GLOUCESTER

1½ **cups/175 g** all-purpose/plain flour
½ **cup/125 g** butter
¾ **cup/200 ml** milk
4 eggs, beaten
1 cup/75 g Double Gloucester cheese, grated
salt
ground black pepper
mustard powder
8 cups/700 g mixed vegetables, cut into thin matchsticks and cooked until tender

Cheese sauce
3 tbs/40 g butter
3 tbs/40 g flour
1½ **cups/360 ml** milk
3 tbs/40 g Double Gloucester cheese, grated

Serves 4–6

1 Make the gnocchi: sift the flour 2 or 3 times and keep on a sheet of paper. Melt the butter in the milk and bring to the boil.

2 When boiling remove from the heat and add the flour all at once and beat until smooth. Cool.

3 Add the eggs gradually, beating well after each addition. Add cheese and seasoning.

4 Form the gnocchi into small shapes using 2 teaspoons and drop them into a large shallow pan of boiling salted water. Simmer the gnocchi very gently for 10 minutes.

5 For the cheese sauce: place all the ingredients in a small saucepan and heat, stirring continuously until the sauce thickens, boils and is smooth.

6 Drain the gnocchi on a dry folded tea cloth. Place the vegetables in a buttered ovenproof dish and cover with gnocchi. Pour the sauce over and sprinkle thickly with more cheese if liked.

7 Bake at 350°F/180°C/Gas Mark 4 for 30 minutes.

LEICESTER CHEESE PUDDING

8 slices wholemeal bread
4 tbs/50 g butter
1 tsp made mustard
2½ **cups/225 g** Leicester cheese, grated
4 eggs
⅔ **cup/150 ml** milk
½ **tsp** salt
¼ **tsp** ground black pepper
¼ **tsp** freshly grated nutmeg

Serves 4

1 Toast the bread on one side. Trim off the crusts and set aside.

2 Cream the butter with the mustard and spread on the untoasted sides of the bread. Cut into fingers.

3 Set aside a quarter of the cheese. Arrange a layer of toast fingers, toasted side down, in a buttered ovenproof pie dish and sprinkle with some of the remaining cheese. Cover with a layer of toast and continue in this way ending with a layer of toast.

4 Beat the eggs and milk with the seasonings. Pour over the dish and leave to stand for 20 minutes. Sprinkle with the reserved cheese.

5 Bake at 375°F/190°C/Gas Mark 5 for 40 minutes until the top is well browned.

ZUCCHINI/COURGETTES AU GRATIN

1 lb/400 g zucchini/courgettes, sliced
¼ **tsp** salt
⅔ **cup/150 ml** freshly boiled water
1 egg
⅔ **cup/150 ml** heavy/double cream
3 tbs/25 g Cheddar cheese, grated
ground black pepper
1 tbs/15 g butter

Serves 4

1 Put the zucchini/courgette slices in a frying pan with the salt and water Cook over moderate heat until the water has almost evaporated.

2 Mix the egg, cream and half the cheese together. Season with pepper.

3 Slide the courgettes into an overproof dish and pour the cream mixture over. Sprinkle with the remaining cheese. Dot with butter.

4 Bake at 400°F/200°C/Gas Mark 6 for 10 minutes or until just set and golden. Serve with roast meat or poultry, grilled meat or fish.

PASTA AND CAULIFLOWER CHEESE

1 medium cauliflower, broken into florets
¼ lb/125 g cooked pasta spirals
3 tbs/40 g wholemeal flour
3 tbs/40 g butter
1¾ cups/450 ml milk
1¼ cups/125 g Cheddar cheese, grated
salt
ground black pepper
1 tbs/15 g wheatgerm
2 tomatoes, sliced
sprigs of parsley

Serves 4

1 Cook the cauliflower in boiling water for 8 minutes, until tender. Drain. Mix the pasta and cauliflower in an overproof dish.

2 Place the flour, butter and milk in a saucepan and heat, stirring continuously until the sauce thickens, boils and is smooth.

3 Cook for 2 minutes. Remove from the heat, stir in most of the cheese until melted. Season to taste. Pour over the pasta and cauliflower.

4 Mix the remaining cheese and wheatgerm and sprinkle over the top. Broil/grill until golden. Garnish with tomato and parsley.

BAKED CHEESE SOUFFLÉ POTATOES

4 medium baked potatoes
2 eggs, separated
6 tbs/50 g Cheddar cheese, grated
2 scallions/spring onions chopped
freshly grated nutmeg
salt
ground black pepper

Serves 4

1 Cut a slice off the top of the potatoes. Scoop out the cooked potato from the shells leaving about ¼in/6mm round the outside. Mash the potato flesh.

2 Stir the egg yolks into the mashed potato with the cheese, scallions/spring onions and seasoning.

3 Whisk the egg whites stiffly and fold into the mixture. Spoon it back into the potato shells and place them on a greased baking tray.

4 Bake at 400°F/200°C/Gas Mark 6 for 15–20 minutes until the filling has risen and is golden brown on top. Serve at once.

Pasta and Cauliflower Cheese

*Mozzarella and
Mushroom in Choux Cups*

PARSNIP TOMATO AND CHEESE CASSEROLE

$1\frac{1}{2}$ **lb/700 g** parsnips, sliced thinly
$\frac{1}{2}$ **lb/225 g** tomatoes, sliced
$1\frac{1}{4}$ **cups/125 g** Gruyère cheese, grated
salt
ground black pepper
$\frac{2}{3}$ **cup/150 ml** unflavoured/natural yogurt

Serves 4
1 Place a layer of parsnips into an ovenproof casserole. Cover with a layer of tomato slices. Sprinkle with some of the cheese and seasoning.

2 Repeat the layers, finishing with a layer of parsnips and reserving 2 tablespoons of cheese.

3 Spread the yogurt over the top and sprinkle over the reserved cheese.

4 Cover the dish and bake at 375°F/190°C/Gas Mark 5 for 40–45 minutes until the parsnips are almost tender. Uncover the dish and bake for a further 10–15 minutes, or until the top is crisp and browned. Serve hot with rice.

AUBERGINE LAYER BAKE

$1\frac{1}{2}$ **lb/700 g** eggplants/aubergines
salt
ground black pepper
$\frac{1}{2}$ **cup/125 g** butter
1 onion, chopped
1 clove garlic, crushed
15 oz/425 g can tomatoes
$\frac{1}{2}$ **tsp** dried oregano
$1\frac{3}{4}$ **cups/175 g** Mozzarella cheese, sliced
$\frac{1}{4}$ **cup/25 g** fresh bread crumbs

Serves 4
1 Slice the eggplants/aubergines thinly, sprinkle with salt and leave in a colander for 1 hour. Rinse and drain. Dry on kitchen paper.

2 Heat 2 tablespoons butter in a saucepan. Fry the onion until softened. Add the garlic, tomatoes, oregano and seasonings. Stir and simmer for 15 minutes.

3 Heat the remaining butter and fry the eggplants on both sides until golden. Drain on kitchen paper.

4 Arrange the eggplant slices, tomato mixture and cheese in layers in an ovenproof dish, finishing with a layer of cheese.

5 Sprinkle with bread crumbs and bake at 350°F/180°C/Gas Mark 4 for 40 minutes. Serve immediately.

MOZZARELLA AND MUSHROOM IN CHOUX CUPS

2 cups/500 ml water
2 cups/225 g butter
2½ cups/275 g flour
pinch salt
5 eggs, beaten
1¼ cups/125 g Mozzarella cheese, grated
pinch cayenne pepper
1½ lb/750 g button mushrooms, sliced
1 onion, chopped
¾ cup/175 g butter
fresh chopped tarragon
1 cup/225 ml heavy/double cream
10 slices Mozzarella cheese

Serves 10
1 Place the water and butter in a saucepan and heat until the butter melts. Bring to the boil and add all the flour at once. Beat until the paste comes away cleanly from the sides of the pan.

2 Allow to cool slightly. Gradually beat in the egg to give a smooth glossy paste. Add just enough to give a paste that holds its shape. Stir in the grated cheese and cayenne.

3 Pipe the paste with a star tube round the edge of 10 buttered dishes. Bake at 375°F/190°C/Gas Mark 5 for 20 minutes until crisp.

4 Fry the mushrooms in the butter and season. Spoon into the centre of each cup.

5 Stir some tarragon into the cream and place a spoonful on top of each dish of mushrooms. Top with a slice of cheese and bake at 350°F/180°C/Gas Mark 4 for 5 minutes. Serve immediately.

LANCASHIRE STUFFED BELGIAN ENDIVE/CHICORY

6 heads Belgian endive/chicory, trimmed
1 small onion, chopped
2 tbs/25 g butter
1½ cups/75 g mushrooms, chopped
salt
ground black pepper
3 tsp mixed chopped fresh herbs
2 tbs/30 g fresh bread crumbs
1¼ cups/125 g Lancashire cheese, crumbled
1 tbs/15 g butter, melted

Serves 6
1 Blanch the Belgian endive/chicory in boiling water for 3–4 minutes, then drain and dry. Split each head lengthways through and lay in a buttered ovenproof dish.

2 Fry the onion in the butter until soft. Add the mushrooms and cook for 2 minutes. Turn into a bowl. Add the seasoning, herbs, bread crumbs and cheese.

3 Spoon on to the Belgian endive/chicory and top with the melted butter. Cover and bake at 375°F/190°C/Gas Mark 5 for 20–30 minutes.

4 Serve hot with a homemade tomato sauce.

BAKED CABBAGE

¾ lb/350 g green cabbage, shredded
⅔ cup/150 ml unflavoured/natural yogurt
⅓ cup/50 g sultanas
⅓ cup/50 g peanuts
salt
ground black pepper
6 tbs/50 g Cheddar cheese, grated
freshly grated nutmeg

Serves 4
1 Place half the cabbage in an ovenproof casserole. Spread half the yogurt over it. Sprinkle with the sultanas and nuts. Season.

2 Top with the remaining cabbage and cover with the remaining yogurt. Sprinkle with the cheese and a little nutmeg.

3 Bake at 400°F/200°C/Gas Mark 6 for 15–20 minutes until the top is lightly browned.

MEXICAN BEANS WITH CHEESE

2 lb/900 g red kidney beans, soaked overnight
4 large onions, chopped
4 cloves garlic, crushed
2 chili peppers, sliced
3 tbs/45 ml oil
2 lb/900 g tomatoes, finely chopped
1 tsp dried oregano
1 tsp salt
1¾ cups/175 g Cheddar cheese, diced

Serves 6–8

1 Drain the beans and cover with fresh water. Bring to the boil and boil rapidly for 10 minutes. Simmer for a further 20 minutes. Drain.

2 Fry the onions, garlic and chilies in the oil in an ovenproof casserole dish until the onion is softened.

3 Add the beans and continue to fry until they are heated through. Add the tomatoes, oregano and salt. Cover and continue to cook over a low heat until the tomatoes are pulpy.

4 Stir the diced cheese into the beans. When simmering, cover and bake at 300°F/160°C/Gas Mark 2 for 3 hours.

BEAN SOUP WITH MOZZARELLA CROÛTES

$\frac{3}{4}$ **cup/175 g** red kidney beans
$\frac{3}{4}$ **cup/175 g** navy/haricot beans
$\frac{3}{4}$ **cup/175 g** black eye beans
$\frac{3}{4}$ **cup/175 g** flagolet beans
10 cups/2 litres vegetable stock
10 cups/2 litres water
2 sticks celery
2 carrots
1 onion, studded with cloves
14 oz/400 g tomatoes, skinned and chopped

English Apple Fondue

Croûtes
14 oz/400 g onions, chopped
2 cloves garlic, crushed
4 tbs/50 g butter
20 slices French bread
2½ cups/250 g Mozzarella cheese, sliced

Serves 10

1 Soak the beans in plenty of water overnight. Place them in a pan of fresh water and bring to the boil for 10 minutes. Rinse in fresh water.

2 Put the beans in a deep pot and pour on the stock and water. Add the celery, carrots and onion. Bring to the boil and simmer for 3 hours.

3 When the beans are tender, remove the celery, carrots and onion and add the tomatoes. Reboil and adjust the seasoning.

4 Make the croûtes: fry the onion and garlic in the butter until soft. Purée and spread on the bread. Top with the sliced cheese. Float the croûtes on portions of the soup and flash under the broiler/grill to melt the cheese. Serve immediately.

ENGLISH APPLE FONDUE

1 clove garlic, halved
2 cups/500 ml apple juice
1 tbs/25 g cornstarch/cornflour
$\frac{1}{4}$ **tsp** mustard powder
$\frac{1}{4}$ **tsp** paprika pepper
7½ cups/700 g Cheddar cheese, grated
4–6 dessert apples, peeled, cored and cubed
celery sticks
cauliflower florets
French bread, cubed

Serves 4–6

1 Rub the inside of an earthenware fondue pot with the cut sides of the garlic.

2 Mix a little apple juice into the cornstarch/cornflour, mustard and paprika to form a smooth consistency.

3 Warm the remaining apple juice in the fondue pot. Gradually add the cheese, stirring continuously over low heat until melted.

4 Stir in the cornstarch/cornflour mixture and bring to the boil. Stir off the heat for a further minute until smooth.

5 Transfer the pan to a spirit lamp or fondue burner, set on a large table mat on the dining table.

6 Serve cubes of apple, or pieces of celery or cauliflower and cubes of bread to dip in the hot cheese sauce.

Salads

CHICKEN SALAD

3 cups/350 g cooked chicken, diced
1 cup/125 g cooked brown rice
1¼ cups/125 g Blue Cheshire cheese, cubed
2 dessert apples, cored, diced
6 radishes, sliced
2 sticks celery, sliced
3 tbs/25 g white raisins/sultanas
⅔ cup/150 ml unflavoured/natural yogurt
1 tbs/15 ml mayonnaise
sliced red apple, to garnish

Serves 4

1 Combine the chicken, rice, cheese, apples, radishes, celery and sultanas.

2 Mix together the yogurt and mayonnaise and fold into the salad mixture. Serve garnished with red apple.

CHEESY RICE SALAD

1 cup/175 g long-grain rice
15 oz/425 g can red kidney beans, drained
7 oz/200 g can pineapple cubes, drained
7 oz/200 g can sweetcorn, drained
1 green pepper, cored, deseeded and sliced
2 sticks celery, chopped
1½ cups/225 g Double Gloucester cheese, diced
salt
ground black pepper

Serves 4

1 Cook the rice in boiling salted water until tender. Rinse and drain thoroughly. Cool.

2 Add the beans, pineapple, corn, pepper, celery and cheese. Mix well and season to taste.

CAESAR SALAD

olive oil
3 cloves garlic, crushed
4 large thick slices bread, cut into cubes
2 Romaine/Cos lettuces, chilled, torn into pieces
1 egg
1 lemon, juice only
16 anchovy fillets, cut into pieces
6 tbs/50 g Parmesan cheese, grated
salt
ground black pepper

Serves 6

1 Heat 4 tablespoons of oil in a frying pan with 2 crushed cloves of garlic. Fry the bread cubes until crisp and golden on all sides, adding more oil as needed.

2 Drain the croûtons on kitchen paper. Rub a salad bowl with the remaining garlic clove.

3 Toss the lettuce with 8 tablespoons olive oil until thoroughly coated. Boil the egg for 1 minute. Break the egg over the lettuce, add the lemon juice, anchovies, cheese and seasoning.

4 Toss together until well mixed. Add the croûtons and toss in. Serve immediately while the croûtons are still crisp.

Chicken Salad

Oriental Mozzarella Salad

RED, WHITE AND BLUE SALAD

1¾ cups/175 g Blue Cheshire cheese, diced
½ lb/225 g black grapes, quartered, seeds removed
1 round lettuce, shredded
2 firm pears, peeled, cored and sliced
1¾ cups/175 g White Cheshire cheese, crumbled
2 red apples, cored and diced
1¾ cups/175 g Red Cheshire cheese, coarsely grated

Dressing
¼ cup/60 ml salad oil
salt
ground black pepper
2 tbs/30 ml apple juice

Serves 8–10

1 Arrange the Blue Cheshire and grapes in the base of a glass salad bowl. Top with a layer of lettuce. Arrange the pears on the lettuce and sprinkle over the White Cheshire.

2 Cover with more lettuce, arrange the apple on top and sprinkle with the Red Cheshire. Garnish with any remaining fruit.

3 For the dressing: whisk all the ingredients together well and serve with the salad.

HAM AND PASTA SALAD

¼ lb/125 g pasta shells
½ lb/225 g ham, diced
1¾ cups/175 g feta cheese, crumbled
3 sticks celery, chopped
½ red pepper, cored, deseeded and chopped
4 scallions/spring onions, chopped
2 tsp made mustard
⅔ cup/150 ml mayonnaise

Serves 4

1 Cook the pasta in boiling salted water until just tender. Drain and cool.

2 Stir in the ham, cheese, celery, pepper and scallions/spring onions.

3 Mix the mustard and mayonnaise and pour over the salad. Toss lightly together.

ORIENTAL MOZZARELLA SALAD

3¾ cups/350 g Mozzarella cheese, diced
11 oz/300 g bean sprouts, washed and drained
1 small bunch radishes, sliced
¼ lb/100g white grapes, halved and deseeded
¼ head Chinese leaves, shredded
⅓ cup/120 ml vinaigrette dressing
salt
ground black pepper
red chicory/radichio leaves

Serves 4

1 Toss all the ingredients together except the radichio leaves which are used to decorate the edge of the serving dish.

2 Pile the salad on to a serving plate and serve chilled.

CHEF'S SALAD

½ lb/225 g cooked gammon or ham
1¼ cups/125 g Danish Blue cheese
½ Romaine/Cos lettuce, shredded
1 bunch radishes, sliced
¼ cucumber, sliced
1 onion, cut into rings

Dressing
pinch mustard powder
salt
ground black pepper
pinch sugar
¼ cup/60 ml salad oil
2 tbs/30 ml wine vinegar

Serves 3–4

1 Cut the gammon into thick strips and cube the cheese. Arrange the salad ingredients in layers in a glass bowl.

2 Make the dressing: place the seasonings in a bowl, blend with the oil, gradually beat in the vinegar and pour over the salad.

GREEK CHEESE SALAD

1½ cups/225 g feta cheese, diced
1 cucumber, diced
1½ lb/700 g tomatoes, skinned and chopped
12 black olives, stoned

Dressing
1 tbs/15 ml wine vinegar

¼ cup/60 ml olive oil
pinch dried oregano or mint
ground black pepper

Serves 6

1 Place the salad ingredients in a bowl. Whisk together the dressing ingredients and pour over.

2 Turn to coat and serve with crusty bread.

DANISH POTATO SALAD

1 lb/450 g cooked new potatoes, cubed
1 cup/125 g cooked chicken or ham, cubed
4 scallions/spring onions, finely sliced
7 oz/200 g can sweetcorn, drained
¼ lb/125 g black grapes, halved and deseeded
½ cup/50 g dried apricots, chopped

Dressing
1¼ cups/125 g Danish Blue cheese, crumbled
2 tbs/30 ml mayonnaise
3 tbs/45 ml light/single cream
2 tbs/30 ml milk

Serves 6

1 Mix together all the salad ingredients.

2 Soften the cheese in a bowl. Beat in mayonnaise, cream and milk to give a smooth dressing. Season to taste.

3 Pour dressing over potato mixture and turn gently with two forks to coat. Serve with crisp lettuce.

Danish Potato Salad

Derby Rice Salad

the cream cheese, a pinch of cayenne pepper and the chives.

3 Add the cooled, dissolved gelatin and stir the mixture for a few minutes. Fold in the mayonnaise and cream.

4 Pour into the mould and chill until set. To serve, dip the mould in hot water for a few seconds and turn out on to a serving plate. Garnish with radishes.

DERBY RICE SALAD

1 cup/175 g long-grain rice
4 tbs/60 ml vinaigrette dressing
6 tbs/50 g Sage Derby cheese, diced
6 tbs/50 g Leicester cheese, diced
1 stick celery, chopped
2 scallions/spring onions, chopped
4 dates, sliced
$\frac{1}{4}$ lb/125 g ham, chopped
8 oz/227 g can pineapple slices, drained and chopped

Serves 4–6
1 Cook the rice until just tender, drain, rinse well, then toss in the vinaigrette dressing. Cool.

2 When cold, mix in the remaining ingredients Alternatively, omit the ham and press the salad into a ring mould. Turn out and fill the centre with rolls of cold meat.

CHEESE RING

2 tsp oil
1$\frac{3}{4}$ cups/175 g dolcelatte cheese, crumbled
2$\frac{1}{2}$ cups/225 g cream cheese
cayenne pepper
1 tbs/15 ml fresh chopped chives
1 tbs/15 g unflavoured gelatin/ gelatine dissolved in 2 tbs/30 ml hot water
$\frac{2}{3}$ cup/150 ml mayonnaise
$\frac{2}{3}$ cup/150 ml heavy/double cream
6 radishes, sliced, to garnish

Serves 6
1 Grease a 1 quart/900 ml ring mould with the oil.

2 Push the dolcelatte cheese through a sieve. Beat in

FRENCH BEAN AND CAERPHILLY SALAD

$\frac{1}{2}$ lb/225 g green/French beans
2$\frac{1}{2}$ cups/225 g Caerphilly cheese, diced
1 small red pepper, cored, deseeded and sliced

Dressing
$\frac{1}{2}$ cup/120 ml salad oil
2 tbs/30 ml wine vinegar
salt
ground black pepper
paprika pepper
1 tbs/15 ml cream

Serves 4
1 Cook the beans in boiling salted water until just tender. Drain and cool.

2 Mix the beans and cheese. Whisk all the dressing ingredients together and pour over the beans.

3 Turn into a salad bowl and scatter the pepper rings on top.

SPINACH AND DERBY SALAD

2 lb/900 g fresh spinach, trimmed and blanched
$\frac{1}{4}$ cup/60 ml salad oil
salt
ground black pepper
1$\frac{3}{4}$ cups/175 g Derby cheese, cubed
2 tbs/30 ml mayonnaise, diluted with a little hot water

Serves 4
1 Drain and refresh the spinach in cold water. Press between 2 plates to remove excess moisture. Place in a wide bowl.

2 Using 2 forks to help separate the leaves, dress the spinach with salad oil, salt and pepper. A little lemon juice may be used to season the salad.

3 Place the spinach in a serving bowl. Mix the cheese with the mayonnaise and extra seasoning and spoon on top of the spinach. Serve chilled.

MUSHROOM AND LEICESTER SALAD

4 cups/225 g cup or button mushrooms
¼ cup/60 ml salad oil
salt
ground black pepper
1¼ cups/125 g Red Leicester cheese
3 tsp fresh chopped parsley
2 tsp fresh chopped chives
1 tbs/15 ml wine vinegar

Serves 4

1 Thinly slice the mushrooms and place in a wide bowl. Add enough oil to coat them. Season with salt and pepper.

2 Cut the cheese into strips and add to the mushrooms with the herbs and vinegar. Toss together and put in a salad bowl. Cover and chill before serving.

SUFFOLK HAM AND PEAR SALAD

⅔ cup/150 ml apple juice
1 tbs/15 ml thin honey
½ lb/225 g new potatoes, cooked and sliced
6–8 oz/175–225 g ham, cut into strips
2 tomatoes, cut in wedges
6 oz/175 g thin baby carrots, sliced
2 tbs/30 ml fresh chopped parsley
1¼ cups/125 g Double Gloucester cheese, diced
2 pears, peeled, quartered and cored
1 cup/75 g Cheddar cheese, grated

Serves 6

1 Mix the apple juice and honey together in a large bowl. Add the potatoes, ham, tomatoes, carrots, parsley and Double Gloucester cheese. Mix well.

2 Place salad on a serving dish. Slice the pears and arrange them on top and finally sprinkle with the grated cheese.

French Bean and Caerphilly Salad (top left); Spinach and Derby Salad (top right) and Mushroom and Red Leicester Salad (bottom)

Desserts

CREAMY APPLE TART/FLAN

Pastry
1 cup/125 g all-purpose/plain flour
1 tbs/15 g confectioner's/icing sugar
6 tbs/50 g unsalted butter
1 egg yolk

Filling
⅔ cup/150 ml heavy/double cream, whipped
6 tbs/50 g Wensleydale cheese, crumbled
3 dessert apples, cored
butter
castor sugar

Serves 4–6

1 Make the pastry: sift the flour and sugar into a bowl. Rub in the butter. Add the egg yolk and work to a firm mixture.

2 Roll out and use to line a 7in/18cm tart pan/flan tin. Line with foil and bake at 425°F/220°C/Gas Mark 7 for 15–20 minutes. Remove the foil and bake for a further 5 minutes.

3 Cool the tart/flan case. Stir the cheese into the whipped cream and spread in the base of the tart/flan. Chill.

4 Slice the apples directly into a pan of cold water. Bring to the boil and drain immediately. Refresh in cold water. Drain.

5 Arrange the apple slices over the tart. Brush with melted butter and sprinkle thickly with sugar. Place under a hot broiler/grill until the sugar melts and browns. Chill well before serving.

RASPBERRY AND REDCURRANT PIE

2 cups/225 g wholemeal flour, sifted with a pinch of salt
½ cup/125 g butter
6 tbs/50 g Cheshire cheese, finely grated
1 lb/450 g mixed raspberries and redcurrants
1 tbs/25 g soft brown sugar
1 tbs/15 ml cold water
milk to glaze

Serves 6–8

1 Rub the butter into the flour. Stir in the cheese and just enough iced water to make a firm dough.

2 Chill for 30 minutes. Roll out three quarters of the pastry and use to line a pie dish. Fill with fruit, sugar and water. Use the remaining pastry to make a lid. Place on the pie, trim and seal the edges. Flute the crust.

3 Brush the pie with milk and chill for 20 minutes, then bake at 375°F/190°C/Gas Mark 5 for 40 minutes. Serve hot or cold.

APPLE AND CHEESECRUST PIE

Cheese pastry
1½ cups/175 g all-purpose/plain flour
½ cup/125 g butter
1¼ cups/125 g Double Gloucester cheese, grated
1 egg yolk
1 tbs/15 ml water

Filling
2 lb/900 g dessert apples
4 tbs/50 g butter
3 tbs/40 g soft brown sugar
pinch ground cinnamon
1 lemon, grated rind of half and all the juice
castor sugar

Serves 6

1 Make the pastry: sift the flour into a bowl and rub in the butter. Stir in the cheese. Mix the egg yolk and water and add to the bowl. Mix to a firm dough. Chill for 30 minutes.

2 Peel, quarter and core the apples and cut each quarter in half. Fry in the butter, dusting with the sugar. Place in a shallow pie dish with the cinnamon, lemon rind and juice. Cool.

3 Roll out the pastry to fit the dish. Make a crust round the rim of the dish, brush with water and lay the lid over it. Press to seal and flute the crust.

4 Brush the pie with water and dust with sugar. Bake at 375°F/190°C/Gas Mark 5 for 20–30 minutes. Serve with cream.

PEACH CHEESE PIE

Base
½ lb/225 g shortcake cookies/biscuits, finely crushed
4 tbs/50 g butter, melted
1 tbs/15 ml golden syrup
¼ tsp ground cinnamon

Filling
15 oz/425 g can peach halves
1¾ cups/175 g Blue Brie cheese, derinded
1 tbs/15 g castor sugar
1¼ cups/300 ml heavy/double cream,
whipped

Serves 6–8

1 Mix the crushed cookies, butter, syrup and cinnamon. Press into the base and up the sides of a buttered 8in/20cm pie dish.

2 Drain the peaches reserving 2 tablespoons of juice. Soften the cheese in a bowl and beat in the reserved juice and sugar. Beat in all but 3 tablespoons of the cream.

3 Reserve 1 peach half and chop the remainder. Stir into the cheese mixture. Pour into the pie case.

4 Decorate with the reserved peach, sliced, and the cream. Chill before serving.

GRANNY'S PUDDING

1½ lb/700 g cooking apples, cooked
and pulped
¾ cup/175 g castor sugar
2 eggs, separated
1¼ cups/125 g Double Gloucester
cheese, finely grated
3 tbs/25 g flaked almonds

Serves 6

1 Place the apples in an 8in/20cm tart pan/tin. Sprinkle 2 tablespoons of the sugar over.

2 Whisk the egg yolks with 2 more tablespoons of the sugar and stir in the cheese. Spread over the apple and sprinkle with the almonds.

3 Whisk the egg whites until stiff, fold in the remaining sugar. Pipe over the cheese mixture to completely cover it.

4 Bake at 350°F/180°C/Gas Mark 4 for 15 minutes. Serve hot.

TANGY APPLE PIE

2 cups/225 g all-purpose/plain flour
pinch salt
½ cup/125 g butter
2 tsp castor sugar
1 tbs/15 g custard powder
3–4 tbs/45–60 ml milk
1 lb/450 g cooking apples. peeled,
cored and thinly sliced
3 tbs/25 g white raisins/sultanas
1 cup/75 g Lancashire or
Wensleydale cheese,
grated
¼ cup/50 g soft brown sugar

1 tbs/15 ml unflavoured yogurt
milk

Serves 6

1 Place the flour and salt in a bowl. Rub in the butter. Stir in the castor sugar and custard powder and enough milk to form a firm dough.

2 Roll out the pastry and use half to line an 8in/20cm pie plate.

3 Mix the apples, sultanas, cheese, brown sugar and yogurt and place in the pie dish. Use the remaining pastry to make a lid for the pie. Seal and flute the crust. Brush with milk.

4 Bake at 400°F/200°C/Gas Mark 6 for 30 minutes. Serve hot with cream.

GINGER CHEESECAKE

½ cup/125 g butter
6 tbs/75 g castor sugar
3 tbs/45 ml black molasses/treacle
6 oz/175 g ginger cookies/biscuits,
crushed
1 tsp lemon juice
½ cup/50 g confectioner's/icing sugar,
sifted
4 tbs/50 g white raisins/sultanas
½ cup/75 g unsalted peauts, roasted
and crushed
1½ cups/150 g Cheddar cheese, finely
grated
1 cup/250 ml heavy/double cream,
whipped

Serves 4

1 Melt the butter, castor sugar and molasses and stir in the cookie/biscuit crumbs. Press on to the base of a 7in/18cm cake pan/tin and leave to set.

2 Fold the lemon juice, confectioner's sugar, white raisins/sultanas, nuts and cheese into the cream. Spread over the pie crust and chill until set.

SYRUP CHEESECAKE

6 tbs/75 g butter
⅓ cup/90 ml golden syrup
1¼ cups/150 g all-purpose/plain flour
1 tsp cornstarch/cornflour
1 egg, beaten
1 large lemon, grated rind and
juice
⅔ cup/150 ml milk
2 tsp unflavoured gelatin/
gelatine
2½ cups/225 g cream cheese
⅔ cup/150 ml heavy/double cream,
whipped

Serves 6

1 Grease a 7in/18cm loose-based springform

pan/tin. Cream the fat and one third of the syrup, mix in the flour.

2 Spread this mixture over the base of the pan. Bake at 325°F/160°C/Gas Mark 3 for 30 minutes until light brown. Cool.

3 Blend the cornstarch/cornflour and egg. Add the lemon rind. Boil the milk and stir gradually into the mixture. Return to the pan and stir over a low heat until thickened. Cool.

4 Dissolve the gelatin in 2 tablespoons of the lemon juice. Whisk the cream cheese with the remaining golden syrup. Whisk in the cold custard and gelatin.

5 Stir in half the cream and pour over the base. Chill. Decorate with the remaining cream.

CHESHIRE CHEESECAKE

$\frac{1}{2}$ **lb/225 g** graham crackers/digestive biscuits, crushed
$\frac{1}{2}$ **cup/125 g** butter
$\frac{3}{4}$ **cup/175 g** castor sugar
$2\frac{1}{2}$ **cups/225 g** Cheshire cheese, finely grated

Danish Pavlova

2 **tsp** custard powder
2 eggs, beaten
$\frac{2}{3}$ **cup/150 ml** whipping cream
1 **tbs/15 ml** lemon juice
$\frac{1}{2}$ **tsp** vanilla extract/essence
$1\frac{1}{4}$ **cups/300 ml** sour cream
4 strawberries
1 kiwi fruit

Serves 6–8

1 Mix the crackers/biscuits with the butter and 1 tablespoon castor sugar. Press on to the base and sides of an 8in/20cm loose-based springform pan/tin.

2 Bake at 325°F/170°C/Gas Mark 3 for 5 minutes. Cool.

3 Beat together the cheese, half cup of the sugar and custard powder. Add the eggs, cream and lemon juice. Beat until smooth. Pour into the crust.

4 Return to the oven and bake for 35–40 minutes. Remove from the oven and cool for 15 minutes. Beat the remaining sugar, vanilla and sour cream together and pour over the cheesecake.

5 Turn the oven up to 425°F/220°C/Gas Mark 7 and bake for 15 minutes. Cool then chill. Decorate with strawberries and kiwi fruit.

BAKED CURD CHEESECAKE

$\frac{1}{4}$ **lb/125 g** shortcrust pastry
2$\frac{1}{2}$ cups/225 g curd cheese
$\frac{2}{3}$ **cup/150 ml** unflavoured/natural yogurt
$\frac{1}{4}$ **cup/50 g** castor sugar
1 tbs/25 g cornstarch/cornflour
$\frac{1}{2}$ **cup/75 g** white raisins/sultanas
1 lemon, grated rind and juice
2 eggs, separated

Serves 6–8

1 Use the pastry to line the base of an 8in/20cm loose-based cake pan/tin. Line with foil and bake at 400°F/200°C/Gas Mark 6 for 15 minutes. Remove the foil and bake for a further 5 minutes. Cool.

2 Make the filling: blend the curd cheese and yogurt. Add the sugar, cornstarch/cornflour, sultanas, grated lemon rind and juice. Beat in the egg yolks.

3 Whisk the egg whites until stiff. Fold into the cheese mixture. Pour into the cake pan/tin and bake at 350°F/180°C/Gas Mark 4 for 30–35 minutes. It should be just set and the top, golden brown. Cool before serving.

DANISH PAVLOVA

3 egg whites
1 cup/200 g soft brown sugar
1 tsp cornstarch/cornflour
1 tsp wine vinegar
1 tsp vanilla extract/essence
1$\frac{3}{4}$ cups/175 g Blue Brie cheese
1$\frac{1}{4}$ cups/300 ml heavy/double cream
1 lb/450 g fresh fruit

Serves 6–8

1 Whisk the egg whites until stiff. Slowly whisk in the sugar. Mix the cornstarch/cornflour, vinegar and vanilla and whisk into the mixture.

2 Turn the mixture onto a baking tray lined with non-stick baking paper and spread it out to an 8in/20cm circle, making a slight wall on the outer edge.

3 Bake at 275°F/140°C/Gas Mark 1 for 1 hour. Turn off the oven and leave the meringue to cool completely in the oven.

4 Thinly slice the rind from the cheese and beat until soft. Lightly whip the cream, stir in the cheese and whip until stiff. Chill.

5 Just before serving, cut the fruit into bite-sized pieces. Reserve some to decorate and pile the rest into the centre of the meringue. Cover the fruit with the cream and decorate with the reserved fruit.

BLACK CHERRY CAKE

15 oz/425 g can pitted black cherries
4$\frac{3}{4}$ oz/135 g pkt blackcurrant jelly
18–20 lady fingers/sponge fingers
2$\frac{1}{2}$ cups/225 g Cheddar cheese, finely grated
2 cups/500 ml heavy/double cream, whipped

Serves 6–8

1 Drain the juice from the cherries and make up to 1$\frac{1}{4}$ cups with boiling water. Pour over the jelly and stir until dissolved.

2 Pour a thin layer of jelly into the base of a 7in/18cm cake pan/tin and chill until set.

3 Decorate the base with a few of the cherries. Carefully stand the sponge fingers round the edge of the tin with the curved sides against the tin.

4 Fold the cheese into two thirds of the cream with the remaining cherries and jelly. Pour into the cake tin and allow to set. Trim the biscuits to the level of the mixture.

5 Dip the pan in hot water and turn the cake out. Decorate with the remaining cream.

WENSLEYDALE APPLE CAKE

2 cups/225 g self-raising flour
$\frac{1}{2}$ **cup/125 g** castor sugar
$\frac{1}{2}$ **tsp** salt
$\frac{3}{4}$ **cup/175 g** butter
1 egg, beaten
$\frac{1}{4}$ **cup/60 ml** milk
3 medium apples, peeled, cored and sliced
1$\frac{1}{4}$ cups/125 g Wensleydale cheese, grated
$\frac{1}{2}$ **tsp** ground cinnamon lemon juice

Serves 6–8

1 Place the flour, half the sugar and salt in a bowl. Rub in two thirds of the butter. Add the egg and milk and mix to a soft batter.

2 Spread into a well buttered 8in/20cm cake pan/tin. Arrange half the apple slices on top and sprinkle with the cheese.

3 Add the remaining apples and sprinkle the rest of the sugar and cinnamon on top. Dot with the rest of the butter and a little lemon juice.

4 Bake at 400°F/200°C/Gas Mark 6 for 45 minutes. Cool, turn out on to a wire rack until cold.

COEUR A LA CRÈME

2½ cups/225 g cottage cheese
⅔ cup/150 ml heavy/double cream
⅔ cup/150 ml sour cream
2 tbs/25 g castor sugar
2 egg whites

Serves 6

1 Sieve the cottage cheese and stir in the creams. Mix in the sugar. Whisk the whites stiffly and fold in.

2 Press the mixture into 6 individual heart-shaped moulds that have holes in the bottom for the mixture to drain. Put the moulds on a deep plate. Or, line a sieve with cheesecloth/muslin and set it over a bowl. Press the mixture into the sieve.

3 Place the moulds or the sieve in the fridge and chill overnight. Turn out and serve.

PASHKA

(Traditional Russian Easter dish)

2½ cups/225 g cottage cheese
⅔ cup/150 ml sour cream
2 tbs/25 g blanched almonds, chopped
3 tbs/25 g candied peel
⅓ cup/50 g raisins
½ lemon, grated rind only

Serves 4

1 Sieve the cottage cheese and beat in the sour cream. Add the almonds, peel, raisins and lemon rind.

2 Mix well. Line a sieve with cheesecloth/muslin and stand over a bowl. Turn the mixture into the sieve. Leave to stand in the fridge for 12–24 hours to drain. Serve.

CASSATA ALLA SICILIANA

7½ cups/700 g fresh ricotta cheese
1 cup/200 g sugar
5 oz/150 g candied lemon peel
¾ cup/125 g cooking chocolate, chopped
4 tbs/60 ml rum
14 oz/400 g sponge cake or ladyfingers/sponge fingers

Serves 6

1 Cream the ricotta until very smooth. Add the sugar, 1 tablespoon of the rum, candied peel and chocolate.

2 Sprinkle the remaining rum on the ladyfingers/sponge cake fingers and use to line the base and sides of a mould or soufflé dish.

3 Fill the mould with the ricotta mixture and chill for at least 3 hours. If you wish to unmould the cassata, line the mould with wax paper brushed with rum.

THE "GUESS-WHAT'S-IN-IT" FUDGE

3½ cups/450 g confectioner's/icing sugar, sifted
½ cup/125 g butter, softened
1¼ cups/125 g Derby cheese, very finely grated
1 tsp vanilla extract/essence
3 tbs/25 g cocoa powder

Makes 1½ lb/700 g

1 Place all the ingredients in a large bowl and mix together thoroughly. Knead to a smooth ball.

2 Divide the fudge in half and shape into 2 rolls, each about 14in/35cm long. Wrap and chill.

3 Cut into even slices and serve.

STRAWBERRY BABAS

1 lb/450 g strawberries, hulled
⅓ cup/75 g castor sugar
¼ cup/60 ml orange liqueur
1¾ cups/175 g Petit Suisse cheese
¾ cup/75 g confectioner's/icing sugar, sifted
⅔ cup/150 ml heavy/double cream
6 individual babas
orange juice

Serves 6

1 Toss the strawberries in the sugar and liqueur and allow to stand for 1 hour.

2 Beat together the cheese and confectioner's sugar until fluffy. Whisk the cream and mix it lightly into the cheese. Chill.

3 Carefully scoop out the insides of the babas to leave firm cases about ⅓in/1cm thick.

4 Drain the strawberries. Measure the juice and make up to 1¼ cups with orange juice.

5 Saturate the interiors of the babas with the juice. Reserve some of the cheese mixture for decoration and use the remainder to fill the cases. Divide the strawberries between the cases.

6 Decorate with the reserved cream and chill briefly before serving.

Mozzarella and Fruit

MOZZARELLA AND FRUIT

1 pineapple, skinned and cored
20 strawberries, sliced
3 kiwi fruit, peeled and sliced
6 cups/600 g Mozzarella cheese, sliced
mint leaves

Serves 10

1 Slice the pineapple allowing 1 thin slice per person. On each plate alternately layer the pineapple, strawberries, kiwi fruit and cheese.

2 Decorate with mint leaves and serve.

CHEESE AND FRUIT BRÛLÉE

¼ lb/125 g grapes, deseeded
½ lb/225 g dessert apples, peeled, cored and chopped
3 tbs/45 ml lemon juice
4 tbs/50 g seedless raisins
1 banana, sliced
2 tbs/25 g brazil nuts, chopped
1¼ cups/125 g Wensleydale cheese, coarsely grated
2 cups/500 ml heavy/double cream, whipped
½–¾ cup/125–175 g light brown/demerara sugar

Serves 4–6

1 Mix the grapes, apples, lemon juice, raisins, banana, nuts and cheese. Place in an ovenproof baking dish.

2 Spread the whipped cream on top and chill for 2 hours. Cover generously with sugar and broil/grill intensely until the sugar caramelizes. Serve immediately.

BANANA CHEESE WHIP

4 bananas
1 orange, juice only
⅔ cup/150 ml unflavoured yogurt
2½ cups/225 g curd cheese
honey

Serves 4

1 Mash the bananas with the orange juice. Beat the yogurt with the curd cheese until smooth. Combine the two mixtures.

2 Add honey to taste. Spoon into individual dishes or glasses. Serve chilled.

Cheese and Wine

In the 1970's the fashion for "cheese and wine parties" reached its peak
of popularity. Sadly, these two partners often made an unhappy
combination. Cheese and wine are not automatically compatible.
Certain cheeses however do beautifully complement particular wines.
This is a general guide for serving, but naturally, with a little experience
and imagination the field can be widened by personal preference.

Rather than be bewildered by choice, firstly decide which takes priority, the cheese or the wine? If you've tracked down some exquisite cheese that you hope to savour in isolation from other food, the wine can be chosen to match either its character or birthplace. On the other hand, if you've managed to lay hands on a truly fine wine, the cheese should be suited so as not to distract from the wine. It is disappointing to pay a high price for good wine and then to drink it with a pungent cheese that takes over the palate and every other sense. Pay heed to quality always.

Strong, pungent cheeses require young, full-bodied red wines or a sweet, white wine. Soft cheeses, and those of more refined flavour, call for quality and age in the wine.

Often, both the wine and cheese will be ordinary. This makes the choice a little less vital and some interesting combinations are suggested below. Experiment with mild cheeses and lesser known types. Try sweet wines with the richer cheeses, sharp whites with Fromage Frais. But do take care with classic combinations like Blue Stilton and vintage port for example. Good port needs no complement, excellent Stilton likewise. Drink port with Stilton by all means but choose a relatively young tawny, a good ruby or late-bottled kind. The cheese benefits from the sweetness and strength of a fortified wine, but it can spoil a fine vintage port.

Another interesting guide can be to combine the native cheeses with the wine of a particular region. Choose the humbler country wines to serve with the local cheese. The great wines of a region usually have far less in common with the local cuisines. Where wine is not made, try the cheeses with the traditional local beer or cider.

Appenzell light fruity reds, Merlot, Beaujolais

Asiago lively full-bodied Piedmontese reds

Banon dry delicate Provençal whites, reds or rosés, Cassis, Gigondas, Côtes de Provence, Chinon

Bel Paese light rosés, Valpolicella, Barbera, Chianti

Bleu d'Auvergne Saint Pourçain, Cornas, Châteauneuf-du-Pape

Blue Cheshire reds from Burgundy or the Médoc, Australian reds, Chilean Cabernet, port

Blue Stilton tawny port, good amontillado sherry, Dão, red Rioja, Barolo, Hermitage

Blue Wensleydale St-Emilion, lesser Médocs

Bondon Touraine Sauvignon, (Normandy) cider

Brick full fruity reds, beer

Brie Sancerre, Frascati, Médoc, Bordeaux reds, Côtes du Roussillon

Brinza beer

Caciotta Chianti

Camembert white Burgundy, Rhine whites, claret

Cantal Gaillac red, Chinon

Cheddar any red wine – the better the Cheddar the better the wine – Burgundies, Châteauneuf-du-Pape, Barolo, Zinfandel, tawny ports, beer, real ale

Cheshire Beaujolais Villages, Loire Gamay

Chèvre French country reds

Coulommiers Nuits-St-Georges

Crottin Sancerre, Chablis

Danablu full-bodied reds, clarets, Burgundies, Rhône reds, Rioja

Edam light fruity reds or whites, beer

Emmental fruity reds or whites, Nierstein, Bourgogne-Mâcon, Champigny, Fendant

Esrom any light to solid red depending on age of cheese

Feta dry Greek whites, retsina, ouzo

Fontina Merlot, Pinot Grigio

Fourme d'Ambert Condrieu

Friese Nagelkaas beer, whisky

Fromage Frais Soave, Anjou Blanc, Vinho Verde

Gammelost strong reds

Gaperon Corbières

Gjetost strong black coffee, akevitt

Gorgonzola Barbera, Barolo, robust Sardinian or Provençal reds

Gouda Beaujolais Villages for young cheeses, full-bodied reds for mature ones, beer

Gruyère Rhône white or red, light fruity Neuchâtel, Pinot Noir

Handkäse beer, cider, apfelwein

Havarti dry light whites, lager

Herve full-bodied reds, Cornas

Kashkaval light dry whites, beer

Leiden Beaujolais Villages, strong dry whites, gin, beer

Liederkrantz powerful reds, Rhônes, Riojas, beer

Limburger full-bodied reds, Châteauneuf-du-Pape, beer

Livarot Morgon, Calvados, cider

Manchego Rhone reds, Riojas

Maroilles Champigny

Mascarpone Moselle, light sweet whites

Monterey Jack Chardonnay, light whites, dry reds

Mozzarella Chianti

Munster Gewürztraminer, Pinot Noir

Mycella strong full reds

Olivet Gigondas, Morgon

Parmesan Chianti, Lambrusco, Sangiovese

Pecorino full Sicilian reds

Piora Pinot Noir

Pont l'Evêque Corbières, Côtes du Roussillon, cider

Port-Salut white Rhône, Fronsac reds

Raclette dry whites, Savoie Blanc, Fendant, beer

Reblochon Beaujolais, Muscadet, Chablis

Rollot St-Emilion

Roquefort minor Sauternes, Monbazillac, Rhône reds

Royalp fruity reds, rosés

Sage Derby strong bitter beer

Samsø light reds and whites

Serra Vinho Verde

Taleggio light reds, Valpolicella, Chianti

Tête de Moine Fendant

Tilsit light fruity reds, fresh whites, tawny port, beer

Vacherin light reds, rosés, Chinon, Côtes de Beaune

Mont d'Or Cabernet

Valençay dry whites, light fruity reds

Weinkäse Moselles, Rhine whites

INDEX

The index is divided into two parts: the first consists of an A-Z of worldwide cheeses and the second contains recipes divided into categories.
All illustrations are in **bold**.

CHEESES

RECIPES

APPETIZERS AND STARTERS

BISCUITS/SCONES

CAKES

CHEESECAKES

DESSERTS

DIPS

FLANS/TARTS

FONDUES

LOAVES AND ROLLS

MAIN MEALS

CREDITS : RECIPES

Biss Lancaster plc: 103; British Meat Recipe Service: 58–63, 59, 61, 75, 84; British Sausage Bureau: 73; Cheeses of England and Wales: 44, 45, 46, 47, 50, 52, 53, 61, 65, 66, 67, 70, 71, 72–74, 76, 78, 80, 83, 84, 85, 86, 89, 92, 98, 100, 101, 102; Dairy Diary: 45, 48, 51, 70, 88, 91, 93, 97; Danish Dairy Board: 48, 50, 52, 56, 58, 62, 75, 77, 80, 82, 99, 102, 105; Dairy Produce Advisory Service: 47, 57, 60, 64, 66, 67, 69, 70, 74, 84, 91, 94, 95–97, 107; English Cheese Council: 49, 54, 55, 56, 66, 68, 70, 72, 77, 81, 82, 84, 85, 86, 88, 89, 90, 91, 96, 97, 103, 107; Mazola Corn Oil: 82; Mushroom Growers' Association: 50; National Dairy Council: 100; Pasta Information Centre: 75;

Recipes on pp. 50, 64, 82, 83 derived from Elisabeth Ayrton's *English Provincial Cooking* (Mitchell Beazley, 1980); Recipes on pp 77, 78, 80, 89, 95, 99 derived from Colin Tudge's *Future Cook* (Mitchell Beazley, 1980).

CREDITS : ILLUSTRATIONS

Archives Editions Atlas: 30, 32, 38, 39, 41T, 42; British Bacon Bureau: 63; British Meat: 59, 61; Cheeses of England and Wales: 3, 6, 7, 46T, 53B, 65B, 73T, 78, 101; Danish Dairy Board: 28, 37, 48, 58, 62B, 75, 77, 81, 99 104; Dutch Dairy Bureau: 9; English Country Cheese Council: 10TR, 24, 87, 108; Farmhouse English Cheese Bureau: 10, 11; Francois Gothier, Ardea London Ltd: 8; Milk Marketing Board: 45, 49, 57, 64T, 67B, 68T, 69B, 74T, 83B, 88, 90, 93, 94, 96, 97, 98, 107; Mushroom Growers' Association: 51; National Dairy Council: 85B, 100.

T = Top   B = Bottom   TR = Top Right